HOW TO CATCH
BIG PIKE

Also available from Constable & Robinson

Getting Started at Fly Fishing for Trout
Fly Fishing for Salmon
Flyfisher's Chronicle

HOW TO CATCH
BIG PIKE

All the insight and technique you need to catch bigger pike,
whatever the location

PAUL GUSTAFSON

with GREG MEENEHAN

A How To Book

ROBINSON

ROBINSON

First published in Great Britain in 1997 by Collins Willow, an imprint of
HarperCollins Publishers, London
This edition published in Great Britain in 2016 by Robinson
1 3 5 7 9 8 6 4 2

A CIP catalogue record for this book
is available from the British Library.

ISBN: 978-1-84528-604-0 (hardback)

Designed and typeset in the UK by Baseline Arts Ltd, Oxford
Printed and bound in China

Robinson
is an imprint of
Little, Brown Book Group
Carmelite House
50 Victoria Embankment
London EC4Y 0DZ

An Hachette UK Company
www.hachette.co.uk

www.littlebrown.co.uk

*This book is dedicated to my mother and to my son, Mathew,
without whose support, encouragement and patience it would never
have been written.*

*I should like to thank Steve Kilbee for putting up with me
during countless fishing expeditions, and Fred Buller and Alwyne Wheeler
for their invaluable advice and support.*

*And not forgetting Peta Lloyd, Paul Burton, Graham Bowerman,
Katie Hedin and Austin Ashman, whose help over the years has
been much appreciated.*

CONTENTS

PHOTOGRAPHS SUPPLIED BY:

Adrian Abib; Gord Burton; Al Rawlings; Gerald Stratford; Pete Climo and Bob Jones; Mick Willis; Bob Church; Pure Fishing and Abu. Garcia; S.M. Group Europe Ltd. Plymouth; Martin Founds and Anglers World Holidays; Kalle Hedin and nedredalalven.se; Robert Glenn and E.P. Barrus Bicester; Pete Shefford; Fred Buller, Berkley; Delkim UK, Greys; Eddie Turner; Geoff Adams; Greg Meenehan; Colin House; Dennis Fogden; Jan Eggers; Gavin Harker; Richard Hawkins; Dean Eades and birdmad.com.

ACKNOWLEDGEMENTS

The author would like to thank:

John M. Casselman, Department of Biology, Queens University, Ontario, Canada; Bruno Broughton, Fisheries Management Consultant; Jim Diana, Professor of Fisheries and Aquaculture, University of Michigan; Dr Allen Messenger and Dr Charles Anderson, Minnesota; David Solomon, Centre for Limnology, University of Wisconsin–Madison; Titus Seilheimer, Fisheries Specialist, Wisconsin; John Solomon and David Lyons; John Zafaradl, Robb Cuss, Pure Fishing and Abu Garcia, Greys and Berkley; Fox International; Delkim UK; Lynx UK; Humminbird Fish Finders and S.M. Group Europe Ltd. Plymouth; E.P. Barnes, Bicester; Anglers World Holidays; Visit Sweden and nedredalalven.se; Visit Scotland and Francis Allan; Tourism Ireland; Loch Lomond and the Trossachs National Park; German Tourist Board; Natural History Museum, Oxford; Blinker Germany; Angelica Stepp and Fisch und Fang Germany; Mads Grosell and Svendsen Sport Denmark; Glowtec; Lyon Tikka Headlamps and Petzl; Malcolm MacCormick; Reuben Heaton UK; Gordon Forester and Liz Bates, Bay Tree Guest House Loch Lomond; Nim Singh and Visit Canada; Pat McLoughlin (Fishing in Ireland) and fisheriesireland.ie; John Boyle and Eamon Grey, The Breffni Arms Hotel, Arvagh, County Cavan; Tim Small and Lechlade Trout Fisheries; Terry Eustace and Gold Label Tackle UK; Nicky Webb; Sean Long; Collin Wiggins; Norman Hawes; Chris Martin; Colin Hoey; Nick Howland; Robbie Brightwell; John Searl; Chris Tarrant; Stuart Earp; David Duffes; Kalle Hedin; Dean Eades; Dean Burman; Pete Mowy; Mike Wells; Phil Grant; Partridge of Reddich; Owner Hooks; Solar Tackle UK; Alan Gibson; *Anglers Mail*; *Angling Times* and Mick Rouse; Pete Coogan Abu Garcia Service; John Zafaradl.

DVDs by the author include *How to Catch Bigger Pike, How to Catch River Pike* and *Paul Gustafson's Pike Fishing in Ireland*.

FOREWORD

BY FRED BULLER

Paul Gustafson is a distinguished and hugely erudite pike angler who, for decades, has seriously sought scientific explanations to further his practical knowledge of pike behaviour. When you look and listen to his DVDs or read his books, however experienced you may be, you are bound to find explanations for, and solutions to, problems that have dogged you for years.

Paul's account of how to locate the biggest pike in a fishery, before describing the best way of catching it, is probably his greatest gift to other fishermen, notwithstanding his precise advice on how to apply various clever techniques that help the determined pike angler to achieve greater success.

A study of Paul's existing books and DVDs might lead you to believe that there isn't much more to learn – that would be a delusion. What Paul sets out to teach his readers in his new book, *How to Catch Big Pike*, is how to catch *Esox lucius* in temperate freshwater habitats throughout the northern hemisphere, wherever the species is to be found. Accordingly, his coverage can be described as global.

Paul Gustafson is an experienced biologist as well as a gifted angler and researcher, which gives his work unmatchable authority.

INTRODUCTION

Izaak Walton called it 'the tyrant of the rivers, or the fresh-water wolf, by reason of his bold, greedy, devouring disposition.' Dick Walker said that whenever he hooked one he felt as Jorrocks did towards his horse when he said: 'Come hup, you hugly brute!'

No other British freshwater fish species has the same aura, creates so much fear and commands so much respect as the pike. It has lived in Britain for millions of years, been the subject of tales that have been handed down for centuries, and been a part of epic battles that have lived on in the memories of generations.

Huge, glass-cased specimens glare down from walls the length and breadth of Britain, with cold, staring eyes and rows of saw-like teeth, defiant even from beyond the grave.

It's the biggest native freshwater fish in the British Isles and a species that anglers long to catch, and talk about in reverential tones. We may rule on land, but the pike is all-powerful beneath the waves, fearless and with neither adversary nor equal.

It's been said that you can't love pike; that they have cold, black hearts and that even the very best pike anglers can do no more than understand them. Yet anglers devote their lives to studying them, and some write books to explain the attraction they hold, to reveal what was hitherto unknown about these majestic fish, and to show how they can be outwitted.

But who is caught, then? The wily pike or the enthralled pike angler? The writers of books about pike, or the readers of them? For when a fascination for the species they call the king of freshwater fishes bites, it bites deep and doesn't ever let go.

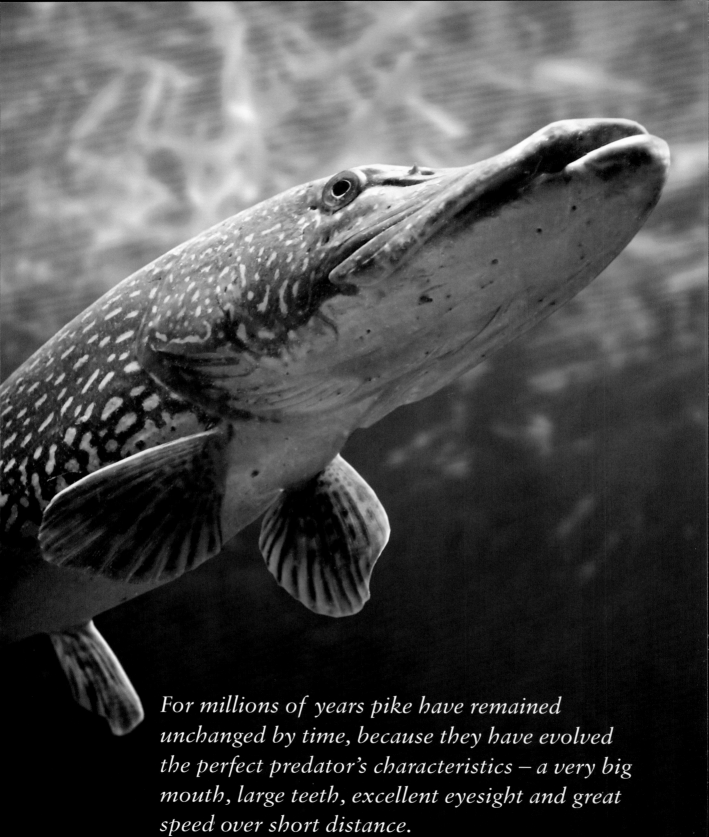

For millions of years pike have remained unchanged by time, because they have evolved the perfect predator's characteristics – a very big mouth, large teeth, excellent eyesight and great speed over short distance.

FIRST STEPS
A PIKE FISHING APPRENTICESHIP

EVERYONE'S PAST HAS A PROFOUND EFFECT ON THEIR PRESENT AND FUTURE, and for anglers this is particularly true. From the first day that we pick up a rod and the first fish that we see and catch, we learn lessons that stay with us for the rest of our lives. The circumstances of every capture are stored in the memory and brought into play when a similar situation occurs. Perhaps without being aware of it we are calling on experiences that stretch back to our earliest days to solve the latest fishing puzzle.

My first days of fishing were spent sitting alone beside a stretch of water, watching what was going on beneath the surface and seeing grown-up anglers leave home at dawn to return much later weighed down with their catches. I was fortunate in that a lake lapped against the shore just a hundred yards from the bottom of my parents' home at Hinksey, in South Oxford, and it was there that I caught my first pike.

Every capture stays in the memory, whether it weighs 5 lb, like my first fish, or 35 lb, like this one, my personal best.

My fishing had been for perch, bream and eels, until one day in autumn I got up early, collected my Pegley Davies rod and a bucket of minnows, which I had left to stand under a dripping tap in the bath, and ran down to the shore. There were two green angling punts moored at the lake, and my tactic for catching fish was to drop a livebait on a size 6 hook against the side of the punt and let it swing under. Almost invariably it would be taken by a perch, sometimes a big one. But this morning when I tried this approach nothing happened, so I pushed the punt a little way out. As the boat moved, I saw the tail of a huge fish lying below. I lowered the bait where I thought the head should be, and the minnow was taken.

The pike I caught was only about 5 lb, but I can still remember the excitement of its capture and the sense of discovery at seeing my first one. Despite the years that have gone by and the number of pike I have seen and caught since, every one I catch reminds me of that fish, and the species still holds the same sense of wonder for me that I experienced on that day.

Throughout the summer, I went down to the shore early in the morning to sit and watch a large pike that would swim over the concrete shelf at the water's edge when the sun was out. I never fished for it. It used to fascinate me just to watch it, and I was quite content to sit there for hours.

I was once there when two men came back in a boat for their Sunday lunch after setting out early. Children weren't allowed out on the water in the punts, so they held a fascination for us, and we waited eagerly to see what the anglers

Ondex spinners.

had caught when they returned. I watched the two men come ashore on this occasion, and they had two very big pike in the bottom of their boat. These fish dwarfed my five-pounder, and I remember thinking that fish of that size were entirely out of reach for someone like me. I couldn't believe I would ever catch a fish that big.

I believe I owe my original instinct for fishing to my father, a keen and skilful angler whose favourite species became mine. One of my earliest memories is sitting with him while he was fishing for eels on the River Severn, near my birthplace at Shrewsbury, and then when we moved to Oxford with my four brothers I watched him fishing the Thames for eels and spinning for pike. To a young boy who wanted to explore the lake at the back of the house, but who had limited resources, spinning was a cheap and effective way of catching fish. All the money from my paper round went on lures – Ondex, Voblex and wooden, jointed plugs – and all of my spare time was spent fishing. With school friends I learned all the best lies on the lake, and practised casting until I could put a plug or spinner on a sixpence. Five of us fished a group of shallow lakes linked by a stream. These held huge numbers of small pike, and our early success with these fish and the lessons we learned by pooling our knowledge encouraged us to try further afield. With a haversack and a net we would spend days on a lake or cover miles of the local stretch of the River Thames and the tributaries that flowed into it.

There were older boys among my fishing friends, and when they learned to drive we went further afield, piling into an old VW Beetle. We fished the Evenlode at Woodstock and King's Weir on the Thames just outside of Oxford. With the broadening of our horizons, the fish became bigger, and the number of species increased. By 1972, I had caught pike to 14 lb from the Evenlode, perch to 3 lb, and chub to 4 lb 11 oz, all on spinners. We would have carried on spinning to the exclusion of all other methods if it hadn't been for the influence of a character we met who made regular appearances in our lives at intervals as the years went by.

He was an Irish navvy – we nicknamed him 'Pikie' – who worked now and then on the roads and lived in a hostel in Oxford. His tackle consisted of a big pike 'bung' float, size 2 single hooks, 35 lb line on a big sea reel and a heavy rod. Yet he caught plenty of fish.

Pikie seemed to be on the river almost every day, always in one of his favourite spots. He used to arrive in old, scruffy clothes and a tatty black mac that he wore on even the hottest day, and a rickety old bike that carried him and his battered tackle to the bank. His trademark was his constantly runny nose with a dew drop on the end, and this kept putting out the cigarette stub, rolled from black shag, that was always pressed between his lips. He was forever trying to re-light this cigarette, his enormous, shovel-like hands shielding the lighted match from the wind, only to have it put out again when the next nose drip fell. He seemed ancient to us, but when he died not long ago he was said to be in his eighties, so at the time he must have been no more than in his late fifties.

I remember watching the pike in Hinksey ditch, which ran along the bottom of my parents' garden. They would come to spawn in early spring, grouped in a shallow bay, very visible from the bank, and we would cast to them for ages to get them to take a spinner or a plug, but without success. Pikie saw us struggling to catch these fish and suggested we get some livebaits and try with them. We came back the next day with a bucketful of lovely dace we had caught, and the first bait we cast among the pike was taken straight away. The fish weighed over 16 lb, a personal best, and we had four other doubles that morning.

I learned how to catch pike that weren't interested in chasing our spinners by using dace livebaits, and had my first success on a deadbait by accident, using a bait that had been allowed to lie on the bottom in a shallow bay while I ate my sandwiches. It was taken by a pike of 19 lb, still one of the hardest-fighting fish I have ever hooked.

Spurred on by this success, I tried to find out more about the method from angling books in the library, but little had been written about deadbaiting by the early seventies. Later when I talked to other anglers, Fred J. Taylor and Bill Giles among them, it was surprising how many had had the same experience, landing their first fish on a deadbait by accident.

As with the discovery of livebaiting, we became convinced that deadbaiting was now the key to success, and decided to spend a lot of our time fishing with them. We struggled for many months, because we didn't understand that deadbaits should be used when you have a good idea of where fish are, and not just cast at random. We used to hurl them out in what we thought were likely-looking spots, but our sense of fish location was not great. It was only when we began plumbing depths and working out why pike were in some swims and not in others that we started to achieve consistent success.

A breakthrough came when we brought all three methods together. One of the best ways of locating fish was, and still is, spinning, and yet spinning didn't always take fish. Follows, swirls and plucks were often all that we could provoke with artificial bait. But once we had found pike-holding areas, we could use livebaits or deadbaits in the same spot, and this improved our catches immediately.

Spinning is a very good exploratory method because it will work straight away, but fish wise up quickly and success will be short-lived. However, the knowledge of holding areas that spinning provides should enable you to catch larger fish when you change to a bait.

With the addition of deadbaiting to our armoury of methods came the need for stronger rods. I knew a couple of lock keepers who built their own, and when

I had saved up the £25 each for two, ten-foot, 2.5 lb test curve Bruce and Walker fibreglass blanks, I pestered them until they agreed to make them up for me.

I can still see those men now, huddled in the keeper's hut on a cold winter's day with the heater going full blast, whipping these rods and drying the varnish in front of the fire because I wanted to use them straight away.

But the confidence they gave me was immense. Before this, I had experienced problems with the reel falling off the worn cork handle of my old rod – something that cost me several big fish. But these new deadbait rods had screw reel fittings, the first ones I had ever used, and armed with them I felt I couldn't fail.

I also caught a lot of pike after dark, particularly in summer, when sport could be slow during the day but came alive at night. Perhaps the best night-fishing water we came across was the Big Coloured Pit, so called because it was still being

There are bigger pike in the UK than the current record. One of 40 lb was once found dead at Boulters Weir.

worked for aggregate and had the clarity of soup. It was very deep – twenty-two or twenty-three feet in places – and fished in the daytime by South Cerney AC, who held matches there. They were after the bream, and regular angling pressure pushed the shoals far from the bank during the day. When the matchmen packed up and it got dark, the bream came in for leftover bait and groundbait and to feed at the bottom of the shelf. The pike followed them. The bream always headed for one or two spots, so location was simple. I fished it with two friends, Steve Kilbee and Nick Webb, and in one session I had fish of 21 lb, 23 lb, 24 lb and 18 lb within twenty minutes. Other waters produced fish only at certain times of day, and you could set your watch by some feeding spells. Once you got to know when they were, you could be at various pits at the hot times and catch big fish from several waters in one day, utilising fishing time to the maximum.

I even hooked a monster on the Thames. A good roach and bream angler, Norman Howes, helped me find it. He told me about a swim where he had fished for barbel and how he had been playing one of 8 lb when it had been taken by a pike that he estimated at over 30 lb. I fished the swim and, after catching a couple of pike, had the big one on. But the hooks pulled and I was left wondering just how big it was. Two anglers on the far bank saw me playing it. The following weekend when I went back for another go, they were in the swim. I asked them how they had got on and they said they'd caught the big one that I had lost the week before. I asked them if they still had it, hoping they'd put it in a sack ready for a photograph. They pointed to an immense body on the grass. It weighed 34 lb 8 oz, and they'd killed it to have it set up. I found out later that, when they were told it would cost several hundred pounds to be done professionally, they threw the pike in a dustbin. I told them what I thought of what they had done, and how long a fish of that size takes to grow to such a weight, but it was all in vain. The damage had already been done. Word spreads quickly when you're catching fish, and other anglers appear at the water even when you think you've kept things quiet. The next thing the banks are lined with anglers and the fish take a hammering. When they come under extreme pressure, pike stop feeding during the day. They learn not to pick up deadbaits. They feed less frequently, and less food means they lose weight.

Perhaps this is why I like to fish waters unknown to other anglers, like the one that gave me my personal best of 35 lb. And perhaps it's why I like the Scottish lochs – their remoteness, their wildness and the sense of isolation that is part of the experience of fishing them. To see a Scottish pike hit a sink-and-draw bait in shallow water and turn and dash through weed, shaking its head from side to side and tail-walking to crash down into thirty or forty feet of water, is an incredible experience. There's nothing as exciting as that.

Pike – the mystery and the myth

A measure of success, no matter how small, is crucial in the early stages of any angler's development if he is to stay a fisherman for life. Looking back, I realise I had just the right amount at just the right time. Too many failures in a row would have drained my confidence, but on the other hand too much success would have taken away the challenge. A good fish followed by a few 'blanks' and then another good catch, and the lessons that came with each session, kept my enthusiasm simmering.

When I try to analyse what attracts me to pike more than any other fish, I can only think that it's the enigma of the species. For millions of years they have remained unchanged by time, because they have evolved the perfect predator's characteristics – a very big mouth, large teeth, excellent eyesight and great speed over short distance. They are hunters and foragers, just as we are, and rule beneath the water's surface without any natural enemies, just as we do on dry land. Perhaps that is part of the fascination, that and the stories and speculation about how big they grow.

We know there are much bigger pike in this country than the present record of 46 lb 10 oz. It wouldn't surprise me to hear of a 55 lb fish from a food-rich still water with a good supply of game and coarse fish and no angling pressure. If the two or three waters that have this potential were opened to pike anglers at the right time of year, who knows what could happen?

Essentially, rods perform a simple task. Choose one with the right strength of blank for the size of bait you will be using and you won't go far wrong. Three budget-priced rods, even in glass fibre, that cover three different tasks are better than one expensive carbon rod.

CHAPTER 2

RODS, REELS & LINE

I CAN REMEMBER A TIME WHEN A ROD was just a rod, not a fashion statement. The colour didn't matter so long as it did the job of putting a bait in the right place, and a fish on the bank.

Today, you get laughed off the water if your rods don't match, aren't worth at least £100 each and aren't displayed in all their glory on a stainless-steel, designer-label rod pod.

I can't be doing with all of that. You won't find me polishing rods lovingly in the evenings. To me, they are tools, and if they get knocked about in the process, so be it.

I haven't taken my rods apart at the joints in fifteen years, and I probably couldn't get them apart if I wanted to. I haven't got time to put them away neatly in rod bags and holdalls. They go straight from the garage on to the roof rack of my car. When you have very little time available to you, you don't waste precious minutes tackling up and down.

A 25 lb 8 oz pike caught on a half mackerel cast seventy yards. Heavy deadbait rods should be capable of throwing big baits a reasonable distance.

(From top to bottom): Fast taper, semi-fast taper and compound taper rods for distance work, medium range and close work respectively. A soft action rod is more forgiving at close range.

Essentially, rods perform a simple task. Choose one with the right strength of blank for the size of bait you will be using and you won't go far wrong.

Three budget-priced rods, even in glass fibre, that cover three different tasks are better than one expensive carbon rod.

If you are in doubt as to what to go for, err on the powerful side, because then you will stand a better chance of landing a good fish. But ideally, three types of rod will cover every pike fishing situation you are likely to encounter.

The heavy deadbait rod

A heavy deadbait rod should be capable of throwing out big baits like jack pike, large mackerel and big coarse fish. It should be able to cast a 1 lb-plus fish up to thirty yards, and make a very good rod for long-range casting, throwing a half mackerel seventy or eighty yards.

I use my own brand of carbon Kevlar rods with three-and-a-half and four-pound test curve. They are heavy, but they sit on rod rests for most of the day so it's not as if you have to hold them for long. My own PG brand have quite soft actions, despite being semi-fast taper, and is sensitive and responsive when fish are being played. These rods are not 'broom handles', so they are sympathetic with smaller fish.

A big pike may run a hundred yards or more with a jack pike sideways in its mouth before stopping and turning the bait. If you are going to be able to pull the hooks out of the skin of the jack, which is fairly tough, into the mouth of the quarry, which is quite bony, you need a rod heavy enough for the job. Mine have a 4 lb test curve, semi-fast taper and are twelve feet long, two-piece, with a butt ring, three stand-off intermediate rings, and a tip ring. For long casting I find that the fewer the rings the better, because friction is reduced. Rings no longer need to be numerous so the line follows the curve of the rod because, unlike the old chrome rings, good-quality modern rod rings won't get grooved by line. The rings on mine are Fuji three-legged that will stand up to knocks.

Don't be tempted into thinking that standard carp rods can do the job just as well. They are simply not powerful enough, because they are designed for throwing 2 oz and 3 oz leads. As pike anglers we are throwing 4 oz, 5 oz and 6 oz mackerel or a 12 oz pike as bait. Pike rods and carp rods are different animals, and you can't cut corners by getting them to double up.

Multi-purpose medium-range rods (far left and right) that I use for most of my fishing and lightweight spinning rods to work plugs.

Playing a mid-twenty on a medium-range rod. The through action of these models makes them a pleasure to play fish, yet there is plenty of power to spare if needed.

The medium-to-close-range rod

The next rod in the trio is a medium-to-close-range, eleven-foot, two-piece model with a 3 lb test curve and a compound taper or 'through' action. Mine are made by Abu. These are ideal for flicking out small baits under-arm on rivers, and are the rods I use for most of my fishing. They're much lighter and easier to handle. I sometimes have a rod in my hand for nine, ten or eleven hours at a time, and can use one of these all day without it becoming uncomfortable. I can feel every knock and tap from a pike. They are even better when used with a multiplier.

I also use one for sink-and-draw fishing with trout or roach of 4 oz or 5 oz, and for livebaiting, though this rod will fish small mackerel, sardines and coarse baits perfectly well. It's a good all-round, multi-purpose deadbait rod for medium-to close-range work. The rings are Fuji.

I have considered using lighter rods, but when you have to bully fish to keep them out of snags on weir pools or play them near sharp rocks on a big water, you can't stop them on anything lighter.

The light rod

The only time I would use a rod of less than a 3 lb test curve would be to do some light spinning, which is something I like but don't get enough time to do. I would use one of Abu's spinning rods for this type of fishing, part of a range I have designed with through actions, that perform well in a variety of situations and can be used equally well with multipliers or fixed-spool reels.

The right fittings

The biggest single bonus of making up your own rods is that you get exactly the fittings and dimensions that you want, from the number

DON'T DISREGARD FIBREGLASS

On the subject of rod-making materials, I think it's high time there was a glass fibre revival, like there has been for LP records. Glass fibre was consigned to the scrap heap long before it had outlived its worth, and I for one wish I'd hung on to my glass-fibre rods.

It is still pleasant to play fish on a glass rod – it performs exactly the same tasks as carbon, and for one third of the cost. It may be heavier, but deadbait rods will be left in rests most of the day anyway. What's more, it takes knocks far better than carbon, which makes it ideal for boat fishing.

I moved on from fibreglass because carbon blanks are very slim in diameter and suit my small hands slightly better. I can see rods becoming even lighter, thinner and, perhaps most important of all, more robust. The best may be still to come. I also think we will see more anglers turning to telescopic rods, as the quality has come on in leaps and bounds. Some are superb, with an excellent action, very compact, ideal for when you haven't got a lot of space, easy to carry and quick to set up.

One development I have yet to see made commercially available is a one-piece rod, which would be welcomed by anglers like myself who never break theirs down. The weak point in any rod is the joint, or joints, and having tried a one-piece and found the action far superior to any two-piece I've used, I'd like to see them on sale. I don't know how many anglers would buy one-piece rods if they were commercially available, though I'm watching developments with interest.

and spacings of rings, down to your name on the butt. I have built all of my own rods, and the last one took me just forty-five minutes to ring and varnish. One thing that I never do is put my name on a rod. I was put off the practice many years ago when a bailiff came round to where I was fishing and told me it was a private water. He looked at my rod and wrote something down. 'I'm going to report you, Terry Eustace!' he said and walked away. I've always been fond of Terry's Big Pit Pike Rods, but prior to that it was because they were excellent fishing rods, rather than their usefulness in getting me out of a tight spot. I never did find out whether Terry at Gold Label Tackle got his collar felt for that!

The reel fittings I plump for are Fuji 18FPS screw reel fittings, which hold the reel securely without any chance of it dropping off. Add to that Fuji abbreviated rubber handles, which are warm to the touch, easy to maintain and non-slip, and Fuji butt caps, and that's it. As far as I'm concerned, cork handles are a thing of the past. They become dirty very quickly, get damaged, and the cork absorbs water.

I go for rod rings with a very large diameter, as the larger they are, the longer they will take to block with ice in bad weather. I smear Vaseline in the rings in winter when conditions are bad.

Some anglers have strong views on whether rods should be finished with matt or gloss varnish. Mine have an anti-flash finish, but I'm not sold on the idea that it makes much difference. I don't think a pike can see the glare of a rod while investigating a bait eighty yards from the bank. And even if it can, who knows whether a flash attracts pike, as it does on a spinner? In the end it's a question of taste.

The right reels

I can sum up the current state of reel design and manufacture by passing on two facts. The first is that the overwhelming majority of anglers want a reel to be black. The second is that tackle companies continue to make reels in silver, gold, electric blue, bright red and just about every other colour they can think of, decorated with crimson, white and yellow flashes.

Pike anglers want reels with big-drummed spools so that they can use them to cast deadbaits reasonable distances. They want handles that are durable and will stand up to regular use. And they want a free-spool facility. But manufacturers don't give them what they want, right across the range of tackle. Instead, they come up with gimmicks like reels with double handles and numbered clutch systems matched to breaking strains. Only when the companies start asking anglers what they are looking for in a fishing reel and listening to their answers will we get something that meets all of our needs. Anglers are only too happy to tell them, and it's the companies who are listening that are doing the best business.

I use multipliers for a lot of my fishing because they suit certain styles better than fixed-spool reels, but for years I argued for a multiplier that allows you to back-wind. You can convert most multipliers to back-wind by removing the anti-reverse dog mechanism, but I wanted an Abu 6501C3 that had started life with a purpose-made back-wind and was made for left-hand wind and finished in black. I designed it and submitted the proposal, and finally, after all the discussions and negotiations, Abu have brought it out. It is the first sizeable multiplier to allow back-winding while playing a fish and, I believe, a major step forward in reel design.

The heavy mob

Just as there are rods that are heavy, rods that are medium-weight and rods that are light, so reels can be categorised and matched to a rod of the appropriate class. A heavy reel on a light rod will make it butt-heavy and ruin the action.

The heavy reels I use for medium-to-close-range work are Fox Stratos 12000FS Bait Runners. These are big, meaty reels that wouldn't look out of place sea fishing. They take 200 to 300 yards of 15 lb line – much more than you need for most styles of pike fishing, apart from drift fishing, or extreme-range casting with frozen deadbaits and 3 oz leads.

The wide spools are very long and tapered, so that more line is laid close to the surface, enabling longer casts to be made. Metal spools are more robust than carbon or plastic, which I have had explode into fragments under pressure.

I load a bulk of old line, topped with 140 yards of fresh, strong monofil for deadbait fishing, so it almost reaches the spool lip. When the line is worn, after about six weeks, I turn it round by winding it on to a spare spool, so that the end that was buried is now uppermost.

Extra-large spools can be bought, capable of carrying enough line to allow a float to be drifted out 200 yards or more, but I'm not prepared to fish more than 150 yards out because tackle control and effective striking then become a problem.

These big reels have fairly fast line pick-up, which you need for when fish run towards you. Wind down quickly and strike early, so that fish don't damage themselves by swallowing the bait.

A few reel grumbles

Large torpedo handles offer a good grip on cold days and help with cranking into big fish. As you will have gathered, though, I don't like double handles. They get in the way, and I don't find them of any benefit.

Clutch drags are one of my pet hates. I never use them when pike fishing, preferring to screw them down solid and back-wind on powerful fish. When you wind down to strike a run from a pike, you need solid resistance to get those hooks home into that hard, bony mouth. If the clutch slips then you are going to lose that fish. It's even worse when fishing at range, with enormous line stretch to overcome. You may get away with a bit of clutch slip when fishing for soft-mouthed species like carp and barbel, but not pike. For my money, a clutch on a pike reel is about as useful as holes in a waterbed. You can get rid of the anti-reverse while you're at it, too, as it's no use to anyone who back-winds.

What I do like on reels is the free-spool facility, a trend set by Shimano's Baitrunner reels, and I would love to be able to buy a reel of similar size to those mentioned with a free-spool facility. Anglers have been asking for that combination for a long time, and I know of at least one company that has recently experimented with a reel along similar lines.

The original Baitrunner reel, the Shimano GT, has a spool and handle that is in my opinion just not man enough for the job of serious pike fishing. I've managed to bend mine out of shape, and while I'm quite hard on gear, strapping it to the roof of the car fully made up, I don't think this reel can take the knocks.

The light brigade

The other fixed-spool reels I use are from Mitchell, which have metal spools, are light in weight, and pleasant to fish with. I tend to use these for spinning, because multipliers don't cast light baits or spinners well.

If you are fishing with anything less than 2 oz you would be better advised to use a fixed-spool reel. A multiplier will never run as freely as a fixed-spool with very light casting weights, because the weight of the lure won't overcome the inertia and friction when a spool turns on a spindle. A fixed-spool creates very little friction because line peels off the front.

Keep 'em clean

Unless you are one of the conscientious few, it's probably quite a while since you cleaned and oiled your reel. Reel maintenance is one of those things that all of us know we should do, but few of us find the time for, no matter how many articles we see about stripping down a reel and giving it a spring clean. I'm no exception. It isn't until the reels sound a bit rough that I'll take the side plate off and give the insides a light greasing and a drop of oil ... which happens only about once every five or six years. It's worth taking the trouble, though. At the very least a noisy reel is annoying to use, and at the worst it could seize up while you are playing a fish. Then it will be the bad workman who is to blame, not his tools.

MAGNIFICENT MULTIPLIERS

There's only one choice of reel for me for boat fishing, and that's a multiplier. It is much lighter, much easier to control using your thumb, and has a much more suitable retrieve rate than a fixed spool. It fits your hand like a glove, and is light enough to use for the twelve or fourteen hours that summer fishing can involve. With my thumb on the spool, I can feather the cast so that it lands lightly on the water, and feel every knock and twitch as the bait trundles along.

When lure fishing there's no danger of line-twist ruining sport, and when casting repeatedly for sink-and-draw fishing, line wear is reduced. Multipliers are ideal for the heavy lines needed when fishing snaggy water because they cast them so much more easily than fixed-spool reels. And when it comes to maintenance, it's a simple matter of taking off the side plate.

Most have level-winds to lay line evenly across the spool, and slow retrieve rates, so you are forced to reel in at the correct speed to suit a fluttered bait. There's no real need to cast far when fishing from a boat, so a fast-retrieve reel isn't necessary, except on the odd occasion when fish run towards you.

When multipliers were designed it wasn't with pike in mind, and so there are features on them that are not best suited to pike fishing, like star drags and clutches, and a permanent anti-reverse. I hope that the reel I designed for Abu will eliminate these problems. Abu have the best on the market at the moment, the Ambassadeur 6501C3, which is left-handed and, in right-hand wind, probably the most popular reel in America. It is better suited to pike fishing than the 7000, which is too big, and the 3000, which is too small.

Abus are still precision-engineered and of superb quality. They are not cheap, but you get what you pay for. I haven't had to oil mine since I bought it more than twenty years ago, and it still works as smoothly as it did at the start. They can take about 200 yards of 13 lb line, but I only put about 140 on because I know I won't need any more. You can buy spare spools for them and carry these loaded with fresh monofil or braid.

Ignored by the majority of anglers in favour of fixed-spools, multipliers are easily the best choice for boat fishing and, with a little practice, are a joy to use. Double-sided tape should be added to the spools when using braid.

A reputation for being difficult

A lot of people are put off using multipliers. They have preconceived ideas about how difficult they are, and soon get into trouble. The younger you are introduced to them the better, because they do take a little getting used to, but my son got the knack in ten minutes.

The way you hold the rod when using one is another reason why some people turn up their noses. But, contrary to what people believe, it's just as comfortable to use the rod upside down as the other way up. You only need look at what sea anglers catch to realise that it works.

Most freshwater fishermen hold the rod in their right hand and wind with their left. That's what anglers want – it's the way they use a rod with a fixed-spool reel. Yet manufacturers still produce multiplier reels that force their customers to swap hands when playing fish. We want to use our strongest hand to put pressure on the fish, but the handle is usually on the right.

Abu are one of the few firms producing multipliers that can be used the 'right' way round. It's time common sense prevailed and anglers were offered a product that lets them fish in the way that suits their natural preferences. The ideal reel would be ambidextrous, but so far that hasn't got further than the drawing board.

I also use multipliers for fishing livebaits from boats, though the bait should be larger than an ounce or two, as multipliers don't cast well with anything less.

The only other reel I have seen used for pike fishing is the Alvey centre-pin, which is best suited to trolling with lead-core lines. These have wide drums to prevent line-twist, which can put kinks in the wire. Anglers like Gord Burton use them regularly, but I don't. I get by with a multiplier for lead-core work, but centre-pins are something I intend to experiment with in the future.

Getting on the right line

Line has a different role to play in pike fishing than in most other branches of the sport, because the fish is so far from the bait it seldom sees it or comes into direct contact with it.

There's no tactical dilemma involved in pike fishing. In other branches of angling using heavier line means getting fewer bites, and using lighter line can mean landing fewer big fish. In pike fishing, though, casting and playing fish are the prime concerns, and so the requirements of pike anglers are different from those of carp anglers and match and pleasure fishermen. With a 30 lb wire trace on the end, there's no need to use a light main line to try and fool fish into taking the bait. I have used lighter lines when long casting is required, and then I have gone down to 12 lb main line with an 18 lb shock leader, but that is only when the features I want to reach are out of 15 lb line casting range.

What qualities should line have? I look for one with a good wet knot strength, and I look for high resistance to abrasion, as many of the lochs and gravel pits I fish have rough boulders and bars that can sandpaper line to ribbons in a very short time.

I look for a line with a high resistance to ultra-violet rays, which will cause an invisible weakening, particularly when fishing on long sunny days in summer. And I look for a line with a resistance to wet oxidation, which causes it to deteriorate.

Although the thickness of line is not a prime concern, I like a line that doesn't glare or reflect light, with potentially fish-frightening consequences. But while a line doesn't necessarily need to have a low breaking strain to be effective, I like it to be fine in diameter because this aids long casting, allows better bait presentation and reduces line drag when fishing on rivers.

Line diameter is something that has improved in leaps and bounds in recent years, to the extent that we're almost spoilt for choice. But the greater choice of lines has led to a wider range being stocked by tackle shops, and so some are left on the shelf for longer.

When I buy line, I get it from the biggest, busiest tackle shop I can find, as I know that if I get a spool that's been on the shelves for months from a shop with a low turnover it could have lost as much as one-third of its stated breaking strain. And that loss is invisible. You pull some off the spool and it looks fine. It's only when you part company with a fish, and afterwards test some on a spring balance, that you realise your 12 lb line is breaking at 9 lb. Old line deteriorates fast when exposed to daylight, and a couple of outings can make its breaking strain drop dramatically. It's high time sell-by dates were introduced by fishing line manufacturers, with anything left on the shelves after the date has expired put in a bargain bin so that anglers can make allowances for strength loss and buy much heavier than they need.

What standard monofilament do I use? In the early days I used Platil, and then moved on to Maxima, which sinks well for deadbait fishing but doesn't take the knocks, especially when over gravel bars or submerged islands. I then experimented with American lines, as the firms over there carry out a lot of research on how well lines stand up to wear and tear. I now use Berkley Iron Silk in 17 lb for gravel pit fishing, but bump it up to 20 lb for weir pools and lochs, and it's 20 lb that I put on my multipliers.

Berkley Iron Silk has excellent wet and dry knot strength, is very resistant to abrasion and very limp. It winds on to a reel almost perfectly straight out of the box. I buy it in 775 yard spools, and it isn't a great deal more expensive than its competitors. I use Iron Silk for all my dead bait fishing and apply a drop of washing up liquid to make it sink.

Braided lines

The recently-developed HPPE braided lines have a big future for pike anglers. I first tried them a couple of years ago when a few brands were imported from America, but they weren't right: they were prone to snapping on the cast or on the strike, and suffered from bedding in on the spool. But in the past few months as I write, the quality has improved enormously, and there are now several brands that are ideal for some types of pike fishing. The chief attributes braids have over monofilament are their excellent abrasion resistance, their knot strength and the fact that they don't deteriorate in ultra-violet light. They are more sensitive when playing fish, having little or no memory, and a much finer diameter than monofil for the same breaking strain. I use two makes: Berkley FireLine and Berkley Gorilla Braid.

When fishing in strong winds or currents, a fine-diameter line can make tackle control a great deal easier. When drifting a bait under a float, you can get the tackle to where you want it more quickly with fine line because there is less drag. When fishing into a headwind, a livebait can be worked out from the bank without tiring.

The abrasion resistance of braids makes them excellent for sink-and-draw fishing, where repeated casting can damage lines. And braided lines don't need greasing to float, which makes them ideal for livebait fishing as they do not weigh the bait down like thicker, heavier mono, and so allow it to work for longer.

Right: American lines have benefited from the research that has gone into how they cope with wear and tear.

Below: Berkley Trilene Big Game monofil line, which is coloured sorrel, is manufactured especially to cope with the stresses that fixed-spool reels exert during casting, retrieving and landing fish.

The main drawback of braids is that they are not suitable for deadbait fishing because they float, which means they get towed by currents and pulled out of position by floating debris, and the bait gets dragged into weed. If you have to keep adjusting the line, you will keep pulling the bait out of position.

Also, the fine diameter causes problems when casting big baits, as this can make the line cut your finger like cheese wire, and also give friction burns. But if you are using a multiplier, and casting a sink-and-draw deadbait, the spool takes all of the weight of the bait and the thrust of the cast, not your finger.

Can pike see colour?

As far as line colour is concerned, the only thing I know for certain is that the cone cells in a pike's eyes are highly sensitive to red, green and yellow in the spectrum, but least sensitive to blue. So baits dyed red, green and yellow should, in theory, be a good idea, as should lines that are blue.

Or perhaps it is better to use a line that is visible than one that is invisible: a completely clear line would be a disadvantage as fish that swim into line they can't see become spooked, whereas ones that swim round line are not. And no matter how visible or invisible a line is, it is always the wire trace that pike are more likely to see as they decide whether to take a bait.

I do know that if you use highly visible lines when boat fishing you are alert to the danger of a fish running into another of your lines. And from the experiments that I have conducted, I haven't found brightly coloured lines – fluorescent green, orange or yellow – present any pike-scaring problems or offer any disadvantages. I use the Berkley Extra Tough in fluorescent green whenever I'm fishing several rods on outriggers from the back of a boat, and I would recommend it for this.

Treating them right

I dress lines for livebait fishing with Mucilin grease to make them float, whereas deadbait lines are treated with neat washing-up liquid and Fuller's Earth, for the opposite effect.

Trying to pick line quickly off the surface when float fishing, then finding it has sunk into the weed is on a par with trying to sink a deadbait line that refuses to cut through the surface. Treating lines makes fishing less frustrating and improves tackle control. I mark the spools and keep them separate so they don't get mixed up.

At the sharp end

Some waters have underwater contours like the surface of the moon. If I'm forced to fish around gravel bars, submerged islands and rocky drop-offs, all of which can be fish-holding features, I run my fingers along the line at regular intervals during the session to search for signs of wear. If I find the tell-tale signs of abrasion – any

TYING THE KNOT

The strongest knot I know of for joining line to the eye of a swivel or hook is the Grinner. And likewise, the Double Grinner is the strongest for joining two pieces of line. When Fred Buller lost his legendary big pike on Loch Lomond, he didn't know that blood knots and half bloods strangle the line and decrease its diameter locally, weakening it so that it parts at less than the stated breaking strain. Granted, it's more difficult to tie a Grinner, but it is well worth the effort as it comes close to retaining all of the line's strength. We are indebted to Dick Walker for giving us a knot that can do that.

The only times I tie a knot other than Grinner or Double Grinner is when joining line to the base of an empty reel spool, when I use a half-blood knot, and when tying a stop knot out of pole elastic, to set the depth of a sliding float. Since I have never had a fish take the last coil of line from my reel, I can say with hand on heart that this join has never let me down.

Top: The three-turn stop knot. Some people use monofil, but I don't like the thought of squeezing the line, so for me it has to be a soft piece of pole elastic every time.

Centre: The straight half-blood – simple to tie, but strangulation of the line against the eye is likely to lead to parting company with a big fish.

Bottom: Dick Walker's Grinner knot – well worth learning as it comes closer than any other design to preserving 100 per cent line strength.

roughness to the touch or signs of shredding – I change the line, swapping spools with one ready-loaded. It's not worth risking losing a big fish for the sake of a spool of line costing £3 or £4.

In the USA, you can buy a neutral-buoyancy line that is oval in diameter. It cuts through the surface layer but stays just sub-surface. It's useful for fishing deadbaits in snaggy areas and on big waters with a lot of 'chop' and surface drift. On Scottish lochs, the line needs to be kept high in the water if tackle losses are not to become a nightmare, especially when legering. I've seen anglers lose fish after fish with a standard rig that takes line along the rocky bottom. Estate lakes, which are shallow and have a strong undertow that pulls line away from where it was cast, might also be easier to fish with such a line. I can see a great deal of scope for anglers here with this neutral-buoyancy line when someone decides to import it.

Lead-core lines

When trolling over deep water is the only way of getting in touch with fish, I carry a lead-core line. The brand I use is made by Normark and sold in 100-metre lengths, marked off in a different colour every six metres to give a rough idea of the fishing depth. I have added to the markings by putting a dab of Tipp-ex every five feet to give a better guide to how deep my bait is running when the line is out behind the boat.

It is made of thin lead, coated with a braid 'skin', and keeps the bait deep. Trolled baits have a habit of riding up to the surface. Lead wire is ideal for this, if a little unwieldy to use. The only thing to watch for is kinks, which can cause the core to fracture if it is bent against itself too severely, and though line strength is not an issue, these sections won't run through the rod rings smoothly.

Trolling would never be my first-choice fishing method. When I fish a big water, I head for areas where I expect a big pike to be. I would much prefer to fish for that pike in a way other than trolling, but when there is nothing to help me locate fish, or they are not where I expect them to be, I will resort to it in order to cover water and find fish in an otherwise barren expanse. Once they are found, I will anchor and fish a static line with a deadbait, to my mind a more enjoyable way of catching pike. There are those who enjoy trolling and have honed it to an art form, but for me it will always be something of a last resort. I believe the sort of fish I am after would prefer to pick up a static, dead or dying fish it finds rather than use precious energy chasing a moving bait. But make no mistake, trolling has accounted for some very big pike. If a bait flutters past a pike at the right depth and speed, the fish may not be able to pass up the meal. So the trolling gear goes with me.

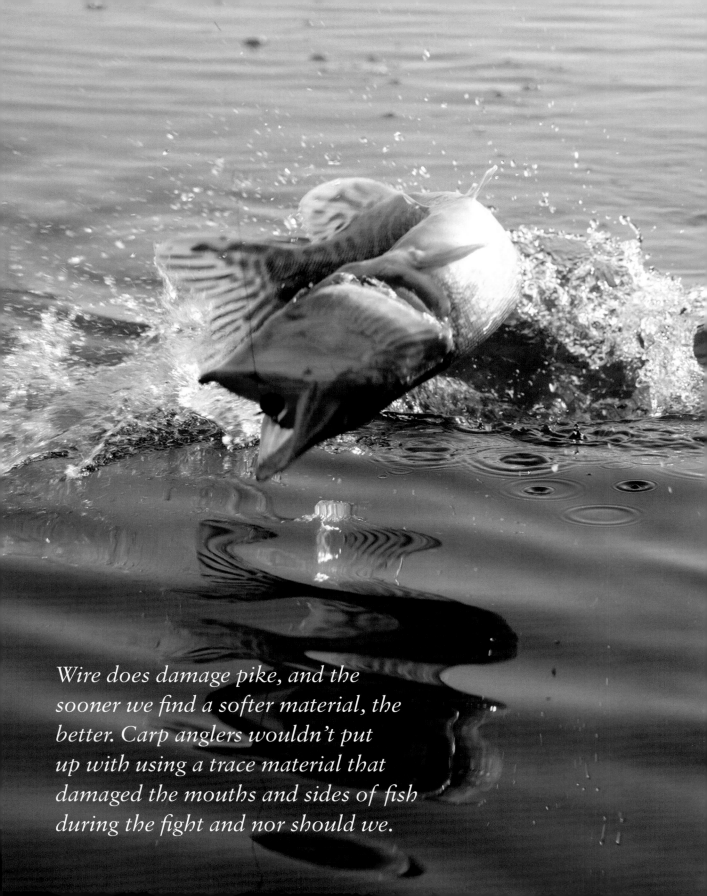

Wire does damage pike, and the
sooner we find a softer material, the
better. Carp anglers wouldn't put
up with using a trace material that
damaged the mouths and sides of fish
during the fight and nor should we.

CHAPTER 3

TERMINAL TACKLE

I HAVE TO PUT HAND ON HEART and admit that I hate making wire hook traces. Some people love all that fiddling with bits and pieces, like making model aeroplanes from plastic kits, but for me trace-making's a means to an end. I'd rather be fishing. For that reason I tend to make my traces robust, so I can get them to last longer without kinking or wearing, and I won't have to sit down with the crimping pliers and box of bits quite so often.

Ways with wire

Wire is inherently unreliable stuff. If you get a kink in it, it breaks, and at way below the unkinked strain. Anglers who use light wire to improve presentation have to put up with it going as curly as a pig's tail, useless for fishing, after landing one or two pike. So I never use less than 30 lb breaking-strain wire, preferably titanium. I used to fish with 20 lb wire, but it cost me a lot of fish because it kinks so easily. I don't believe I've caught fewer fish since switching to 30 lb. Even this thick wire has a diameter less than the equivalent nylon. It's not as supple as line, I'll grant you, but pike don't seem particularly fussy about what comes stapled to their food.

Single-strand and multi-strand titanium wire.

Wire does damage pike, and the sooner we find a softer material, the better. Carp anglers wouldn't put up with using a trace material that damaged the mouths and sides of fish during the fight and nor should we. But in recent years there have been huge developments in the production of wire, and I now use the 30 lb titanium wire almost exclusively as it does not kink and lasts for an entire season. I'd still like to see the tackle trade come up with something better, however, and judging by the leaps forward being made in the manufacture of monofilament and braided lines, I think it won't be long before there is a more fish-friendly and practical alternative to steel wire.

Trace dimensions

Most of the traces in my bag are between eighteen and twenty inches long, with a few of fourteen to sixteen inches for free-roving livebait rigs. If the trace is too long with a livebaiting rig, the bait will be so far from the lead – which should be keeping it at the ideal depth – it may start riding up in the water. This can be counteracted by pinching a couple of swan shot on the trace to hold the bait down, but shorter traces solve the problem. The only ultra-long traces I use are for fishing the boulder-strewn waters of Scottish lochs, and then the traces will be twenty-four inches long, merely to provide a longer, abrasion-resistant link.

If I'm using an uptrace for paternostering – see the diagram in Chapter Nine on page 167 – to protect the line from being bitten through, the hook trace will be only about nine or ten inches and the uptrace the same. When livebaiting, the bait on a long trace can swim up in the water and tangle with the nylon above

CRIMPING OR TWISTING

As Shakespeare might have said, had he been an angler: to crimp or not to crimp, that is the question. Whether 'tis nobler to squeeze short sleeves of soft metal onto one's trace to secure hooks and swivels, or to twist the wire round itself after heating the end with a match.

I always crimp. It's stronger than twisting and has never let me down, though the way you crimp is important. I flatten the crimp in the middle, and don't flatten the ends, so that if the hooks or swivel get bent back during the fight, there's room for the wire to move freely. Crimp too tight to the ends and the wire can fracture.

I use copper crimps made by Abu and a pair of crimping pliers with teeth of various sizes to match the size of crimp. It's important to pass the wire through each crimp three times: once on the way to the hook, once on the way back from the hook, and then once again, with a short section of the free end

Left to right: twisted trace; crimped spinning or lure trace with large loop; trace crimped too closely to eye of treble which is likely to break; trace correctly crimped to swivel.

doubled back inside the crimp to tuck it out of harm's way. The end of a piece of wire is extremely sharp and capable of giving you a nasty cut if it catches your hand. It will also pick up weed and debris, so tuck everything in before you squeeze the crimp tight.

Perfect traces rolled up ready to go. I will take up to fourteen titanium traces with me, wound on a flexible rig roll and held in place with mapping pins. A cold river bank is no place for trace-making.

the uptrace. If a pike graps it then, it's goodbye to your rig, and perhaps goodbye to a pike, condemned to a lingering death. The traceshould also be shorter than any weak 'paternoster' link that runs from swivel to bomb. If the bait reaches the sanctuary of the bottom, it will lie still and defeat the object of livebaiting.

Trace-making is fiddly enough at home, but on the bank it's almost impossible, especially in cold weather. I take plenty of rigs, far more than I will need, wrapped around flexible Gordon Griffiths' rig rolls and pinned down with mapping pins. If I'm heading for a water, such as a weir pool, where on a good day a catch of a couple of dozen pike could be on the cards, I will take forty traces with me to allow for those that will get kinked or lost.

The only time I don't use rig rolls is when fishing in Scotland, or when it's raining, as rigs kept in a roll will get wet and have to be taken off and dried. For these occasions I use a plastic rig bin, which stops them getting wet and rusting.

Buy the best hooks

I've tried a lot of hooks in my time, but there are only two makes that have never let me down – Partridge and Owner Extra Strong in size 6 and 8 for both live- and deadbaiting. The size 6s are for jack deadbaits, and the size 8s are my standard hooks for mackerel, sardines, coarse fish and small livebaits.

I occasionally use Partridge Parrot Beak single hooks, through top and bottom lips of sink-and-draw baits, or through the root of the tail of a sardine, but I like the improved hooking capabilities that come from having two treble hooks. I also

Top: Wire traces with owner and Partridge hooks attached.

Above: Owner and lynx treble hooks make excellent stingers for large synthetic lures.

use the Parrot Beak single on traces for a trout livebait, using it with two trebles. The single goes in the dorsal fin, the bottom treble in the flank and the treble in the middle is left loose as a flier for better hooking.

When wobbling a trout deadbait, I use a size 4 or 6 single Parrot Beak through the top and bottom lips of the trout to retain it, and then push an elastic band over the point and past the barb to keep it in place. The other hook on the trace is a size 8 treble, which goes in the flank. It's important that the single hook goes through both lips of the trout, or the mouth will be forced open on the retrieve and presentation will suffer. If the mouth is open, the bait will spin, whereas I want it to flutter from side to side. And in snag-ridden areas, there is less chance of a single hook getting caught up than a treble, with its two free prongs.

I also use Partridge Grey Shadow hooks for the Niflor Teflon coating that stops them from rusting. They've got longer points, slightly bigger barbs and wider gapes, which makes them excellent for livebaiting as they help retain the bait far better than hooks with micro-barbs. I also use them for bigger coarse-fish deadbaits because they retain them better than the Extra Strong Outpoint trebles.

They are very good on plugs and spinners, which are prone to attract rust. Few plugs come with the right size and quality of hook attached, and one of the first things I do when I buy plugs is change the trebles. Some anglers claim hooks should not be changed on plugs because those fitted give the plug its fish-attracting action. Plug firms put on hooks of a reasonable price and quality, but no better, and I would always improve the hooks with something similar that doesn't impair the action.

Many anglers now use semi-barbed treble hooks in preference to fully barbed but I have lost too many fish on semi-barbed. With the rigs I use, a run is struck immediately in 80 per cent of situations. Pike won't be taking the bait deep into their throats and there shouldn't be any fear of fish damage. With my instant-strike rig, pike are generally hooked neatly in the corner of the mouth.

You might think that one swivel is as good as another, but eye design is what holds the key.

1: Diamond-eye swivels squeeze the line into a tight area at the base of the eye as it's being tied on, decreasing the diameter locally, which may lead to crack-offs.

2: I now use power swivels for nearly all of my pike fishing.

3: Snap links that work on the keyring principle are well made and shouldn't let you down…

4: … But you can't play safer than with a Mick McMahon design of link.

5: Berkley black barrel swivels are built to withstand a 60 lb pull.

6: Snap links on the loop and eye principle have lost me big fish.

Sturdy swivels

You wouldn't think swivels could vary much, but they do. Diamond-eyed swivels are bad news in my opinion, because there isn't enough room for line to seat itself. It gets squashed into a tight area at the base of the eye as it is being tied on, and when the knot is drawn together, that shortage of space decreases the diameter of the line locally and leads to crack-offs.

Good swivels should rotate under pressure, but a lot of them grate and don't have much mobility. A barrel swivel should have a snug fit between the eye's stem and barrel, so that dirt and grit can't get inside the barrel and cause wear. The ones I use are Berkley black barrel swivels or power swivels, which are 60 lb breaking strain.

A float for every occasion

To say that pike floats are a bit behind the times is rather like saying greenheart has probably had its day as a rod-building material. Pike float design is in its infancy. Look in a pike angler's tackle box and you will probably see two types of float – thick fat ones, and long thin ones. Imagine a match angler going fishing armed with just two types of float. 'I've got my thick fat ones and my long thin ones, so nothing'll get past me today!'

The concave surfaces of a fluted EVA foam float trap the current, sending it downstream more rapidly than a round-bodied float, imparting more movement to the bait than a standard float.

As every matchman knows, to float fish effectively you need a range in different shapes and sizes to catch fish in a variety of conditions and on several different waters. A pike angler is no different. His float has the job of taking a bait to where he wants to send it, acting as a bite indicator and supporting a bait in the water. There ought to be a huge range in the shops, enabling anglers to present baits perfectly, but the truth is, there are few different shapes for sale, and anyone who wants something a little different has to make his own.

That's what I do for most of my fishing. I tend to use small floats, as much of my fishing is deadbaiting, and floats for that style don't need to be big. *Fishing Gazette* 'bungs' have had their day. The only times I would use a big float are when fishing at range, when fishing on large, windswept waters like lochs or loughs, and in turbulent water below weirs, where visibility becomes a problem.

The colour depends on the direction of the sun and the intensity of the light. With the light coming from behind me or from one side of me, I usually opt for orange-topped or red-topped floats. I don't find yellow easy to see. When the light is coming straight towards me and everything is in silhouette, I go for black, and when it is late in the evening and the light is fading fast, I change to floats with isotopes, especially if I'm planning to fish on into the darkness.

But one thing all of my home-made floats have in common is a tough coating of two-pack epoxy resin, so that they will take all the knocks that occur when driving from water to water with rods strapped to the roof rack, or when they're lying in the bottom of the boat where they may get stepped on.

The fluted balsa or EVA float

These have an advantage over round-bodied floats in that it has concave surfaces, which help send a bait downstream against an upstream wind. With a fluted balsa, the current gets trapped in one or more of the flutes and sends the bait on its way. Fluted floats also give a bait a bit of movement, which adds to its pulling power. I use them in two-and-a-half-inch, four-inch and eight-inch sizes.

Fluted floats with concave surfaces are ideal when fishing rivers.

The round polystyrene float

This is a bit smaller than a golf ball, and is a sliding float used in still waters to hold up a live 3 oz to 4 oz trout or a deadbait. Some are made from ping-pong balls, which are cheap to buy and take paint well, making them very visible. Mine are red on top and brown on the bottom. I like to use them on backwaters of the Thames and the big marinas, where the flow is not strong and they can be used to carry a biggish bait slowly through a swim and right under the noses of hungry fish.

The cigar-shaped float

This is the one for trotting slowly in fast water. I use it as a sliding float for livebaiting. It's also good for fishing very deep water and tripping a bait through. Made of expanded polystyrene, mine are in three sizes, four to eight inches in length. I couple the size of the float to the size of the bait. For most of my fishing I use one of about four inches long. Too big a float and a pike can't pull it under; too small a float and you get false bite indications from the bait. At the lower extreme, I have presented a tiny roach or gudgeon for pike swirling through shoals of fry by using a two-inch cigar float taking a single swan shot.

Pike are very delicately balanced in the water and if a float is too big it will upset this balance when they mouth the bait and move away with it, pulling them off keel and causing them to drop it. Sometimes they will be so hungry they won't care, but on critical days when they are feeding half-heartedly, the size of the float can make a big difference.

Fluted float, self-cocking big water float, Eddie Turner plastic and trolling float.

The self-cocking float

For deadbait fishing on a Scottish loch I use these in a fat, cigar shape about seven or eight inches long and an inch and a half in diameter. They have to be this big to be seen above the waves. This design is attached bottom-end only as this makes them easier to cast long distances. Bottom-end attachment is too sensitive for livebait fishing, as the float gets pulled under and gives a lot of false indications. My self-cocking floats have a brass stem to add weight.

The sunken paternoster float

This is round, all-black, made of polystyrene, and of a size appropriate for the size of the livebait. It will hold a bait off the bottom where the pike can see it easily. However, there are ways of controlling the position of a bait without using a sunken paternoster.

This is one for special circumstances only, when a pop-up won't do the job, or for holding a bait in a known hotspot just beyond snags while keeping the line away from the tops of the obstructions.

The luminous float

If you haven't tried float legering at night, you haven't sampled one of the most exciting ways of catching pike. Seeing a luminous float slide away, and striking into a powerful fish somewhere down in the inky depths, adds a completely new dimension to your fishing.

My floats for this are cigar-shaped or round-bodied, depending on the location, painted with luminous paint and with slots drilled in them to take night lights – usually isotope Betalights because they last the longest and so are cheapest in the long run.

Balloons

Finally, although I don't use drifter floats, if I want to get a bait out quickly into unfished water and have the wind at my back, I will resort to taking a few balloons with me and using them to drift the bait out. They get out a lot quicker than with a drifter and, after I have struck the balloon from its paper-clip attachment, I can go round to the opposite bank at the end of the day and pick the balloons up.

Stainless steel deadbait wobble bars

A lot of anglers are frustrated inventors. If they're lucky, a tackle manufacturer may take an interest in the idea and offer to pay royalties on each one sold. I've been fortunate enough to have had a couple of home-made products I've used for years produced commercially. The stainless steel deadbait wobble bars and the deadbait support links are two examples.

I first used deadbait wobble bars in 1970 for fishing sink-and-draw. The early ones were made out of a length of mild steel cut to a size to suit the bait, had a hole drilled in them for the trace and were pushed inside the bait through the mouth. They were attached to the trace by a link of wire, which was fixed to the eye of the top treble, leaving both sets of hooks free to be pinned to the bait in places that gave it a good action. If the bait got lost, the wobble bar came back because it was firmly attached to the trace by wire. I've since used them to catch a huge number of pike, the biggest one 35 lb, which took a 4 oz brown trout fished sink-and-draw in three feet of water.

The advantages of having a weight inside the bait and not running on the line are that when you are reeling in, all of the action goes into the bait and not into a lead weight, which will swing from side to side. Leads make it difficult to cast accurately under trees, and have a habit of becoming snagged when fishing over boulders.

Above: With a stainless steel wobble bar, all of the action from the rod goes into the bait and not into a lead weight swinging loose on the line.

Below: A Cox & Rawle leger boom will prevent tangles when deadbaiting without creating resistance that might make a pike drop the bait.

You can fish at different depths and in restricted areas near to snags with a wobble bar, letting the bait flutter under obstructions, and when you hook a pike you are far more 'in touch' with the fish. It is particularly good for fishing in weir pools or anywhere where a lot of water needs to be covered. On gravel-bottomed rivers, a bait can be bounced along and made to look natural.

Dinsmore sell the stainless steel bars in 0.5 oz, 1 oz, 1.5 oz and 2 oz sizes for different sizes of bait, for working the bait deep or fluttering it across the surface. For a 5 oz roach I would use a 1 oz bar, and for an 8 oz chub a bar of 1.5 oz.

Deadbait support links

The deadbait support link, made by myself, is a very light, black plastic hook that takes all of the weight of the bait off the trace by using a spare loop of line, thus allowing the treble hooks to be pinned lightly into the bait and struck out cleanly. A full description is given in a Chapter 9, page 160.

Greys and Cox & Rawle running ledger booms and links.

Cox & Rawle leger booms

When the coarse fishing market can't provide me with what I want, I look to other branches of the sport, and this is how I came to use a sea fishing boom for pike. I wanted one that would prevent tangles when legering a livebait or deadbaiting in rivers. I don't like having a metal swivel running freely on the main line, causing abrasion.

The Cox & Rawle boom consists of a length of plastic tube through which the line runs. It offers less resistance to a taking fish than pulling line through the eye of a swivel. It's particularly useful on silty waters when you don't want the line and trace being pulled into mud by the lead. The lead is attached to a snap link at one end of the boom and the other end is stopped on the line by a bead and a swivel. I use 0.5 oz to 1.5 oz leads with it. It's the best anti-tangle boom I have come across. I don't know why they don't market it for freshwater fishing as well.

It's easy to overcomplicate rigs with a lot of unnecessary 'furniture' on the main line and trace, but unless the result is tangle free then your original aim won't be achieved.

The best in beads

Dinsmore make a huge selection of beads, but I use two – both black, one with a very small hole and used above a sliding float, so that it doesn't jump over the stop knot; and a larger one to keep a boom or lead clear of the knot where the main line is tied to the swivel of the wire trace. I use plastic and rubber, both of which work well, but I haven't found floating beads to be of any extra benefit.

Lots of leads

Leads, like anglers, come in all shapes and sizes: some slimline and built for speed, and others short and dumpy. The question is, do we need so many alternatives? The shape and size of the best lead are dictated by the contours of the swim to be fished, the strength of the flow, if any, and the distance to be cast. In some swims a quarter-ounce drilled bullet will suffice, but in others a 2.5 oz Arlesey bomb will not be enough.

Generally, I use Arleseys half-ounce up to 2.5 oz with link swivels attached. If I want to hold bottom in an open area, then I use a lead flattened by putting it in a vice and hitting it on both sides with a hammer. There are a multitude of shapes, powder coatings and anti-tangle devices, and no doubt some of them work, but I don't believe in complicating rigs unnecessarily because the less there is to a rig, the less there is to go wrong. I see very little advantage in using tubing. The leger boom mentioned is important, as it holds the lead away from the main line. But use whatever you are confident with, and worry about what does and doesn't work when things start to go wrong.

A weak link

Snap links come in two types; those for people who like to live dangerously, and those for people who play safe.

Some designs of snap link have been known to open when fish were being played. You need to look for links that cannot be pulled open by exerting pressure on the line. I will only use black Berkley Mick McMahon link swivels, which are Cross-lok designs and will never open by rod pressure alone.

Above left: Wobble bars and swivels.

Above right: Crimping pliers and crimping sleeves Greys.

Proof that the deadbolt support link works. A fish of 18 lb 8 oz caught at ultra-long range on a half mackerel.

I don't even use them for attaching plugs, when snap links are at their most useful. I prefer to form a large, open loop in the trace wire, going through the plug's eye, because the greater the amount of movement the lure is allowed, the better the action. Many anglers who use plugs and lures don't realise how much they are impeding the action of their artificials by using link swivels. A big loop is a lot more successful, believe me.

Weaker line

I always carry a spool of old, weak nylon, of about 8 lb breaking strain, for making the loops that lasso the tails of bait fish and support them on deadbait rigs, and also as a weak link to the lead when paternostering.

Boxes within boxes

A big box means peace of mind. Everything I need for the day goes into one big Plano box. It's well-made, and doesn't allow small items to jump from one compartment to another because the compartments fit snugly against the lid. It carries all of my terminal tackle for all my fishing, and I know that if I've got this box, I've got all the items I may need.

The box within the box is a Plano transparent one with individual compartments, each of which contains the necessary items for making up traces – trebles, crimps, swivels and deadbait support links on link swivels, as well as beads and anything else tiny that threatens to roll away if given too much space.

I take it with me in case of emergencies and can lift it out and take it indoors when the dreaded time comes to make some more traces.

Drop-in Plano tackle box which contains all of my terminal tackle.

I look at as many examples of one product as I can find, buy the best I can afford and look after it. If it's well made it will be a joy to use and will enhance the angling experience, if not your catches.

CHAPTER 4

TOOLS & ACCESSORIES

W HEN IT COMES TO ACCESSORIES there is as much opportunity for bewilderment as in any other area of tackle.

Go into your local specialist tackle supplier and you will enter an Aladdin's cave of camouflage-coloured luggage, electronic wizardry and success-rate-upping gadgetry all designed if not to catch fish, then at least to catch anglers. It would be simple for us to turn our backs on all of it and say that none of it will help put more fish on the bank, but the truth is that in enabling us to use our time on the bank more efficiently, these products do make a difference to our level of success. The knack is in being firm about what is and isn't needed, and then sorting the best and most reliable items from the dozens of similar items made by different companies.

Forceps, compass, Depth-o-plug and wire cutters.

I try to have a firm idea of what I want before I go into a tackle shop, and then match what is available to what I had in mind. Tackle dealers can be very persuasive and suggest that the alternatives they do have are just as good. You need to be brave, turn down something that is second best, and go elsewhere until you find what you need. I look at as many examples of one product as I can find, buy the best I can afford and look after it. If it's well made it will be a joy to use and will enhance the angling experience, if not your catches. Below is a list of what you would find if you rummaged around in my accessory bag.

Reuben Heaton depth-o-Plug and thermometers.

The Depth-o-Plug

Starting with the business end of the list, a Depth-o-Plug, produced by Reuben Heaton, is essential for anyone tackling a new water who doesn't want to resort to guesswork. It will help you to plumb depths to decide where to fish without having to resort to a pike float and sliding stop knot.

Basically, a Depth-o-Plug is a plastic tube with a scale of depth readings marked on the side. It goes on the end of your line and can be cast up to 70 yards. When it comes back, the level of the water inside the tube can be read against the scale to tell the depth at the spot where you have cast. You then pour out the water and cast elsewhere.

Reuben Heaton also produce a Depth-o-Thermometer which can be cast out, giving the angler very accurate temperature readings. On a new water I like to work my way round the major swims, measuring the depth at regular intervals from one side of the swim to the other and back towards me, looking for any sudden drop in depth or rise on to a plateau. Make a note of any variation, how far out and at what angle, and also jot down the average depth so that you know the deepest swims on the water, for when the weather turns cold. It's surprising how many anglers can't tell you what depth of water they are fishing in, or even which area of the lake is deep and which is shallow. Without this kind of information, you're relying on guesswork.

All of this work can be carried out in the close season, or when you have a couple of hours to spare after work. It needn't encroach on fishing time. This will give you an advantage over other anglers as you build up an intimate knowledge of the contours of the water to stand you in good stead later on.

Wide selection of alarms

Carp and pike anglers now have a bewildering array of bite alarms to choose from, with every imaginable function from simple red and green lights and a latching device that keeps them on after the line has stopped moving to 50-metre paging devices which allow you to nip into the bushes to answer the call of nature without missing a run.

I tried a lot of alarms before I picked one that was reliable, robust and provided me with everything I needed. Then I bought six of them and I've been using them ever since. That was thirteen years ago, and now they look bruised and battered, and have plenty of dents and scratches because they stay on my buzzer bars from one season to the next, but I wouldn't be without them. They are the original Optonic alarms converted by Delkim, and if you are buying alarms now, Delkim produces an alarm that is just as good. The battery can now be changed without dismantling the whole alarm.

Delkim bite alarms are probably the most reliable on the market.

The alarms take extension leads which run to a sounder box that I hang in my car for night fishing when I can park near the water in foul weather. But the sounder box certainly isn't an alarm clock for when I go to sleep, which for caring pike anglers is the nearest thing to a criminal offence. They have volume and tone controls for when I want to keep noise to a minimum. Then I will turn them down as low as I can and sit close by. On normal volume, and with regular use, I usually get twelve to fourteen weeks out of a set of batteries.

On gravel pits, where there is no flow and little debris to foul the line, I use Backbiter alarms and fish with the bale arms of my reels open. However, on rivers these keep getting set off by the current, so I use the Delkims and the Baitrunner facility on my reels with the bale arms closed.

Rod rests and buzzer bars

Most of the time my alarms are attached to rod rests rather than buzzer bars, because it is only when I have a great deal of space, such as on a large, open gravel pit, with pure gravel banks running for hundreds of yards, that I can angle the lines anywhere I want from the side-by-side arrangement without interference from bankside vegetation.

Stainless steel Butt-cups hold rods firmly in position.

On gravel pits and still waters with no flow or debris, anglers like Eddie Turner use backbiter alarms.

My buzzer bars are made of stainless steel, which takes the knocks. The front bar measures fourteen inches and the rear bar ten inches. This gives me a V formation, with the rods pointing at different angles.

I like to keep the tips of the rods apart to cut down on tangles. When a fish kites towards the second rod, I have a few seconds more to sink the line. I like to have the rod tip pointing towards the bait, to cut down on line drag through sharp angles, but angled rods mean I can position baits further apart.

Overall, I prefer to use single rod rests, because I am less restricted than if I have the rods side by side. A lot of anglers who use buzzer bars let the direction they're set dictate where they will cast. Or if they do put a bait down the bank, the rod's still in their buzzer bar set-up, too far away. A pike will make a beeline for bankside vegetation, and may become snagged before they can apply any pressure to stop it.

The rear rod rest heads I use are stainless steel and U-shaped, made by a friend. They fit the rod butts exactly, so that the rods can't be pulled into the water if the line gets jammed or wrapped round the handle.

My banksticks are made from both aluminium and fibreglass and extend to 36 inches. I won't buy telescopic bank sticks with thumbscrews, as these will seize, break or rust sooner or later and become a source of irritation. Berkley and Solar Tackle sell a telescopic bank stick that locks on a friction principle, so the height can be varied without the need for knobs or attachments.

Eddie holding a 40 lb still water pike.

Carry a notebook

You may not fancy the idea of taking a notebook with you when you go fishing, but if you want to build up an accurate picture of a water's contours, you need to note down the data rather than rely on your memory.

I draw a map of the water and its surrounding area, including inlets, outlets, submerged islands and any feature that will help pinpoint a productive spot on the lake. If I'm keeping an eye on a water where excavation work is still in progress, there may be a chance to take pictures of it before it fills with water, which will be a great advantage in years to come. When it comes to knowing a water's contours, even an echo sounder can't compete with a chance to see a gravel pit before it is flooded.

The weather can help you to get to know a water better. Occasionally you will get a mixture of sunshine and cloud, with the sun bursting through the cloud momentarily at just the right angle to illuminate the contours of a clear water, showing underwater features you didn't know were there. With a notebook at hand you can add these to your plan and investigate them on future visits.

As you catch fish and spot others in the margins, make a note of where you saw or caught them, at what time of day, in what conditions, in which month of the year and on what bait – even down to the water temperature. They need only be brief notes, but they will be enough to point you in the right direction in the future.

Lost without a compass

One of the best ways of locating fish on a gravel pit is to head for the north-east corner, for reasons explained fully in Chapter 7, yet finding these banks will be a problem without a compass. Few anglers, even good ones, carry one, yet you can't tell wind direction accurately without a compass, nor whether a bank is sheltered from cold, easterly winds. Add an arrow pointing north to your map of the water, so that you can include compass bearings in your calculations of where to fish given the wind direction over the previous few days.

When you've decided which bank to try, move in with the Depth-o-Plug and find out if you've got the right depth of water and if there's a feature that may hold pike.

Sunglasses and hat

Sunglasses have a threefold use for anglers, apart from making us look hip and cool. They protect our eyes from reflected glare, they shield them from hooks and other sharp objects swinging around near our heads or flying back towards us when we lose a fish at the net, and if they are polarised, they enable us to cut out surface glare when spotting pike and hotspots. In theory we could do without them, but it's surprising how much of a headache you can get from looking at water all day long. It's a combination of the length of time – anything up to sixteen hours a day in Scotland in summer – the strain of concentrating on a float and the problems caused by glare on the water's surface that cause the headaches and make polarising glasses essential for many fishing situations. There are a lot of good ones around these days, albeit at a price, with Ray-Bans and Optix being as well made as any.

To get the most from the polarising effect you should also wear a broad-brimmed hat or cap, which will shade your eyes and keep your head warm. Baseball caps are excellent for this, and the best ones have neck protectors to keep the sun off your neck. I like to wear a white hat in summer, to reflect the sun, and a camouflage one in winter, but I know some people are sticklers for always turning out in drab colours from head to toe. I was once like that myself. I went through a phase a few years ago of painting every item of tackle I had NATO green, right down to my flask. I even gave my stainless buzzer bars a lick of paint, too, but you live and learn.

BAROMETERS & THERMOMETERS

There's a direct correlation between atmospheric pressure changes, temperature changes and the chances of a successful day's fishing. A glance at the barometer and thermometer hanging on the garage wall every time you go out, and a note of what it read when you were successful, will give you an idea of the best conditions for fishing. Some people have garden ponds and peer into those before leaving to see how active the fish are. Others take the temperature when they arrive, and set great store by the readings at different times of day.

Certain waters respond best in particular temperatures and pressure cycles, and until you make a note of these and compare them with your record of catches, you won't fully appreciate how the pieces of the jigsaw fit together. There won't be one condition that brings pike on the feed on all waters. Each one will be different. But when you know which water will fish best under what conditions you can improve your success rate by letting past experiences of pressure and temperature dictate where you go and when, and what techniques to use.

All the information you can put together will help with the overall picture, and the longer you carry out this research, and the more thorough you are, the sooner you will see a pattern emerging. The most successful anglers only go out when they know conditions are right, and while they may miss out on an odd maverick fish or two that doesn't obey the rules, they will save themselves a lot of time and trouble fishing when nothing is feeding.

After a while you get to know instinctively when conditions are just right, and you are going to catch something. If that happens to be in midweek when you have only a couple of hours to spare, so be it. It is better to fish for two hours when conditions are right than to wait for the weekend and fish all day when they are not.

The trusty Packaseat

Carrying gear to the waterside isn't a problem on a small still water, when a simple carry-all can be used. But for river fishing, when a roving approach is essential, you may only be in a swim for a matter of minutes and move swims dozens of times in a day. Your selection of tackle is scaled down because you're covering several miles of river, but you still need some sort of bag and perhaps a simple seat.

I have a Packaseat, now seventeen years old, and it does both jobs in one. Made on a lightweight aluminium frame, it is large enough to take plastic boxes of terminal tackle, rig rolls, scales, sacks and so on, with pockets for bank sticks, but is still light enough to be swung over a shoulder without weighing me down. The bait – half a dozen mackerel, a dozen sardines and a dozen freshwater fish – also goes inside. As I'm wearing waterproofs, the umbrella can stay at home.

A large part of the enjoyment of river fishing is travelling light and casting as you walk, unencumbered by bedchairs and rod holdalls. Anglers used to fishing still waters often can't make the transition to the roving approach required on rivers. They try to scale down their stuff but they can't bear to leave anything behind. Only when they've walked four miles and are too worn out to stand do they find the resolve to leave some of it behind on future trips or go back to fishing still waters.

More enjoyment can be had by travelling light and casting as you walk, without the clutter of rod holdalls and bedchairs.

Echo sounders and fish-finding devices

I wouldn't be without a fish finder when tackling a big water I know little or nothing about. It's like having a third eye that can see beneath the waves. I use mine to sort out swims on vast strips of water like Scottish lochs or Irish lakes, or very big sections of river.

Most current models come in 20° or 53° transducers, though I find a 20° beam too narrow to give a useful picture, particularly over shallow water. The 53° gives a far bigger window. Sounders work by sending ultra-sonic signals through a transducer mounted on the back of a boat. These bounce back from whatever is below and return to the transducer to be translated into patterns on an LCD screen. Only trial and error will teach you how to interpret what you are looking at.

A fish finder is a must when tackling any big water.

Some offer 3-D viewing, and the latest models have a side scanner that picks up signals from the side of the boat, increasing the area covered, and show objects on screen as hollow fish. Most of them have a grey-line feature that enables the user to tell how solid the bottom is, from soft mud to hard rock or something in between. Their built-in simulators allow someone unfamiliar with them to practise using them indoors until they are proficient enough to benefit when they get out on to the water.

From the LCD readout you can pick out a lot of features. Often, the places that look good from the bank turn out to be too deep or too shallow or have a bottom that isn't to the pike's liking. In lochs, I look for drop-offs near to a feature, or gentle slopes in rivers, and search the area around them or work down both banks of a river, putting the sounder on the left and exploring that side of the river and then coming back downstream on the far side with the sounder on the right.

Pike love snaggy areas because they give them cover from which to spring an ambush, and the closer you can get to these areas without losing tackle, the better. In rivers I like to fish around weed beds, lily pads and debris left over from old weirs, which I can locate with the fish finder. I don't use it to find pike, because there's no way of telling what species you are looking at. You might be dropping your deadbait in the middle of a run of game fish or a shoal of gudgeon.

In the early days, I wrote off areas that didn't show fish on the screen. On one occasion, I drifted over a perfect drop-off on Loch Awe, found nothing, and was tempted to move off to another feature. But I decided to stay put because I knew fish fed there at a certain time in the morning, before moving back out into open water. Right on cue, pike started arriving from other areas of the loch, visiting the swim to feed before moving back out into open water.

Fish finders are only as good as the person operating them, and getting good is a matter of experience. They are no more a short cut to success than learning to cast a long way or devising a new way of presenting a bait. Using them successfully is a skill that's well worth acquiring, and I have no qualms about taking one with me.

Fish-holding features come out of the blue

I use an echo sounder when a bankside feature suggests there could be a fish-holding contour in that area, but I also like to have it switched on while I'm just travelling up-river, because features can turn up in the middle of nowhere.

I once came across an area with a sudden drop in depth on the Thames, where the bottom went from seven feet to fifteen. This depression held a massive head of bream, and it has produced some excellent catches of pike for me, but it was in an otherwise completely featureless and barren stretch of river. I later found out it was the site of an old weir pool that had been dismantled years ago, but if I hadn't had the echo sounder switched on as I motored upstream I would never have found it.

The two models I use at the moment are the Max portable and the 561, both of which can be obtained from the SM Group (Europe) Ltd in Plymouth. They are very reliable, totally water-resistant and very robust. Fitting them is easy and mastering the basics is simple. The real skill comes with practice. Mine runs off a sealed-for-life, 12-volt motorcycle battery, from which it will work for two or three days before needing a recharge.

Is a downrigger worth the outlay?

If you are seriously into trolling – and there are a lot worse ways of searching a large expanse of seemingly featureless water – it may be worth investing in a downrigger.

Basically a downrigger is a device that attaches to the gunwale of a boat, and has a weight that will take a trolled bait down to a pre-set depth and keep it there. It is at its most useful on a concrete-banked, man-made reservoir where the bottom is even, such as the two bowls at Farmoor. If the downrigger has to be adjusted continually to negotiate changing contours it can be awkward to use. I have one that slots into a platform I built on my boat, because I have found downriggers work better when attached at the transom of the boat rather than the gunwales.

On one occasion at a trout reservoir, the pike were feeding 20 feet down in 40 feet of water, and anyone who had a downrigger and could troll a bait at that depth was more successful than those anglers pulling their baits through that feeding layer from below the fish, and only catching one or two.

Canon make the best ones, but they are rather expensive. You'll need to part with £300 for a really good one. This will have a control on it that allows you to regulate how deep your bait is running, something that cannot be achieved with certainty when trolling without such a device. A quick-release stacker, which is a pincer rather like a clothes peg, keeps the line attached to the lead ball at the right depth until a fish pulls it free.

Considering the financial outlay, you will need to be using a downrigger a lot to make it worth the investment. The opportunities to fish even-bottomed waters for pike are rare, and even when they do present themselves it is rarely in the warm weather needed for pike in such deep waters to be active and intercepting a moving bait.

Binoculars for a clearer picture

Binoculars aren't just to watch the wildlife in between action. It's surprising how much more you can observe through a pair of 'bins'. Grebes feeding in one area at distance, fish topping or being chased, or pike swirling, are all valuable clues. If there's a big head of fry on the water and the grebes are staying in one spot, it's a reasonable bet that one or two good pike are around.

On warmer days you may see a dorsal fin out of the water at the back of an island, especially in a flat calm, or a fish strike in the weed, and if you're float fishing you can fish at longer distance without eye strain using binoculars. In the course of a long day it also makes a welcome break to look around the water now and then just to see what's going on.

Mine are fairly cheap Tasco 8 x 30 zip-focus ones. They do the job and stand up to getting knocked around, trodden on and dropped, which happens, inevitably,

MAPS FOR PEOPLE GOING PLACES

You wouldn't expect to find your way around London without a map, yet people go afloat on vast waters like Loch Lomond without one and are surprised when they get into trouble. They forget where they've left the car, or they lose their sense of direction, or perhaps the mist comes down and they go round in circles without seeing land for hours.

There is an excellent admiralty map of Loch Lomond (see Chapter 15, Lochs & Loughs) that charts all the depths and is very accurate. I also use Ordnance Survey maps for any area of the country I am investigating, and these are sufficiently detailed to allow me to pinpoint a water.

For river fishing, Stanfords' map of the Thames shows slipways, mooring points, car parks, lock gates, weirs, access points, footpaths – in fact everything you could want to know when tackling the river as a newcomer. There are other maps that show the features

Maps of Loch Lomond, Glen Orchy and Scotland.

of rivers like the Hampshire Avon, Dorset Stour and River Wye in a similar way.

I coat my maps in clear vinyl so that it doesn't matter if they get wet. As maps are always being bent and folded, this also adds considerably to their life span.

when you're fishing. I don't think it's worth buying expensive binoculars because they come in for so much abuse, but it's definitely worth having a pair of some sort.

The ultimate landing net

Too many anglers have landing nets that will let them down at a critical moment. They wouldn't dream of using old line or rusty hooks, but they keep using the same shop-bought landing net with its frail, worn front cord, and risk losing a big fish when it snaps, leaving them without a net.

I gave up on shop-bought landing nets years ago, and made myself a sturdy net that can be repaired at the water. It has served me well ever since. The arms are made of solid fibreglass, and the spreader block of solid aluminium. Hollow glass-fibre arms snap or get trodden on, and nylon spreader blocks break. I've glued a cat's eye to the block for ease of location at night, and have a slot for an isotope for the same reason.

The arms measure 48 inches each and are made from the tops of two boat rod blanks. The ends of both have aluminium tips glued into them and a cord of 60 lb to 80 lb nylon-coated wire – which will stand up to being prodded into gravel – secured in an aluminium cap that screws on the end. If the cord should break, it can be repaired on the bank by unscrewing one of the ends, unlike shop-bought nets, which cannot be saved. The aluminium tips have two pieces of plastic tubing that bend over them to stop them sticking through the mesh and damaging the net. The net is minnow mesh rather than bream mesh, which is heavy in flowing water, but the finer the mesh, the easier it is to get hooks out. Mine is three feet deep and doubles as a landing net for eel fishing.

The screw-in handle is about five feet long and made of hollow fibreglass, as carbon fibre is more expensive and unnecessary, with an alternative two-and-a-half foot handle for boat fishing. If you still want to struggle on with the cord net you are using, invest in a repair kit, so that if the cord breaks while you're on the bank, at least you won't be left without a net.

When I'm fishing a lure or sink-and-draw style and I'm likely to land a lot of fish that have a flying treble hanging loose outside their mouth, I use a net with a border of three or four inches of a smooth, vinyl material around the rim, which doesn't catch on treble hooks. It was introduced by Abu last year and is the first purpose-made lure net with anti-snag material on the market.

Dual-purpose unhooking mats

If I can get an item to do two jobs instead of one, I will. Keep sacks can double as unhooking mats on a reasonably soft surface like grass, and save on space when you're on the move. The best sort are zip sacks, which avoid all the fuss and time-wasting of draw cords and knots. A couple of firms make unhooking mats

Solid aluminium spreader block and solid fibreglass arms. I gave up on shop-bought landing nets and made myself a sturdy one that is built to last.

and sacks combined, and of these, ones by Wychwood and Specialist Angling Supplies are among the best.

Scales that are man enough

These should be accurate, easy to use and compact, as well as weighing to British record weight. Mine are 120 lb Reuben Heaton, which are all of these things. I've yet to catch a pike that takes them to their limit.

But the future could well lie with digital scales, which are capable of weighing down to hundredths of an ounce. Both Berkley and Salter have brought out a set that weigh in lb and oz as well as kilos. They are strong and accurate and should last a lifetime if looked after.

Sling as a safety precaution

So long as it's big and soft and has two pieces of strong cord attached firmly, any weigh sling will do the job. Mine is made of nylon with a rubber lining and will weigh a fish of over 40 lb. If a fish is particularly large or lively I like to put it back in the sling after weighing and photographing it, and use this to carry it down to the water. It only takes a trip or a stumble with a fish in your hands to lead to an accident that could cost the fish its life.

Reuben Heaton scales and weigh sling.

Essential forceps

In the words of the advert, 'Don't leave home without them'. The safety of the fish you catch depends on your having at least one pair of artery forceps to remove hooks from gristly corners of mouths and inaccessible parts of the throat. My 8-inch and 12-inch forceps go with me on every trip. Both are of the straight kind, as I can't bear curved forceps. Have them ready to hand, use them quickly and get the fish back as soon as you can.

Invaluable knife and scissors

If you're preparing deadbaits like mackerel on the bank you'll need a very sharp knife to do the job. The old saying that it's easier to cut yourself with a blunt knife than a sharp one is very true. A sharp knife requires little effort, so there's less force involved and less likelihood of a slip and an accident.

My teeth will bite through light nylon but I draw the line when it comes to 20 lb, and so does my dentist. A strong, sharp pair of scissors is well worth having.

Hand towel for messy tasks

Some people think nothing of chopping up a mackerel, throwing the head and guts into the margins by hand, and then tucking into their sandwiches. I'm not one of them. I may fish for a week at a time in Scotland, sleeping under the stars, but I still preserve a little self-respect. I always take a towel with me to clean my hands after preparing bait and handling fish. Apart from the hygiene aspect, wet hands on a cold day are as much fun as toothache.

Hands-free torch and headlamp

A hands-free light source makes a big difference when you're night fishing, for everything from unhooking fish to brewing tea. Petzl makes some excellent ones, in Mini, Medium and Mega sizes, with battery packs and headbands. The Medium size seems to have the best battery life. All are waterproof and have a spare bulb in the torch head. I've used them for ten years and would recommend them heartily.

A powerful lamp attached to a motorcycle battery can be an aid to fish location if used in the clear, shallow water of a gravel pit after dark. When you turn on the lamp, pointing it directly down into the water from a boat in the shallows or from the bank, fish big and small are caught in its beam and stunned for a few seconds, like rabbits in a headlight beam. They don't move, and in up to fifteen feet of water you can see several pike huddled in a hotspot that would be well worth trying another time. You even have time to guess their size before they move off. I once found a feature well out in a gravel pit that held six 20-lb pike. I know they were that size because I caught four of them the next day.

This tactic works best from a boat because the water is just a little bit deeper. It needs to be clear, though, but in the right conditions it's surprising how much it will pick up. I will only use it as a last resort, though, when I'm really struggling on a water. I can see the purists among you wincing at the thought of chasing after fish with a powerful lamp, but is a light source any more unreasonable than a boat, for instance? Only you can decide whether or not it's ethical, but if it means the difference between success and failure on a difficult water where location is the key, it takes a strong man to ignore it.

The pike's a victim of a bad press. If he looked as cute and cuddly as a baby seal there wouldn't be a problem. The irony of the image most people have of pike, however, is that, far from being indestructible, armour-plated warriors, they are probably the most delicate of coarse fish.

CHAPTER 5

PIKE

A FRAGILE QUARRY

PIKE HAVE GOT AN IMAGE PROBLEM. It's not their fault, but somewhere along the line people – the non-angling public in particular – have got it into their heads that they are Britain's nearest thing to crocodiles. Tales abound of these monsters of the deep engulfing ducklings, small dogs and the legs of swimmers: myths of huge, black-hearted fish from whom nothing and no one venturing into the water is safe. The only good pike is a dead pike, and anyone brave enough to catch and kill such a tyrant is a modern St George slaying a dragon.

To many, the image of pike is of a razor-toothed crocodile. But removed from the water they are extremely vulnerable.

And the myth persists even among experienced anglers, who should know better. Some matchmen still kill every pike that comes near them, and small boys step on them or kill them rather than face removing the hooks from their fearsome jaws, lined with row upon row of razor-sharp teeth.

The pike's a victim of a bad press. If he looked as cute and cuddly as a baby seal there wouldn't be a problem. The irony of the image most people have of pike, however, is that, far from being indestructible, armour-plated warriors, pike are probably the most delicate of coarse fish. To everyone, anglers included, they look big and powerful, but the truth is that they can't stand rough handling. When removed from the water they are extremely vulnerable, especially in inexperienced hands. And the bigger the pike, the more vulnerable it is.

When to strike

Pike anglers have to take their share of the blame for damaging pike. Part of the problem of their quarry's suffering stems from the fact that pike anglers use big baits that have to be turned by the pike through ninety degrees before they can be swallowed, and so the 'bites' or runs can't be struck immediately. In most instances, runs need to be left for a few seconds to allow the pike to engulf the bait.

There will always be a freak fish that takes a bait straight down, either out of habit or hunger. On some days, pike will wolf baits back, and on others they will rush off some distance with them before swallowing, especially if they have competition from other, perhaps bigger, pike. You can never know for certain how a pike will behave and what mood it will be in, and so accidents are inevitable.

I give pike no more than five to ten seconds before I strike, whether it's a screaming run or just a twitch, but even that can be too long. Judging the strike is a very individual thing. It's something that inexperienced anglers have to learn, water by water, and a certain proportion of the pike they hook are going to suffer because of it. Any system of trial and error will always produce its casualties.

I have fished for pike for most of my life and built up enormous respect for them. I would rather lose a pike, no matter how big, than deeply hook it. I don't like damaging fish, and having to retrieve hooks from deep inside a pike spoils my enjoyment because I have caused suffering – the last thing I want to do. If a big fish throws the hooks and gets free, it can always be caught again, but one that is damaged may be lost for ever.

It isn't the same in carp fishing. Carp don't run the same risk, because single hooks are used and the strike is instant. Indeed, the fish often pricks itself when a bolt rig is being used, and the angler merely finishes the job by pulling the hook home. Treble hooks and time delays are unique to pike fishing, but the caring pike angler will find a way to avoid damaging his quarry.

Why does it happen?

There are three main reasons why pike are deeply hooked:

- Because the run was not struck early enough;
- Poor bite indication or detection;
- A poor rig, with hooks placed too far down a deadbait.

You alone can decide when to strike, and you must examine your motives for waiting longer than normal. As far as bite detection goes, you owe it to your quarry to use reliable alarms with fresh batteries, and to stay close enough to your rods to reach them quickly.

If you use Backbiter alarms, you should fish a tight line to the run clip so that it will sound at even the slightest dropback run and respond by releasing the line to even a small pluck, before a fish has time to swallow your bait. There are times when that is all the indication you get, and if you don't get a sign that there is interest in your bait, everything may have been swallowed by the time you realise you've got a run.

That leaves rigs, and this is the area that I looked at when trying to overcome the problem of occasional deep-hooked fish. If a rig could be devised that could be struck almost instantly, swallowed baits would be a thing of the past.

I would rather lose a pike, no matter how big, than deep hook it. Causing suffering to one is the last thing I want to do.

FISHING AT RANGE

We needed a rig that could be struck almost instantly, which would turn those aborted takes into captured fish. It was a question of where to place the hooks, so that they could gain a hold in the pike's mouth immediately the bait was picked up.

Fishing at range can also cause a delay to the strike, either through the amount of time it takes to wind down to the fish, or because the strike is ineffectual. A proper striking technique is needed at long range if a fish isn't to gain an extra few seconds and swallow the bait.

After a few seconds, wind down hard, point the rod towards the bait and make a sweeping strike, bringing the tip of the rod from the surface of the water upwards. This will pick up any slack line and take a considerable amount of stretch out of it, too. The clutch should be locked solid to avoid any slipping of the spool, which would lessen the impact.

One strike may not be enough at range. The process may need to be repeated to keep in touch with the fish, by pointing the rod at the bait again, winding down and making a second, full sweep. Only then will you be in full contact with a properly-hooked pike.

At close range, with a softer through-actioned rod, strikes are more of a pull than a sweep, to absorb the shock. Anything more than that can lead to a crack-off on the strike, especially if the fish moves away from you as the hooks go home.

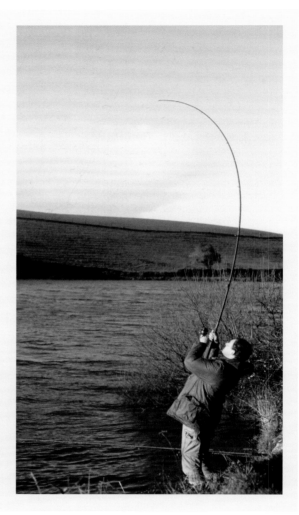

Protection for pike

The motives for developing the instant-strike rig did not spring purely from a need for conservation. Pike on one of the waters I fished with friends were becoming cautious after they had been caught a few times. They would pick up a bait, swim a short distance, then drop it.

The traditional positioning of hooks in a bait owes more to supporting the bait's weight in the cast than hooking a pike on the strike, and doesn't use treble hooks to their full potential.

I've never been happy with the depth to which hooks have to be impaled in a bait in order to keep it in place during the cast. It takes an almighty strike to then pull those hooks clear and into a pike's bony mouth when a run materialises, and at range, it is difficult to apply enough force even to pull the hooks clear of the bait.

We had noticed that a large proportion of the pike we played and lost still had the bait in their mouth, attached to one or more of the trebles. It made me realise that unless the hooks were struck clear of the bait they often failed to take hold in the mouth of the fish, and that if I could find a way of supporting the weight of the bait by another means, the hooks could be nicked lightly into the bait and struck clear. I could also choose where to position the hooks so that an instant strike could be made.

The best way we found of supporting the weight of the bait was with a large loop of strong line. This was passed over the tail of the deadbait with a couple of half hitches to hold it in place. The other end of the loop was passed through

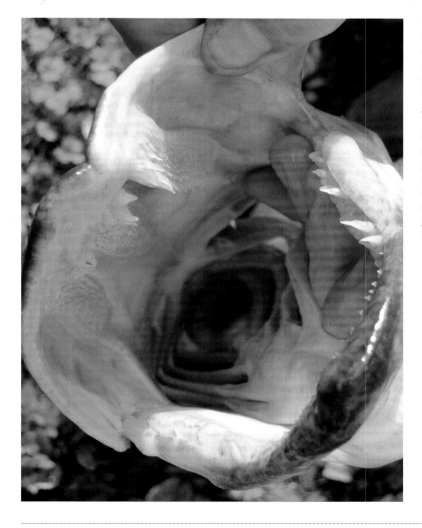

With hundreds of teeth in their armoury, pike don't take any prisoners when their powerful jaws clamp shut. The teeth in the lower jaw puncture the prey's internal organs and the rows of smaller teeth in the upper jaw hold the victim firmly.

one of the eyes of the swivel at the top of the wire trace, and held in place with a piece of folded, soluble PVA tape. The PVA was in place because we didn't want a permanent attachment to the top of the trace, which might get in the way of the strike, but we needed something that would support the bait on the cast.

One early problem was that a lightly hooked bait could get pulled off the hooks when retrieved through weed, providing pike with free meals. There are times when a pike will pick up only one bait all day, so we wanted it to be the one we were using, not one that we had lost. We found a way to avoid leaving the bait behind; by passing the trace through the loop of line attached to the bait, so that when the PVA dissolved and the strike was made, the loop slipped down and caught on the trace and the bait came back.

At the start we used a pair of size 2 Edgar Sealey Parrot Beak single hooks on the wire trace, but lost a lot of fish on the strike. But when we switched to trebles the success rate improved enormously. A pike's mouth is more than a match for single hooks. The bony surfaces offer few hook-holds, and you need more than one point to find a purchase.

But the principle worked. The hooks came out of the bait easily and into the fish, and by positioning them further along the bait, nearer the head, we were able to strike early and get a hook-hold. We could also cast soft baits like sardines further without the hooks pulling out. A few turns of fuse wire around the root of the tail made a holding place for the loop of line.

The only later modification was to switch from PVA tape to a purpose-made deadbait support link at the top of the trace, which supports the loop much better and brings a welcome end to fiddling with soluble tape with wet hands on rainy nights.

Livebaits need longer

No rig is completely 'instant strike', though. The only times when I've stood holding a rod and wound down and struck straight away have been when fishing a tiny livebait in Blenheim, and on Theale Lagoon when fish were preoccupied with taking fry, and then it was because they were engulfing the bait instantly.

In most cases, deadbaits tend to be swallowed sooner than livebaits. Pike know that a fish is dead and is not going to escape, and so they pick it up to swallow it straight away, whereas a livebait has to be caught and killed by grabbing it across the width of its body.

A fish taken head-on is less likely to be wounded fatally at the moment of being seized. Taking a food fish sideways enables a pike to puncture the internal organs, which are located along the belly, with the longer teeth of the movable lower jaw, while the smaller teeth of the fixed upper jaw act as a grip. Only then, when the fish has been killed, can it be turned to be swallowed, usually head first.

For this reason, takes while livebait fishing need to be given a little longer, say fifteen to thirty seconds. The bigger the livebait, the longer you may need to wait for the pike to take and turn it. Occasionally, when I have been fishing with a big roach or bream as bait, I've given runs a bit longer, but if you've ever seen a big pike taking a live fish you'll realise it can make short work of its prey. It may seize and wound a fish before it turns it to swallow its prey, but this happens quickly, before the fish can escape or another pike can move in and threaten to steal the meal.

Watching film of pike feeding in slow motion, I have seen that if the food fish is facing the pike as it approaches, it will try to dodge to the left or right of the pike to avoid being caught. The moment it turns away it is taken most easily, while it is side-on to the pike. Very few fish go upwards and over the pike's head, which is their best means of escape. It's nature's way of providing pike with enough sustenance, just as nature makes roach shoal up for safety in numbers.

Jack deadbaits

The physical size of a 2 lb or 3 lb jack pike bait dictates that any pike eating it has to be given longer, and I have waited from thirty seconds to two or three minutes for a fish to take one properly, depending on what the pike is doing with the bait.

The big difference between a take on a small deadbait and one on a jack pike is that successful hooking relies on your interpretation. When a pike takes a jack it sends vibrations up the line, often quite violent ones, and with experience these can be used to judge what is happening to the bait, and what the pike is doing. At some stage during the head-shaking and jerking on the end, there comes a moment when you just know that the bait is about to be swallowed, and you have to act fast.

The length of time this takes to happen varies from water to water, with the seasons, and with the mood of the fish. Sometimes pike will take the bait back to their lie and turn it and begin to swallow it. I wait for the run to stop, and I've known that to be 80 yards or more. Then I wind down gently to the fish so that I can feel the savage mouthing actions and get an indication of when swallowing is beginning to commence. There are exceptions to every rule, and I have had pike swallow jacks on the spot before now, so you need to be on your toes. No two fish will react in the same way, and no two takes are ever alike.

When a fish runs with a bait, be it a jack pike or a half mackerel, it usually goes directly away from you or, if you are fishing well out, straight towards you. You need to be sure that the bite indication system you choose will register both types of run.

Pressurised pike

Delayed striking isn't the only way that pike may suffer at the hands of unthinking anglers. To suggest that fish suffer from stress may seem like a fanciful notion to many, but there is no doubt that pike will not tolerate overfishing. If pike are caught over and over again and harried, their growth is inhibited. You can see it happen whenever a new water that was previously closed or restricted to pike anglers opens its doors. The first people on the water enjoy the cream of the sport, but then catches tail off sharply as fish restrict their choice of food and feeding times to avoid being caught. On a trout water I fished, the pike started by being caught on deadbaits, then switched to livebaits, and finally restricted their feeding to night time. The fish were still there, but bankside disturbance, baits

An upper twenty on display before it succumbed to angling pressure.

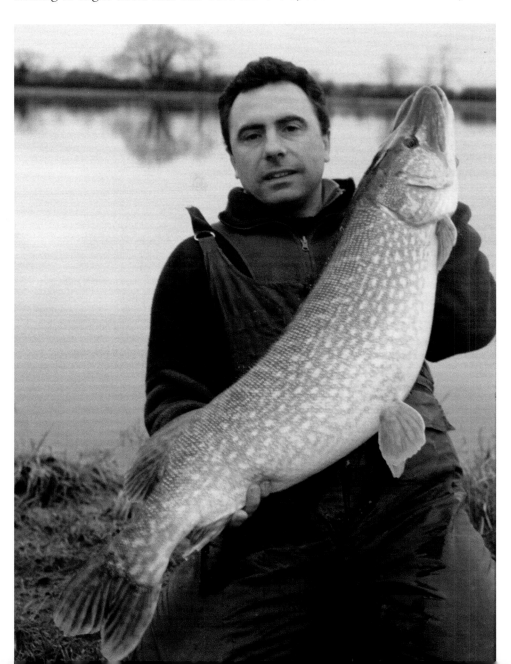

crashing into the water and boats being rowed up and down all contributed to the spoiling of sport.

That's why I don't like fishing public waters. When the Oxford pits became fished really hard, I turned to waters that were more wild and which held pike that hadn't been caught before. I'm not interested in pike that have been caught lots of times by other anglers, only in fresh, uncaught fish.

So what will I do when all of the local gravel pits are being heavily fished? I will turn to the river, which has wild areas that have not seen an angler for years. There is enough water to keep me going until the end of my days, and provide me with good sport and a sense of the unexpected while gravel pit anglers are fishing shoulder-to-shoulder.

At the same time, I keep in touch with the gravel pit grapevine to find out which waters are becoming available. I have no more access to private waters than anyone else, but if I see a likely-looking water that has been left fallow, or hear of one that has potential, I will contact the gravel company to see if I can gain access.

If I can find two or three likely-looking waters, I will concentrate my efforts on these rather than try to spread myself too thinly by fishing a large number inconsistently. It can take as many as three seasons to get the best from a new water.

On a gravel pit still being worked, pike can take refuge.

I have been known to find waters on Ordnance Survey maps and, if they look of a suitable age, find out who owns them and ask politely if I can fish. It's part of the challenge, and fishing a 'virgin' water is a unique and exciting experience. I wouldn't swap these waters for any number of over-fished venues, no matter what their record for big pike.

Private waters are fished on trust, and that's a trust I wouldn't abuse. I have permission to fish three or four extremely good waters, but I do so sparingly. I may only fish them three or four times a season because they just can't stand the pressure, even though no one else fishes them except me.

When you are looking at why pike become stressed by being fished for by large numbers of anglers, you need to examine the place of pike in the underwater world. It is the supreme predator, having evolved over millions of years, the oldest fossil remains, found in western Canada, dating back at least 60 million years. Remains in North Norfolk show there have been pike in Britain for at least 500,000 years, and they have few natural enemies. They used to be taken by osprey, but if you see one of those once in a lifetime you can consider yourself privileged. Pike are at the top of the ecological pyramid, and as such are more vulnerable to what can best be described as emotional stress. The more supreme the predator, the more harm it does to subdue that creature, and to make it aware that it isn't in command. I believe it's like caging a lion.

Less fishing space is better

Pike caught several times will change their feeding habits and seek out a place of refuge, but many gravel pits and lakes offer 'unrestricted access' to their banks. It makes my heart sink when I hear that phrase. If you fish public waters and you want reasonable sport, find one with banks closed to anglers – where there is a nature reserve or an active gravel working – anything to reduce the amount of angling pressure and provide a haven for pike to get away from aerial bombardments with half mackerel all hours of the day and night.

Some waters are so wide that there's a section in the middle that no one can reach, or at least they couldn't until the invention of radio-controlled, bait-towing boats capable of positioning baits accurately at hundreds of yards. Drifter floats can only reach that water on a wind directly out from the bank. Otherwise the middle is a much-needed place of safety for pike, and if there's a safe area somewhere on a water, pike will find it, feeding and staying healthy, and only venturing out when they're strong enough to face the fray again. The fact that the fish on that over-fished trout water I mentioned had changed their feeding habits suggests they had already tried the first alternative of seeking refuge and failed, and were now a long way down the short road to a rather sad, sorry and emaciated end.

Numbers of rods

If a large number of anglers on a water will have a detrimental effect on sport, then a smaller number of anglers armed with a lot of rods will be just as bad.

To some anglers, each rod is like a National Lottery scratchcard – the more they have, the greater their chance of success. But the chances don't always increase in proportion to numbers of baits used. One rod in the right place is better than four in the wrong place, and less likely to disturb the fish.

A lot depends on the type of water. On some I can fish several rods, and on others only one. I have fished with more than two rods on occasion, but that's been when the fishing has been extremely slow. When fishing on a river I'm not prepared to use more than two rods, because the degree of technical difficulty is such that you can't handle more and still fish properly. If you get simultaneous runs on two or three rods when fish come on the feed, you face a dilemma. I've had two rods go at once, so it's going to be a lot worse with multiple rod set-ups.

With two rods, I've been able to pick up one rod, strike it and open the bale arm, then strike the other and play that fish. Once a fish has been hooked it will run off and then, feeling no resistance, stop, which will let you finish with the first fish. But multiply this by five or six and you have a recipe for disaster.

The greater the number of rods fished, the longer it will take to reach them all. In summer, and at night, pike can wolf baits back, and unless you are next to the rod, no more than ten metres away, you will be giving yourself and the pike problems.

Gravel pits usually have only a few hotspots, and a couple of rods presented correctly are sufficient to fish effectively. Large numbers of rod are no substitute for bad angling. Location is everything, and once you have pinpointed the fish then two or three rods are more than enough.

Happy landings

Landing a pike should be a straightforward business, but a lot of people still poke around with the landing net before the fish is ready. It should be submerged, and the fish drawn over it, only when you feel the pike is sufficiently tired to be netted.

Always bring the whole of the fish over the net before lifting. Once the fish is in the net, the rod should be placed on the bank, and the fish lifted from the water by holding on to the mesh or arms, not the net handle, which is liable to snap and let the fish fall to the ground with a bump.

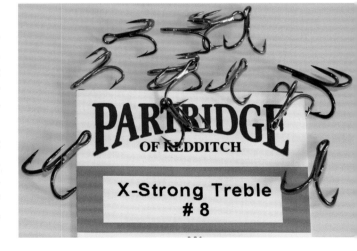

The small barbs and needle eyes on Partridge and Owner trebles are a substantial aid to problem-free unhooking.

SURE HANDLING

Handling pike presents a minefield of problems. The toothsome predator myth which strikes fear into some anglers' hearts, and a good measure of incompetence, cause all the problems.

First and foremost, use an unhooking mat. Every serious big-fish angler should have one. You wouldn't like your skin rubbed around on gravel and neither does a pike. It should have enough closed-cell foam padding – which doesn't absorb water and become smelly – to cushion the fish's body. So long as the design is long enough and soft enough, there's no need for buckles and flaps. I've never seen the point of putting flaps over a fish's body. They serve no useful purpose, and remove the slime that is the pike's protective layer against infection.

If you get caught without a mat, look for an area of soft grass, or use a weigh sling as a substitute. Repeat captures are becoming the norm, and so we are going to have to start taking greater care of the pike we catch or they won't be around for long.

Don't let a pike flap on the bank. The heavier the pike, the greater the chance of it hurting itself, as its body weight can cause damage to its delicate internal organs. If it jerks its head, put your hand under the head like a pillow to stop it hitting the ground, not on top of it, which means pushing one of its eyes against the ground. Ask yourself, 'How would I like it?' and you won't go far wrong.

Unhooking techniques

Big pike are easier to handle than small ones, partly because they tend to be quieter, and partly because there is more room for manoeuvre in their mouths.

Lay the pike on its side and kneel astride it to prevent yourself leaning on it. If you are right-handed, place your left hand under the gill cover at the front of the mouth and, with a firm grip on the lower jaw, gently pull the jaw towards you to open the mouth. That way there's no chance of getting bitten. There's a membrane under the jaw between the bones, so don't put your finger through it accidentally. Your fingers can rest against the membrane, but you shouldn't use any force against it.

Using eight-inch straight forceps, grip the shank of the hook, turn the points towards you, and tug them out. If the hooks are further back in the mouth, insert the forceps between the rows of pink gill rakers beneath the gill covers, being careful not to damage them as they are very fragile, and guide the forceps to the hooks while looking straight down through the open mouth.

If you have managed to deep-hook the fish, and the hooks are out of sight, put the trace under tension against the rod or by being held by someone else, and pull it until folds of skin in the pike's throat are drawn back, and the treble comes into view. Turn the treble upside down and tug it out. If it takes a bit of force to get it out, so be it. Just get on with it. If you can see it, then you can get it out. Whatever happens, if you find yourself in that situation you'll be sure not to let it happen again. If ever there was a deterrent devised for people who leave runs too long before striking, then it's dealing with deeply-hooked pike.

Get a move on!

Wherever the hooks are and whatever the problem, get on with the job quickly and efficiently, as it is better to remove the hooks with a quick tug and get the fish back in the water than to spend a long time teasing free the tiniest shred of skin. If you have someone with you, get them to pour water on the fish to prevent it from drying out.

If you've got a pike gag, throw it away. They do far more harm than good, and are completely unnecessary. Sometimes, while going in through the gill rakers, the back of your hand just brushes them. You may be surprised how much the cuts will bleed. The rakers are coated in an anti-coagulant, which will stop the wound from healing for a short time, but the marks will be no more than grazes and you

A gorgeous 22 lb pike caught from a Thames weir pool.

won't even be aware at first what has happened. If you seem to get cut regularly, buy a pair of gardening gloves and chop off the fingertips so that you can hold the fish firmly but still have the backs of your hands covered.

Everyone gets their fingers nicked or damaged now and then, no matter how experienced or careful they are. It is a good idea to have some plasters with you, because open cuts need to be protected on the bank, especially with Weil's disease around.

Keep pike as still as possible during the whole operation, for their sake as well as your own. The more a fish is allowed to move around, the more likely you or it will become injured.

Beware of flying trebles

You would think that a pike hooked in the edge of the mouth would pose no problems, but get a loose treble wrapped in the mesh of a landing net and you have a situation potentially more damaging than a deeply-hooked fish, as you struggle to get the hooks out of several layers of mesh.

Sometimes you don't see the 'flying' treble until the fish is in the net, and if that happens you should take the fish out of the net before unhooking it. If it spins in the net it could split its mouth on the tight trace or gouge its eye on the loose treble.

If it spins, stop the fish from moving around, cut the line above the trace to get the rod out of the way and, with the pike held securely, get the mesh unpicked as fast as possible. The larger the mesh of the net, the more difficult it is to unravel. Minnow mesh is a lot easier to deal with than bream mesh.

Landing the fish by hand isn't a complete solution, because if that loose top treble snags your jacket or, worse still, the back of your hand, one slip and you could have an angry, frightened, head-shaking fish tearing that three-pointed piece of sharp wire through your hand as it tries to escape. Carry a pair of wire cutters in your pocket. You'll be glad of them.

Be on your guard as the fish begins to tire, and be ready to change tactics from landing by net to landing by hand. Play the fish out so that it isn't too lively in the edge. Small pike, and those to about 15 lb, can sometimes be unhooked over the side of a boat or in the shallows, as they are not going to be weighed or photographed.

With big fish, it pays to use a net, and a good-sized one at that.

Why I won't use barbless hooks

I wish I could recommend barbless hooks as the pike fishing of the future, but, while I have landed quite a few fish on them, I have also lost a good few. I'm not alone in finding barbless hooks difficult to get on with, and there are several famous names in pike angling, in particular Jim Gibbinson and Ken Crow, who have lost one too many fish on them and gone back to barbed. One fish sticks in my memory.

It was a gravel pit fish of about 25 lb, and when it launched itself clear of the water it shook its head and the trebles flew out. With it went all of my confidence in barbless hooks.

I ease my conscience by reminding myself there's a school of thought that claims barbless hooks, whether single or treble, cause more damage than barbed because they penetrate further, pushing deep into the flesh-like needles. I'm not sure whether that's the case, but the fact remains that if you strike a fish early and hook it in the mouth or scissors, you can use whatever sort of hook you want, because that fish isn't going to come to harm.

I would back anyone using barbed hooks and striking quickly over someone using barbless, and saying it doesn't matter how long they wait before they strike. That's something that is heard too often on the bank. A deeply-hooked pike is a mistake, no matter what sort of hooks are being used.

The right weigh

Purpose-made pike weigh slings are a different shape from carp weigh slings. If you are after big pike, you need the proper thing, because folding a fish in half will do nothing for its backbone, and put a strain on its internal organs. If fish were meant to be shaped like boomerangs, God would have made them that way.

Give 'em the sack

Keep-nets are no place for pike. Split fins and sides rubbed raw are the inevitable consequences. If you must retain a fish, a pike sack or tube is the thing to use. I always carry two sacks with me, and they double as an unhooking mat for roving fishing. The big, zipped design is best. A fish can be put in sideways on, and there is no draw cord to tangle. Make sure the sack is big enough: a 20 lb pike will be about 40 inches long. A sack material is soft, but a fish can damage itself by rubbing against a sharp object on the bottom in shallow water. Wade out to deeper water where there is a soft bottom, or tether the sack from a tree branch.

Pike tubes are excellent alternatives, because their rigid frames mean pike don't rub against hard objects, opening areas to infection.

I have seen pike left in shallows overnight, and anglers come back to find herons and cormorants have attacked them. It isn't fair to the fish. If it's a really big pike and you want a photograph in daylight then sack it overnight, but do it properly.

Fish handled carefully will be none the worse for wear. I used to fish a pit where the first pike I caught was almost always the same 8 lb jack. I must have caught it eight or nine times, and I think it knew I wasn't going to harm it. On another water I was chopping mackerel heads off baits and throwing them in the shallows. I caught a pike and unhooked it, and when I put it back, it swam over them, dropped down and picked one up before going on its way. And on the river, I've caught the same fish twice within

If you're going to get passers-by to take catch shots for you, a camera with a programme mode is a must. Anything more complicated is asking for trouble.

minutes. Pike don't have a problem with being caught if they are treated properly and returned immediately. It's mishandling that makes the fish lose condition.

I would liken handling pike to holding a racing pigeon. Put in the hands of someone who knows how to hold it, a pigeon doesn't struggle. The confidence of the handler is transmitted to the bird, and it can sense that it's not going to be harmed. But hold it awkwardly and you transmit your incompetence, and the creature will become agitated. There's a right and a wrong way to do everything.

Posing for passers-by

Pictures are not as important as the satisfaction of catching the fish and putting it back unharmed. It detracts greatly from the pleasure of the capture if a fish is damaged or has problems going back.

If you must take pictures, you owe it to the fish to have everything worked out in advance, and to do the job quickly and efficiently. I have had a Nikon FM2 for twelve years and it stands up to being dropped and stood on, and still produces excellent pictures. I use it for close-up reference pictures of fish for identification, and pictures of waters and features. However, when it comes to getting a passer-by to take a catch shot with it, you can tell by the puzzled look on their faces as they examine the unfamiliar buttons and knobs that things are going to go badly wrong. And they do, regularly. So I've bought an auto-wind, auto-focus Canon A1 Sureshot camera with a self-contained flash, which has a quality zoom lens of 35 to 70 mm, and a programme mode I can set before handing it over. Put it in the hands of someone who knows nothing about cameras, tell him where to stand and what to press, and you will get good results almost every time.

Posing for self-portraits

Self-portraits require a little more preparation. Position bank sticks either side of the frame, just out of shot, and screw the camera into a bank stick with an adapter. A self-timer will give you about twelve seconds to position the fish, which should be laid on a sack with a corner covering its eyes, something that often has a calming effect and stops it moving around. If you catch two fish at once, you could try placing them on your knees, which I did for a self-portrait of two 24-pounders that was considered good enough to grace the front cover of *Angler's Mail*.

When holding fish for pictures, tuck your hands under the pike to show its proportions, without letting your fingers get in the way, and hold it close to you, to protect it if it struggles, and to avoid distorting its size in the photograph. Holding it towards the lens doesn't make it look bigger: it just makes it look weird and out of proportion, and either you or the pike are likely to be out of focus.

Choose a plain background with the sun in your face. Make sure the fish is clean of grass and leaves before you pick it up, and that there are no distracting items of tackle showing in the corners of the shot.

Photos at night are harder to take. You will need to shine a torch on to the fish to focus and compose the shot. If there's a brolly or trees to provide background and reflect the flash, position the shot there, but always keep to distances specified on the flash information, or you risk getting pictures that are too light or too dark.

Many happy returns

When a fish has been weighed and photographed – if it's big enough to warrant that – put it back in the weigh sling and then carry it down the bank to the water. When you put pike back, especially the harder-fighting loch fish, you should hold them in the water for a minute or two while they recover; this stops them from swimming off immediately. In summer, fish will take longer to recover than in winter. At that time they are at their fittest, having had three or four months of good feeding to recover from spawning, and will fight their hardest. Couple this with the fact that oxygen levels are at their lowest and you will see why more time has to be taken.

Summer pike are more active and more athletic, so they are more enjoyable to catch. What they lack in size they will make up for in numbers and enthusiasm, but sacking them for a picture is not a good idea.

Before now I've hooked a big fish in summer and have asked someone to get my camera ready when I have still been playing it. It may have looked like over-confidence, but I wasn't trying to look cool, only save time. Two or three minutes is the maximum time pike should be out of the water in summer, as in these conditions their body temperature is rising all the time.

Try to put them back in calm water, so that they can recover out of any flow. If you try to put them back in fast water they won't have enough energy to fight the current, and will get swept downstream to die, belly up.

The same goes for very cold temperatures, when the air may be down to the minuses. Fins begin to freeze when it gets this cold, so don't mess about with sacks and pictures in these conditions, for the sake of the fish's well-being.

Big pike are rare and beautiful creatures, so let's take good care of them. If we want these fish to grow and give other people enjoyment then we should look after them, and return them in the same condition they were in when we caught them.

*Use gentle hands
to return pike to
the water.*

Pike are basically lazy creatures looking for an easy life. They will seek to gain maximum reward from minimum effort, which means eating bream and roach. So although there are lots of trout, fishing with a trout livebait may not work.

CHAPTER 6

BAIT

The choice of baits available to pike anglers is enormous, and most of them have accounted for a fish or two at some time or other. From strange-looking exotic fish to strawberry-flavoured mackerel, someone, somewhere has tried them all. There's no doubt they will all work on their day, and there will be days when pike will look at only one type of bait in one size and ignore everything else.

But the majority of the time, thank goodness, pike will take the old favourites, and if I were marooned on a desert island that happened to have a pike lake, I should be happy with a bucket of live brown trout and a bag of frozen sardines. Why I plump for these two fish above any others, and when I would ignore them in favour of something else, form the basis for this chapter, for you need to know why pike prefer one bait to another in order to know when you can afford to leave the alternatives at home.

The changing face of livebaiting

There was a time when livebaiting for me meant catching coarse fish in advance of a session. Every piking trip had to be preceded by a few hours with a float rod in the hope of catching enough baits to last the day. It wasn't ideal. There were times when coarse fish were frustratingly difficult to catch, particularly in the depths of winter, and I didn't want to lose a day of pike fishing simply because I couldn't get livebaits.

There had to be a solution, and it came with the rapid growth of trout fishing as a sport and the demand for the species among fish eaters. Trout farms sprang up alongside all of the major rivers in the country, providing perfect livebaits for just a few pence each. These fish are bred for the table, so anglers' consciences are clear as they are not removing precious stocks of native coarse fish. And there are fewer worries with transferring diseases, as trout farms are forever seeking and obtaining fish-moving consents from the Environment Agency.

Rainbow trout make excellent livebaits. They have a firm skin, with scales that stand up to handling and casting, and a soft flesh that is attractive to pike.

They're a good source of protein, and I believe pike find them easy to digest. The fact that we eat trout rather than roach or chub suggests they are a bit of a delicacy. Their only drawback is that they have a tendency to swim high in the water when tired, like rudd, dace and roach, and if that happens they need to be taken off and a fresh bait put on. However, this habit can be used to good effect when legering livebaits, as their desire to head for the surface keeps them off the bottom, and in view of any pike.

Brown trout are just the opposite. Their first impulse is to dive deep, and this makes them the best choice for float fishing, especially over deep water. Very little lead is needed to hold them down, which means they will stay alive for longer and not wear themselves out towing a heavy lead around. Crucian carp, bream and chub have a similar deep-diving tendency.

I am fortunate in living close to a trout farm that has a good stock of various sizes of trout. They also have both rainbows and brownies, and it is the latter I particularly like for fishing in Scotland. Browns are much slower-growing and so are more expensive – 45p each for a 3 oz to 4 oz trout, compared with 30p for a similar rainbow. This is a good, manageable size as, the larger the fish, the more difficult it is to cast and control, and the bigger the float you need. In fact, everything has to be stepped up, and then handling tackle becomes a problem. I buy a couple of dozen trout for a day's fishing, and keep any leftovers alive for the next outing.

Is livebaiting necessary?

Even with the issue of coarse fish removal resolved by using trout, there still remains a question mark over livebaiting. The issue isn't so much a matter of whether it's cruel, which takes us into the realms of the 'Do fish feel pain?' debate, but whether it's necessary. If we can catch pike on deadbaits under any conditions, why not give up livebaiting for good?

Having fished both methods through several decades, I can say with confidence that there are days when livebaits will out-fish any other method. Certainly, on a river when conditions are right, a livebait is in a class of its own. Location is of paramount importance when river fishing, and a great deal more water can be covered with a trotted livebait than with any other method. I can trot a bait up to 80 yards downstream under a float, searching the water as it goes down. It would take me a very long time to cover the same amount of water with a static deadbait.

I'm not what you could call an enthusiastic livebaiter. I would much rather use a deadbait. But I've seen how preoccupied fish feeding selectively can become. I've seen them at Theale Lagoon, crashing frantically into shoals of two-inch roach, mouths wide open, and one pike of over 30 lb in such a feeding frenzy that it beached itself in the shallows. I was able to weigh the stranded fish without having caught it, and it took the scales down to 30 lb 2 oz. Yet the pike refused everything we put in front of them, except small, live fish. There are times when nothing else will work.

The bottom line is, if you don't livebait, you're handicapping yourself. I would like to think I could catch the same number and size of fish on deadbaits as I do on lives, but that's just not the case. There are even some rivers, like the Trent, the Hampshire Avon and the Weaver in Cheshire, on which you would be a lot less likely to succeed with a deadbait.

There are times when pike are in a torpid state, perhaps due to a series of heavy frosts or a prolonged spell of hot weather, and are not interested in feeding. They can often be persuaded to reflex-feed or grab a livebait out of aggression. A livebait must have much the same effect on the pike as a bluebottle buzzing around our heads. Sooner or later we have to strike out at it to bring an end to the annoyance. They will drop the bait as soon as it has been killed, because they don't intend to eat it, but if your hooks are in the right position, and you strike early enough, reflex feeders can be hooked in the lip. A deadbait would have sat there all day without bringing any response.

Pike pick up attractive vibrations from livebaits, and they can feel those movements of the bait at much greater distance than they can see, making livebaits more effective. It always makes me smile when I read that a livebait should behave naturally to tempt a pike. It is precisely because these baits are behaving unnaturally that they are so attractive to pike, or more attractive than a fish swimming free and unrestricted as part of a shoal. Livebaits are vulnerable, and vulnerability to a pike means food.

I've cast a livebait caught from a water teeming with stunted carp and rudd into the middle of a shoal of hundreds of others that were identical, and had the bait taken instantly by a 28 lb pike. There were so many small carp you would have thought it unlikely a fish would pick up mine. But I believe it did so because the bait was behaving unnaturally and giving out involuntary distress signals.

I've even cast baits into dense weed when pike have been lying there, and they have been found surprisingly quickly. I believe they can home in on the tiny movements of the gills and fins of coarse fish using a unique sensory system that they have, known as the neuromast system, which is described in Chapter 10.

If someone comes up with an artificial lure that simulates these vibrations accurately, livebaiting could become obsolete.

What about coarse fish livebaits?
Trout supply almost all of my needs as far as livebaiting is concerned because coarse fish don't lend themselves to being hurled out a long way and cast repeatedly. But when I'm fishing from a boat or on a tributary of a river, and don't need to cast very far, then I will use roach and chub livebaits if I can get hold of them.

Some of the coarse baits I have used have been so big they would make a matchman swear, but big baits catch big pike, and if that is what is required, then I will use them without any qualms. When I have experimented with big coarse baits I have so far found it almost impossible to go too big. River pike feed regularly on 2 lb bream and chub, so providing them with a bait of similar size is only giving them what they are used to.

Frank Guttfield was fishing the Thames a few years ago when a barbel of 6 lb he was playing was taken by a very big pike that grabbed it across the head and the flank. It damaged the barbel so badly that Frank had to finish it off.

I have caught a pike of 26 lb that had a jack of over 6 lb in the back of its throat, and a friend who caught a pike of 13 lb 6 oz could see the legs of a coot sticking up from inside its throat.

I have even had days when trout livebaits have been ignored, but when I put on a roach of 12 oz it was taken straight away. We had thirteen double-figure pike that day, all on big roach, and as soon as we ran out, sport was over. Big coarse baits do work, if your conscience will allow you to use them, and there are certainly times when nothing else will do.

Fish moving orders

Like it or not, bylaws state that you have to get a fish moving order from your local authority, approved by the local office of the Environment Agency, before you can take live fish from one water to another. You must state what you are taking, and where you are going to use them. If you haven't got an order, and you are caught using live fish from another water, there are fairly hefty fines in place to dissuade you from doing so again.

A lot of trout farms now ask for fish moving order documents or consents when you go there to buy fish, and won't sell you trout without a form. Anglers do get away without them, but it is best to obtain one. A single consent covers you for any number of fish for six months, and helps fight the spread of disease around the country. Some trout farms can't issue consents to take live fish because their stock is not designated disease-free.

Legered livebaits

Most of the time, livebaiting means float fishing, but one tactic worth trying is legering with lives. Fished this way they don't move around much, which makes me wonder why they are so attractive to pike. But the movement of the fins and gills is probably enough vibration for a big pike to detect.

The biggest pike often lie near the bottom, and when temperatures are low, they will be in deep water. We want to position a bait where they are lying, and it is easier to do that by legering than by float fishing. A float-fished bait is only

KEEPING & CARRYING LIVEBAITS

When I visit the trout farm, which is only ten minutes' drive away, I take with me two snap-lidded plastic buckets made for beer brewing, each with an aerator pump glued to the top. When I get them home, I transfer the trout to the two five-foot galvanised horse troughs I keep in my back garden for livebaits, and pump air into them through air stones from a power point in my garage. I can keep up to two dozen brownies quite comfortably in each for up to a month.

The important thing to realise is that trout have been fed very heavily on high-protein trout pellets up until the time they were bought, so their stomachs are full. Once I take them, I tend to starve them, for their own good. If I pick them up on a Tuesday and intend to use them that weekend, I won't feed them at all. In the past I have not fed them for two weeks without any detrimental effect. Feeding them causes more problems than not, because as soon as you give them something to eat, the tank becomes filthy. What goes in one end has to come out of the other, and you have to change the water on a regular basis. Without food they can live quite happily on their own body fat for two or three weeks, and probably be healthier when you use them than when they arrived. Trout require clean, well-oxygenated water much more than large amounts of food.

Both of the galvanised troughs I use have pieces of nylon mesh stretched over the tops and stapled to two bits of timber, because I'm not the only fisher in the neighbourhood. I put a dozen trout in one evening and woke up the next morning to find nine lying on the lawn, picked out by cats that had several hours' enjoyable fishing at my expense. I've had a visit from a beady-eyed heron, too, that had my entire stock of brown trout for breakfast.

I have a tiny net from a pet shop to get the little chaps out, and I wouldn't be without it. Any trout left over at the end of the day go back in the troughs. If it's really cold in winter and there is a danger of the troughs freezing over, then I drag them into the garage to stop ice forming on them.

When carrying livebaits to the bank, I use the same buckets, but with only three or four inches of water in the bottom if a long walk is on the cards. Gone are the days when I could lug a full bucket of livebaits across three or four meadows without breaking sweat. Pipe lagging taped to the handle, which is invariably made of painfully thin, rigid wire, makes carrying more comfortable.

Snap-lidded brewing bins and aerators will keep your livebaits alive and lively from fish farm to home and then to the swim. Keep water levels low to lighten the load, or your carrying arm may end up longer than the other.

in the right spot for a moment before the current takes it away or the bait swims out of position, but a legered livebait can be kept where you want it without the need for repeated casting. Often when float fishing fails, legering succeeds, and creates much less disturbance, because a rig only needs to be cast a few times in a morning.

If I know of a holding area and want to keep a bait in that lie or deep hole, then I would use a legered livebait. The outside of a bend in a river or a depression are just a couple of places where legering is a better option than float fishing. In difficult swims with lots of bankside vegetation to hamper casting, legering is again the prime method. Similarly when putting a bait close to snags like a half-submerged tree, or when trying to repeat a good cast, a legered bait is best. There are times when a legered livebait is the only method that will succeed. And my first choice of bait would be a rainbow trout.

Sardines, smelt, sand eels, mackerel, pike, roach and trout. The choice of deadbait is a wide one, and all have different uses on different waters where pike show a preference for one type of bait over another.

Deciding which deadbait

If livebaiting is a useful alternative method for me, deadbait fishing is my bread-and-butter approach. It's the first choice in most situations, and the method from which I gain most satisfaction while targeting big pike selectively.

Yet among many modern pike anglers it is a second-rate technique. Why use a dead fish when you can use a live one? Their image of deadbaiting is 'lob it out and leave it', but to see it as such is to overlook the number of different ways a deadbait can be fished. Just as a good lure angler can search a stretch of water by bringing that lump of plastic or wood to life, so skilled sink-and-draw techniques can cover a whole pool on a river, enticing a pike to take by making the bait flutter and wobble attractively. A lot depends on the choice of species of fish to use as bait, and here I've listed most of the alternatives, along with the times when they are at their best and why.

As a general rule I would say that deadbaits should be killed freshly or have been frozen soon after capture. However, I can't help thinking of an angler of my acquaintance. Everything he fished with was old, so it will come as no surprise to hear that his bait matched his tackle. He's the only angler I've ever met who didn't discard a deadbait when it split, but took out his sewing kit and stitched it back together with wool. You think I'm joking? I only wish I were, and the worst part is he used to catch pike on them, and big ones at that. For Phil, deadbaits could be of any age or freshness, even rancid. For everyone else my advice would be deadbaits should be as fresh as possible.

Freshly killed brown trout make excellent wobbled baits. Trout are very flexible when first killed, before rigor mortis *has set in and they go as stiff as a board.*

Trout have their uses

Having read how highly I rate brown and rainbow trout as livebaits, you may be surprised to discover that I don't use them for static deadbaits. The reason is I don't think they give off a particularly attractive scent when dead, and they certainly don't lend themselves to being frozen. They turn very soft and break up easily, so it's fresh or nothing, and even fresh are second best to other species.

However, when looking for a bait to be wobbled, it's a different matter. Their streamlined shape makes them move through the water very attractively on the retrieve, and their toughness when freshly killed means they stand up well to attack. I have caught four or five pike on the same trout. Brown and rainbow trout are my first choice for wobbled deadbaits, especially when they weigh about 6 oz. I go for a slightly heavier bait when wobbling because a pike has to chase it to take it, often in fast-flowing water, and I believe you need to offer a fish a decent meal to make the reward worth the energy expended.

Trout are very flexible when first killed, before *rigor mortis* has set in, more so than 'big-scaled' fish like roach and chub, and that suppleness gives the bait the movement throughout the body and in the tail it needs to attract the attention of a big pike. Freshly killed trout have been used to good effect at Underbank Reservoir and Damflask, in South Yorkshire, by Tag Barnes and Colin Dyson, fishing twelve feet down in forty feet of water, and the fact that they were freshly killed added to their attraction. I take trout to the water's edge live, and kill them as I need them or just ten minutes before. It's the only way you can ensure your deadbaits are truly fresh.

But sardines are best

So, if trout aren't my first choice for a static deadbait, what is? The answer is sardines. They are by far the best deadbait on rivers, and will on most occasions out-fish anything else. Extremely oily, they give off a superb smell that gets wafted downstream to any feeding pike, drawing it up to the source of the scent. What's more, they are extremely cheap and easily available, bought in kilo bags from your local market for about £2 for fifteen fish. The best ones I have used have been imported from Portugal. You need to make sure they have been separated in the bag, though, because if they have been frozen in one big lump you will have to thaw the whole lot to get at the half a dozen you'll need for a trip. This process of freezing individually is known in the trade as 'freeflow'.

Beware of sardines that were frozen when less than fresh. The best baits will be bright and shiny. If there is a greenish tinge to the underside of the stomachs you know they were frozen after being out of the water for a fair period of time.

I have used sardines and re-frozen them and still caught pike on them on the next outing, unlike smelts, which don't seem to lend themselves to being re-frozen. Mackerel stand up to this treatment OK, though.

If it's fresh sardines you are going for, look at the clarity of the eye to tell how good they are. Blood seeps slowly into the eye of a dead sardine, darkening it, so the more discoloured it is, the longer the fish has been dead. Women in Greece used to give the eyes of fish on the market stalls a poke to make sure they were still attached, because stallholders got to know that the eye was a gauge of freshness and started substituting ones from fresh fish to deceive their customers. Also, give the stomach a prod: a fresh fish has a firm stomach.

The one drawback to sardines is that they can't be cast very far. Their soft, oily flesh breaks up easily, so I try not to use them for long-range fishing on gravel pits, but stick to close-to-medium work. There are three ways in which I fish sardines: float legered out of a boat, legered with a Cox & Rawle leger boom in rivers, and freelined using the deadbait support rig on gravel pits. Sardines are especially good after dark lobbed out under-arm into the margins.

I take the bait to the water frozen in a plastic bag and partially thaw one sardine by dropping it in the margins while I am tackling up. I sometimes pinch a small amount of lead on the trace just above the root of the tail when I use a partially thawed bait, to make sure it has sunk. I put one treble hook through the root of the tail, and pin the other treble in the flank. Using the deadbait support rig enables me to cast sardines further and avoid losing them on the retrieve and giving the pike a free meal.

And mackerel are close behind

The only other deadbait I use regularly is mackerel, which make excellent long-range baits that pike find very attractive. Their aerodynamic shape and extra weight mean they can be cast long distances freelined when frozen. The beauty of freelining is there is nothing to hamper the take or impede the strike, and the fight is not impaired by a heavy lead bouncing on the line.

Mackerel are very robust and stand up well to repeated casting caused by striving for range. If the first couple of casts go astray you can usually have another go without even needing to adjust the hook hold. The best way to mount the bait is with the deadbait support rig, with a loop of strong line around the root of the tail to support the mackerel, and hooks pinned lightly in the skin.

A 30 lb 4 oz South Cerney gravel pit fish caught at range on a half mackerel, followed by one of 26 lb the next day.

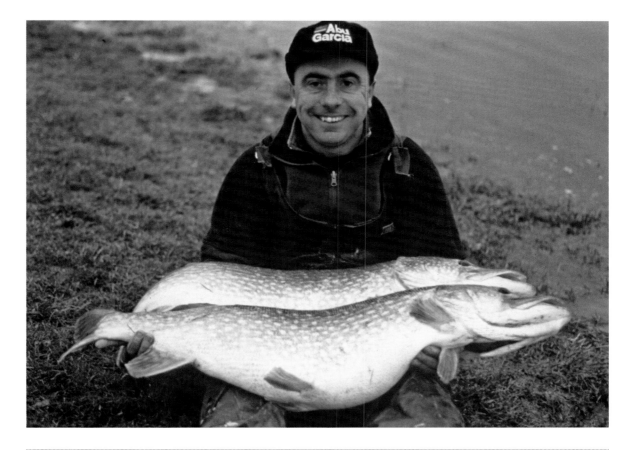

I buy my mackerel in boxes weighing a stone from Greenslade's at Poole Harbour on the South Coast. I buy ten stone at a time, for £4 to £5 a stone. I can pick the size of baits I want and I know they are going to be extremely fresh. Even with the cost of the petrol down there it works out very cheap, and provides me with much better bait than I would get from a fishmonger's, which always seems to have mackerel too big for my purposes.

I ring up Greenslade's in advance and ask them to layer the fish for me and to keep them apart. They have huge freezers down there and will put the fish in the back until there is a cool day, when I travel down to pick them up. It takes me just an hour and a half from Oxford with a good run, and they're still frozen when I get them home. I ask for twelve-inch fish and use three-quarters of that, chopping off the heads to use for pre-baiting. Some of the baits I chop in advance and freeze in bags of half a dozen, but mainly they are frozen intact and the chopping is done on the bank, as they are needed. Any heads chopped off in advance can be thrown into a chosen area of a water I want to fish at regular intervals over three or four weeks leading up to the session. It's surprising how used to that food source pike become. They are waiting and hungry when you turn up with your rods.

Streamlining a mackerel

To prepare a mackerel for fishing, I chop off the head at an angle across the bait and then take off the corner, to give the bait a curved end where the head used to be. This lets more of the attractive juices seep out into the water, and prevents the belly from splitting. I also chop off the tail to within half an inch of the root, which makes it more aerodynamic and less likely to twist on the cast and cause tangles.

Making a mackerel more streamlined by trimming it with a sharp knife will make it fly through the air without twisting when cast, keeping tackle tangles to a minimum.

I will use a mackerel until the belly splits and then chop it up for pre-baiting. Used baits will refreeze, but I don't bother unless I'm short.

I go down to Poole to stock up in July or August, the peak time for English mackerel, and again in the winter. They have supplies all the year round as their boats travel far afield for fish, though it pays to be stocked up in advance of the winter's worst weather as this can keep the boats in port. The boxes of frozen bait go straight into my chest freezer in the garage, apart from the few mackerel that I chop in advance, and some of it stays there for over six months and is still fine to use. My chest freezer is a lot less than full size. If you're thinking of getting a freezer just for bait, don't make the mistake of getting a really big one, as they need to be kept filled to work efficiently.

From the cradle to the grave

Pike first feed on pike from four or five weeks old, and later, small pike get eaten by bigger ones because they are plentiful and easy to catch. By the time it reaches a respectable size, a large pike may have seen off tens of dozens of smaller ones, so they are as natural a food source as any they are likely to encounter. On a water without a big head of coarse fish but with plenty of pike there may be little else in the way of food. In that case big pike will actively seek out smaller pike, and will be in areas where they can obtain them.

Even a 9 lb pike is not safe. This 29-pounder choked to death on its smaller brethren. (Picture courtesy of Oxford University Museum.)

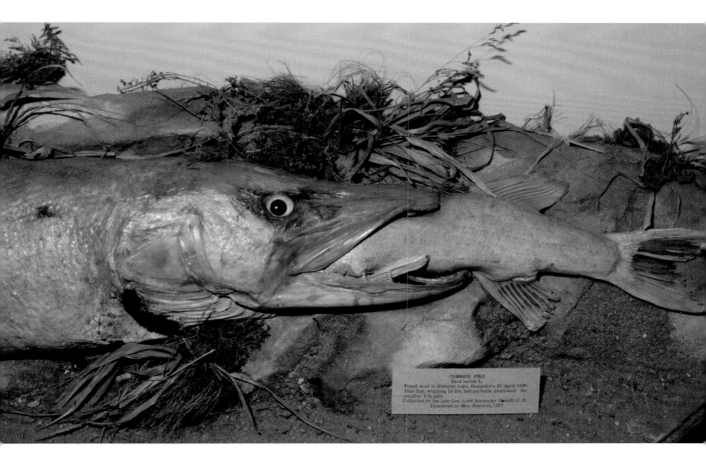

A PIKE WHEN THE TIME IS RIGHT

There are times during the season when a small jack pike will outfish any other bait. At the back end of the season, small male pike are drawn to big, hungry hen fish at a time when they have burned up a lot of energy in spawning. The cock fish can be so preoccupied with the urge to reproduce that they become an easy target. A big hen fish surrounded by males may turn on one and swallow it. The time of year that this happens depends on the location of the water. On English rivers it is usually in February or March, whereas in Scotland it is more like March or April. Big Thames pike are suckers for a smaller pike at this time of the year, and will also seek them out at other times.

When they're in that mood, a jack is the first choice bait. I once caught a 24 lb 8 oz pike from a Thames tributary on one, and at the back of her throat were the remains of another hapless suitor.

It's the distinctive smell of a small pike that triggers the reaction. Some anglers think only a whole fish will work as bait, believing it is the appearance that provokes the feeding urge, but a jack pike will work as bait whether whole, cut in half or even in steaks. To fish a steak, pass a loop of nylon through the cavity where the guts were before they were pushed out, and use this to support the bait on the cast. Shape is immaterial to the attractiveness of the bait. The scent is everything.

An upper double taken on a jack deadbait in March. At this time of year big pike seek out jacks.

On one water I fished there were reeds and rushes just in front of a deep trough, and small pike would sit in the reeds but very seldom venture out into deeper water. I caught one of about 2 lb on a sardine and, as I played it, an incredible bow wave appeared behind the fish, coming right in under my feet. The fish, one of about 13 lb, came shooting across the surface of the water and took the jack, but as it did so a fish well into the thirties grabbed the 13 lb fish across the side.

I knew the hooks were nowhere near its mouth, so I tried to guide the big fish gently towards the net, but as I got it near it let go. Even a 13 lb pike is not safe when a very big one is hungry.

I've come across half a dozen such waters on my travels, and it always takes a while to understand what's going on. All you catch at first on conventional livebaits and deadbaits is small jack pike. The place seems to be over-run with them. You might even give it up as a bad job, but as soon as you offer a pike as a bait, by accident or by design, your results will be transformed.

Having whetted your appetite for catching pike on pike, however, I should warn you that feeding times are a lot less frequent than with standard food items. If a big pike takes an 8 lb jack it could go for three to four weeks without needing to feed again. A pike needs to eat only four to five times its body weight in a year to maintain growth and keep healthy.

Scrape a few scales from a small area of flank when mounting a pike deadbait on trebles. This allows the hooks to be nicked lightly in the flesh and struck clear cleanly.

Start by spinning

I've known waters with just a few large coarse fish that have failed to spawn. The pike were numerous and mostly small and had to feed on each other to survive. On a water like that, I would start by spinning for them, and if I caught a number of less than 1 lb fish I would cut one in half and put it on a deadbait rig.

Pike are very tough-skinned fish, being small-scaled, and they need a bit of attention before being mounted on a rig. I chop off the fins to help with casting and scrape just a few scales from a small area of flank. This allows me to nick one of the hooks of the end treble in the skin. The other prongs sit on scales in an area that hasn't been cleared, so that they skid off on the strike. The other treble goes just in front of the tail root and is also nicked in very lightly.

Jack pike are such a good bait for big fish it is tempting to suggest them as livebait, but experience has proved they are too difficult to catch to order, and even when they can be caught, the tackle has to be stepped up to fish them effectively. Hooks, floats and leads all need to be bigger, and with that increase in size comes a decrease in the chances of success. If jack pike can be caught, though, and there's a pike in the water big enough to make fishing with crude tackle worthwhile, then by all means persevere. If I were going to use one I would keep it well off the bottom, out of the weed, and put it in a position where it could be seen clearly and was very vulnerable. I would also have at least 150 yards of line on the reel, as a pike that takes a jack tends to run and run.

Clive Loveland and Allen Edwards fished for pike out of boats in Knipton Reservoir, near Grantham in Lincolnshire in the late sixties, and landed some huge fish that fired the imagination of pike anglers for over two decades, the biggest weighing 39 lb. I'm sure that if pike were used more widely and more often by anglers we would see some huge fish start to come out.

Eels keep others at bay

As a dedicated eel angler with a fascination for the species, it takes a great deal of provocation for me to end up describing eels as a bloody pest. But that is a measure of how bad the problem has become in Scotland, where it is now impossible to keep a bait intact in the water on days, and nights, when small eels are active.

In certain lakes in summer, eels are constantly making a nuisance of themselves by sucking the guts out of sardines, running away with baits intended for pike and tangling wire traces. There is only one pike bait that they won't touch, and that's another eel.

I'm a member of the Eel Anglers' Club and an ardent campaigner for putting large eels back, but it has become a positive pleasure to me to use a small one as bait in Scotland. Fishing an eel section certainly gets rid of the problem, for while pike have no qualms about eating each other, small eels won't consider eating their own kind, thank goodness. I never go to Scotland now without a couple of dozen eel sections in my freezer box.

Eels have made a particular nuisance of themselves in Scotland by tangling wire traces and taking bait intended for pike.

ROACH HAVE THEIR PLACE

If you'd asked me a short time ago what I thought about roach as deadbaits I would have said 'Not a lot', as I'd never caught anything outstanding on one. But that was before a 26 lb 12 oz river pike took a 1 lb-plus roach I was fishing sink-and-draw.

The truth is, if I had fished roach deadbaits more often perhaps I might have had more success with them (see picture below), but as I am happy using sardines, mackerel and wobbled trout, I haven't felt the need to find an alternative to these baits. But if I were on a water where roach are the predominant species but which wasn't responding to sea baits, I would certainly give one a try.

I've also used them as pop-ups with air injected in their stomach, and swim bladder left intact, to stop them from sinking into blanket weed, creating a highly visible bait. And I use them in the mouths

Avoid bursting the swim bladder when air-injecting deadbaits, as the added buoyancy will help keep it clear of blanket weed on the bottom and visible to passing fish.

of tributaries, or on gravel pits when the sun is out, and pike come up to take plateau feeders. They make good trailing baits, too, towed behind a boat beneath a float, as I've done on Blenheim Palace lake.

Eels are so plentiful in these lochs that pike must feed on them regularly, especially when the eels are congregated in one place when making the most of a large, natural food source, like eggs from spawning fish. They are such a high-protein food that it is too good for pike to ignore, and I'm sure they seek them out at certain times.

Waters in southern England also have large populations of eels. Broadlands Lake has a massive head of eels and brown trout, and plenty of big pike as well. On waters like this, eel sections are well worth a try.

Anything from a 1 lb to a 1 lb 4 oz eel is about the best size, though smaller ones still make good baits. The eel should be chopped into four-inch sections, which can be used over and over again without losing any of their attractiveness. I've caught three or four pike on one eel section, which is about as much as you can ask of any bait.

I mount mine straight on the hooks without using the deadbait support rig, because there is nowhere to put the loop of line. This doesn't matter because an eel's skin is so tough even hooks nicked lightly under it will stand up to the fiercest casting. A 1 lb 4 oz eel is the limit, though. I'm not prepared to use anything of over that size. A 2 lb to 3 lb eel could be twenty to thirty years old, and I'm not prepared to kill something of that age just for an alternative bait.

Perch taken tail first

On the subject of alternative pike baits, it's often vital to match the species being used to the one most common in the water being fished. Perch come into their own as a bait when used on a water where they predominate, but when there are no more perch than normal, they are not as good a bait as a wobbled trout or a legered mackerel or sardine.

The species has made a comeback, and the huge increase in the population in recent times means they have to be considered as a bait as they are bound to figure in the diet of pike. Perch lie in similar areas to pike and live in close proximity to them, so it is no surprise pike target them. Considering how they are valued as a table fish on the continent, it would come as no surprise if perch were to feature high on a pike's menu.

I can remember legering a sardine while fishing with my son on a backwater of the Thames, and watching pike chasing perch but showing no interest in what I was offering them. But when I found a worm under a tree stump, caught a perch on my son's rod, and put that on as bait, it was taken as soon as I cast out, by a pike of 23 lb.

But while they make lively and hardy livebaits, with skins so tough that hooks need only to be nicked in lightly, as sink-and-draw deadbaits they are a dead loss, as they go as stiff as a board as soon as they are killed. And as they don't smell particularly attractive, they don't make very good static deadbaits either.

Incidentally, there's a myth about pike that eat perch, that claims they can only take them down head first. It's not true. Pike can also swallow them tail first, spiky dorsal fin and razor-pointed gill covers and all, though don't ask me how.

Smelt and sandeels

Sandeels make great distance baits, because you can whack them out to features in a way that wouldn't be possible with other species. Their main drawback is that, while they can be freelined at close range, that is about their limit so far as freelining goes, because of their lightness, for they can only be cast short distances without a lead.

Smelts have a beautiful aroma of cucumber, and pink flesh that is very attractive to pike. When popped up they stay buoyant for hours, and they are also good for paternostering. However, once thawed they don't lend themselves to re-freezing, as the aroma disappears and the flesh turns very soft.

All manner of exotics

I'm often asked by anglers whether exotics work for pike, mostly by anglers who seem to think that the unusual makes up for bad angling. It's a popular myth that pike on waters fished hard with conventional baits will respond to strange creatures the like of which they've never seen before. All manner of weirdos, from tropical tank casualties to multi-coloured, spiky-finned sea fish, have been tried, but to the best of my knowledge the anglers using them are still waiting for them to work regularly. The truth is that any bait is only as good as the angler using it.

It's tempting to think that pike on hard-fished waters will respond better to an unusual bait, but on pits in the Oxford area that have been pike fished regularly for over ten years, fish are still picking up mackerel and sardines. If ever there was an argument against popping down to the Asian market for a kilo of lesser forkbeard, or raiding the aquarist shop's dustbin for black bullhead catfish, then that is it.

More important than the choice of bait are the method of presentation and putting the bait in the right spot. It's not the bait that 'blows' on a water, it's the way it is presented, and if a different tactic is used and the bait fished at a different depth or in a different style, then fish that rejected it the first time may be encouraged to take it the second.

Pike anglers can be the worst offenders when it comes to being inflexible in their approach. Many will throw out a deadbait and sit back for hours in the hope of a run, when a paternostered, popped-up or wobbled deadbait would have brought instant results.

Or it could be the time of day: if pike have become wary of feeding in daylight and moved out of range to return at night, then fishing on into the dark could be the answer.

My advice to anyone determined to use exotics is, fish one on one rod and a standard bait on the other, to compare their effectiveness. But personally I wouldn't bother with exotics unless I had first tried a variety of methods of presentation with conventional baits.

Flavouring and colouring baits

Flavoured and coloured baits will always be popular with anglers, but there are other ways of making sure your baits stand out and catch the eye of patrolling pike.

I've never felt the need to flavour or colour my baits, though some anglers do it a lot. If I want a bait that is highly visible, I will use a roach or dace, or pop a bait up, or wobble it to make it stand out more. There are so many ways of making a bait more noticeable that I don't think treating them is necessary.

Some anglers will dye a bait and then fish it on the bottom. I have serious doubts about how much of a bait a pike can see when it is on the bottom. A pike's eyes are set so high on its head that they must lose sight of the bait when they get above it and close to it, which makes dyeing it a bit of a waste of time.

Some anglers swear that adding a coloured, plastic tag to trebles when using livebaits improves their catches. Most of the tags I've seen used have been red, which pike can see very well, but they are equally attuned to picking out greens and yellows. In experiments in Holland, different-coloured lights were shone in tanks, and pike were found to be attracted to those that were red, green or yellow, but least attracted to blue. Red is a colour that occurs naturally on the fins of food fish like roach, and these are used to signal to each other, which means they are very visible under the water, although not visible above the surface by birds and other predators. If they are visible to other roach, they are particularly visible to pike because they hunt from below.

Yet Fred Buller's most successful plug is one that has a green back and a yellow belly, so I believe that any strong additional colour, whether it be red, green or yellow, may enhance a bait's attractiveness.

Of more importance is the size of the tag, because all freshwater is slightly cloudy, and for a pike to see a tag on a bait it needs to be big enough to stand out.

Be prepared for the unexpected

If there's one rule to bear in mind when choosing a bait for pike fishing, it's always expect the unexpected. The majority of pike will take standard baits for most of the time, but there are always freak preoccupations, and fish with stomachs full of strange things. On a water I fished with friends we all found sport slow until a big fish turned up out of the blue caught on a tench, which was only used because of a shortage of bait. Others followed when we tried the bait again, proving it wasn't a fluke. It seemed we were dealing with a preoccupation. They certainly didn't want what we were offering up until then.

Perhaps it was the size of the bait. The tench in that lake were numerous, and all about 1 lb or just over. The fry in Theale Lagoon were only an inch or two in length, yet they were being targeted by pike big enough to make you think they wouldn't consider it worth their while chasing things little bigger than whitebait.

If there's a moral, it's that it's always worth trying a bait that is naturally occurring, even if only as a last resort. If one species of food fish is there in large numbers, then the pike may not need to eat anything else, and this could hold the key to unlocking the mystery of why your line seems glued to your rod rings.

Sometimes it is only when the supply of the chosen food dries up that these fish are caught, having been forced to broaden their diet. There may have been a lot of angling activity on that water for a number of years, yet these fish with tunnel vision as far as food is concerned, many of which are very large, will have avoided capture because no one was using what they were eating.

Pike like an easy life

Trout waters are slightly different. A lot of people, especially fly anglers who see pike as a menace, think that pike in trout waters feed only on trout. But that isn't necessarily the case. If there are many bream or roach in the water, it is a reasonable bet that the pike will take the more vulnerable, slower-swimming coarse fish and ignore the trout. Pike are basically lazy creatures looking for an easy life. They will seek to gain maximum reward from minimum effort, which means eating bream and roach. So although there are lots of trout, fishing with a trout livebait may not work.

In most situations, though, your standard choice of bait will suffice. It's only when pike get locked into eating one species and ignoring everything else that we have to rethink things.

An impressive 23 lb pike – which this author was particularly proud of!

And it's worth remembering that you can take experimentation too far, and neglect presentation and location, both of which are usually of more importance than choice of bait. Faith in the bait you are used to using is the foundation stone of successful fishing.

Upper Thames pike feed mainly on chub, and lower Thames on bream, while Severn or Wye fish take mostly roach, dace and eels. But I would back a sardine or half mackerel against any of these coarse baits in most circumstances. I don't know if it's the stronger smell that sea baits give off, as they certainly must taste different from coarse fish, but, with a few exceptions, sardines, mackerel and trout will score more heavily than any coarse deadbaits.

Just occasionally, though, something unexpected comes to light and makes us realise how little we know about the feeding preferences of pike. Farmoor I is a prolific, trout-fishing-only reservoir with a good head of pike and stocks of roach, bream, chub and perch of a suitable size for food. When big coarse fish die and float to the surface they are often picked out when they wash ashore and given to a local taxidermist, who examines the stomach contents when preparing the body to be set up. Over the course of a couple of years, several sizeable pike were opened up, and all were found to be full to the gills with weed. Farmoor I is a very rich water and the weed is not just empty green stuff, but teeming with larvae and crustaceans. I can only suggest that those pike had cottoned on to the fact that they only had to eat this protein-rich herbage to survive, and so avoid wasting energy chasing food that could swim away. Perhaps there is more to pike diet than we think.

It's a mistake to fish too many waters. The more of them you fish, the less time you will spend on each one and the less well you will get to know each of them. It's best to concentrate on one or two until you know them intimately.

CHAPTER 7

GRAVEL PITS & LAKES

G RAVEL PITS ARE LIKE PEOPLE – NO TWO ARE EVER ALIKE. One will be good in the mornings but difficult in the evenings, and another will be moody in the morning but at its best late at night. But they all have behaviour patterns. Study them carefully and you will be able to anticipate their moods and arrange to be around when they are at their best. If you fish a water around the clock for a number of weeks, you will be able to work out the feeding periods and to be on another water in the quiet periods.

In settled weather at any one time of year, it is sometimes possible to set your watch by the feeding spells of pike. And if you know when to be there, and have access to two or three waters with consecutive feeding spells in one small area, you can be at each one at the 'hot' time and make the most of all of them.

A 23 lb specimen taken on a half mackerel.

A 27 lb 8 oz fish from the Nature Reserve, a water in which the pike fed most often in the afternoon when a south-westerly was blowing.

Perfect timing

At one time I was fishing four waters near Oxford: the Education Pit, the Poplar Pit, the Nature Reserve and the Night Water. All were close to each other and had good bankside access, so I could drive right up to the swims. The fish on the Education Pit fed at first light, for half an hour, and that would be it for the rest of the day. The Poplar Pit normally fished well from 11 a.m. to 11.30 a.m., the Nature Reserve in the afternoons, and the Night Water, logically, at night.

One Sunday a friend, Steve Kilbee, and I decided to have a 'pit crawl'. We started on the Education Pit and had pike of 23 lb, 24 lb and an 18-pounder at first light. We got to the Poplar Pit at about 10.30 a.m. and had pike of 24 lb and 26 lb within the space of forty-five minutes. By noon we had moved down the road to the Nature Reserve, and Steve had one of 26 lb, and that evening we fished the Night Pit and, within fifteen minutes of casting, I had a pike of 19 lb 6 oz. It doesn't happen like that very often, but when it does it's enormously satisfying, and you know you are beginning to get it right.

But it's a mistake to fish too many waters. The more of them you fish, the less time you will spend on each one and the less well you will get to know each of them. It's best to concentrate on one or two until you know them intimately. If you then move on to other waters but find them hard going at first, you can return to the ones you know for a confidence booster.

The popular choice for most pike anglers

Love them or loathe them, gravel pits make up a large percentage of the pike fishing available to most anglers, and as rivers gradually decline in level and quality because of the increasing demand for water, the role they play is likely to increase. To fully understand them you need to know a little of the history of how and why they were created, and how they differ according to the decade in which they were dug.

Most of those we fish now were dug in the 1970s and 1980s, when the building boom was at its height and gravel for roads and houses was in great supply. Rich seams in and around Berkshire, Buckinghamshire, Surrey, Hertfordshire and Oxfordshire were fully exploited by firms like Smiths Gravel, Peter Cullimore and ARC, with the result that large areas of land were turned into pits as companies extracted the gravel. Huge complexes grew up around Reading, at South Cerney, down at Ringwood, and near Staines, as well up in Lincolnshire and down in Kent – anywhere with gravel seams deep enough to be financially viable. Oxford got a ring road to lighten the traffic in the city, and gravel for that dual-carriageway came from pits that have since become famous-name fisheries, like the Thames Conservancy pit (TC) just yards from the road it created, Dorchester Lagoon and Queenford Lagoon.

A gravel pit dug dry, with its furrows and heaps of non-gravel items.

An Oxford gravel pit dug down to its layer of blue clay.

So many gravel pits were dug in the seventies that when they had been worked out, many were left fallow as the extractors moved on to the next. They filled with rainwater and through seepage from underground springs, as the water table that previously infiltrated the gravel returned to its natural level. When winter came and heavy rain made swollen streams and brooks spill over into the pits, a new aquatic environment was born.

How they were dug

The way gravel was extracted has a bearing on the contours of each water. Early pits were dug using drag lines and buckets to scoop up the gravel, creating long furrows side by side, like the lines in a ploughed field. This rather crude method means that pits dug in the sixties and early seventies have furrows along the bottom.

Any non-gravel items extracted were swept to one side in a random pattern, creating contours and bars, later to become important features. But these early pits are very different from later ones that were purposely landscaped by contractors, in line with new regulations.

Later, a more efficient method of extracting gravel was devised, and pits were excavated using mechanical diggers called Traxcavators, which need a dry surface to operate. So those dug in the eighties, right up to the financial crash and the end of the boom in 1987, were dug dry and didn't have furrows.

And now in the twenty-first century, on the few pits being worked, methods are further mechanised, and the bed of the lake is much smoother, rising on to plateaux as the gravel seam lifts, and dropping where it runs deep again.

But no matter how good methods of gravel extraction become, the pits they produce will rarely be more than 30 feet deep, because that's roughly gravel's extreme depth. The majority of pits in the Home Counties and Oxfordshire are between 9 feet and 15 feet deep. In Kent they removed the gravel but stopped when they reached the greensand layer because there was no commercial demand for greensand, whereas in Oxfordshire it was blue clay they hit when the gravel had been taken out.

Pits dug purely for clay differ from gravel pits in that they can be as much as 140 feet deep. Clay occurs in much deeper seams than gravel. These very deep waters only fish well under the warm rays of spring sunshine and when the water has had a chance to warm up by the autumn, but not in mid-winter. A few years ago some friends and I fished Grebe Lake, at Crendon Underwood near Bicester,

Pike from egg stage to three weeks old. After hatching, they attach themselves to weed for several days until their yolk sack has been absorbed and they are strong enough to become free-swimming and start to hunt for food.

which is a clay pit of this depth, and struggled to get a run after November. Timing is the most important factor when approaching clay pits, as the fish are in a state of semi-hibernation in the coldest weather and unlikely to respond.

How they are colonised?

In a newly flooded gravel pit, life enters from feeder streams that bring caddis and crustaceans, hog lice and shrimps – food for the first fish in a new water.

Often, gravel pits are connected by a series of small pipes used to keep the water level at bay while others are being worked. Small fish find their way in when streams flood over fields to one gravel pit, and then all the others become colonised. Damsel flies, sedges and bloodworm spread as adults on the wing, providing an excellent food supply.

Small fish and insects seem to appear almost instantly in recently flooded waters, providing the basis for a new ecosystem of aquatic life. The tiny fish begin their lives in the varieties of marginal weeds that sprout up as the gravel working stops and the water clears, over the course of two or three months. If the pit has been dug dry enough for light to penetrate in the large puddles of shallow water, certain hardy water plants may have got a foothold already. This weed provides the small fish that arrive with food and cover. Tiny fish can live out the start of their lives hidden in weed. Pull some up on any still water in summer and you will find insect life and minute fish sheltering in among the strands.

The plop of small pike

Daphnia multiply and provide food for small fish. Among them will be small pike. After hatching, they stay close to the weed in which they were born and live on a diet of daphnia, plankton and minute crustaceans. From four to five weeks old, they begin to feed on larger prey like chironomids and small fish, including their own kind, and by May and June they are taking large fry. I have often sat by the water in summer and heard the resounding plops of tiny pike taking buzzers and damselfly nymphs off the surface in the marginal rafts of floating weed.

I believe that the first fish to learn to become cannibalistic may become the ultimate survivors. They manage to make it through the first winter by feeding on their own brethren, whereas other young pike often find food hard to come by and their mortality rate is much higher. If the roach fail to spawn one year, then the pike that have learned to feed on their own kind are the ones that will survive. Why some do and some don't is still a mystery. If they get through the first two winters, they are over the most precarious time, and their likelihood of survival improves a great deal. But nature does its best to help them, and its timing is exquisite. When the pike are a couple of months old the roach, perch and bream fry emerge from their eggs when they are of a perfect size for the young pike to eat.

When young pike are ready to leave the margins to seek bigger creatures in the depths, having outgrown the shallow water, they lose the characteristic creamy yellow bars on their flanks. They now weigh about 7 lb, and this change in markings takes two or three years to come about. The bars are replaced by oval, dappled spots better suited to camouflage in the shifting light found in deeper water.

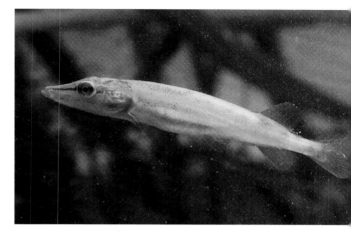

How fast do pike grow?

By the time a water is ten to fifteen years old, with a good fish population, it should contain a fair head of 20 lb pike. I caught a 23 lb pike in a gravel pit and sent a scale from it to Alwyne Wheeler at the British Museum. He counted nine annual growth rings. The rate of growth is speeded up if the gravel pit is linked to older ones by drainage pipes or channels, which greatly aid the spread of fish. But even 50-acre or 60-acre rich gravel pits rarely have more than four or five fish of 20 lb, which is about the upper limit, and there are very few waters with more than this.

Pike weights in gravel pits that aren't artificially topped up with trout or coarse fish seem to reach their size limit at 33 lb to 34 lb. If you've caught one of that weight, you've gone about as far as you can go on that sort of water. It takes a gravel pit with something very special for the weight of its pike to go above that

Sit by the water in summer and you will hear the resounding plops of tiny pike taking buzzers and damselfly nymphs off the surface. The ones that turn cannibalistic first will be the ultimate survivors.

This is my second-best river pike, a 26 lb 12 oz fish taken on a sink-and-draw roach while it was lying close to a bream shoal.

– something like a plentiful supply of bream or a very large head of roach. Some commercially run waters stock large numbers of small food fish, like carp, that make good fodder and improve the growth rate enormously.

There have also been occasions when a pit has been backfilled and all of the fish have been concentrated into a smaller area, creating a bonanza for the pike. If you come across a pit being backfilled, do your utmost to get permission to fish it, because catches can be impressive and location is not a problem.

So, the age of a gravel pit is very important when trying to discover whether it holds big fish, but you can't tell how old one is by the number and size of trees on the banks. If it hasn't been landscaped, there will be very few shrubs. If there are mature willows, then it's a fair bet that it is between fifteen and twenty years old, but don't overlook a water just because it has near-barren banks. Plenty of those sort of waters have produced big pike.

The amount of vegetation overhanging the surface and the clarity of the water dictate whether it is silty or weedy. Water surrounded by trees that lose their leaves tends to be silty and free from weed, because the trees shade the light necessary for weed growth, and their fallen leaves cover the bottom, also hampering growth. Some waters are so narrow and have such a luxuriant growth of trees on the banks that they form a canopy, blocking out much of the light. Less weed growth means fewer food fish and fewer pike.

Open pits may contain one or two small pike, but they are generally likely to be richer. Small open waters can produce big fish, but don't spent too much time on them in the hope that they hold a monster. You'll know within two or three sessions if there's something special in there.

Gravel pits designed for angling

So many gravel pits were dug and left fallow in the seventies that it was possible to investigate them without anyone knowing or caring. The firms were too busy digging gravel to concern themselves about the pits they had left behind. At South Cerney alone there were forty or fifty gravel pits in one small area, all of different ages and many untouched by anglers. All gravel pits produce their best catches in cycles, and those that didn't produce big fish when we tried them could be left for a few years until they were at their peak, such was the huge choice of waters.

But by the time the eighties arrived, purpose-built recreation waters were being created by gravel companies when extraction had been completed, in line with planning regulations and agreements signed when permission to dig for gravel was granted. They landscaped the pits, creating bars and islands for wildlife and nesting birds, planted vegetation above and below the waterline, and flooded them to create wildlife sanctuaries, water parks and recreation centres for sailing enthusiasts, water-skiers and anglers.

Waters that have had little attention from anglers do exist, like the one in Gloucestershire that produced this fish of 24 lb 8 oz.

What started out as an obligation to leave the area looking attractive soon became a chance to respond to a growing demand for sites suitable for outdoor activities. They found that if they built houses in the area, and set up water sports parks for wind surfing and jet-skiing, there was big money to be made at a time when the demand for gravel and the need to dig new pits was falling.

The situation now is that there are fewer new waters being created than for several decades, but the rise in the popularity of pike fishing, as the second most popular fishing species after carp, has meant more anglers pursuing them. Where once you could visit a complex and stroll around several waters trying here and there unhindered, now there's hardly a gravel pit anywhere that hasn't got a line of brollies or bivvies sprouting like green mushrooms from its banks. And on such waters pike won't reach their full potential if they are being caught regularly instead of being left to feed and grow.

Pike-angling pioneers

So the angler who wants good sport has to break new ground if he is to keep catching big pike. He needs to be the first one on a water, he needs to spend a lot of time fishing speculatively, and put up with hours spent trying to get to grips with new places and, unfortunately, he needs to cover his tracks so that others can't follow.

I'm more secretive about location than I used to be. When waters were ten a penny I'd talk openly, but not now. The few pits that allow me solitude are very precious, because I know how hard it is to find new waters.

On my third cast with a sink-and-draw wobbled trout, this incredible pike came after the bait, broke the water as it took it and tore off. It pulled the scales down to an incredible 35 lb.

I like fishing pits that haven't seen an angler. Their challenge is a large part of the attraction of pike fishing for me. And once I catch the fish I'm after, I seldom go back. The challenge is in finding somewhere untouched, exploring it, calculating the age of the pit and its potential, getting permission, working out how to tackle it, plumbing depths, finding features, calculating where the fish should be and putting them on the bank, hard-fighting and fin-perfect, untouched by any other angler.

For me, the preparation and planning is as exciting as the fishing, and the catching is just the icing on the cake. But when you land a fish from that type of water, having done your homework, you do get an incredible amount of satisfaction. You don't get this if you let others do the preparation work for you, and just cast out and reel the fish in without understanding why you have caught it.

Waters that have had little attention from anglers do still exist. We once found a place so overgrown we had to cut our way through brambles and hawthorns to get to the bank, and then there were no swims or footpaths to make things easy. Yet it produced pike in the upper twenties for us.

I believe that almost all of the fish I have landed have never been caught before. You can often tell when a pike has been handled – abrasion marks down its side from hooks or wire, an old wound in the area of the jaw where a small layer of scar tissue has healed, or fins split by mishandling. But virgin waters aren't easy to find. In many cases it takes more ingenuity and perseverance to get access to an unspoilt water than it does to catch the fish that are in it.

In search of new waters

Every close season I look at new waters and search for pits capable of producing big fish, using Ordnance Survey maps for the area. Often they are the most remote, as this stops them from getting other anglers' attention.

My biggest pike came from a gravel pit I saw while driving around looking at waters. It was close to a stream, so I thought it might have a good head of eels and food fish, and it looked quite old, judging by the size and maturity of the trees around it.

I knocked on the door of an old cottage nearby, and asked the man who answered it if he knew anything about the gravel pit nearby. He said it belonged to him but he didn't have any fishing on it. I told him I was interested in pike and explained that I wouldn't abuse his permission, drop litter, make a noise, drive

Fish of 24 lb 12 oz and 24 lb 8 oz in consecutive casts from a clear gravel pit.

on the land or do anything that would abuse his trust, and any fish caught would be put back. He was a nature lover and had had the water dug initially to attract wildlife and birds. He didn't need money from anglers, being a rich land owner, so he had everything to lose and nothing to gain. He said he would think about it for a few weeks, and I arranged to contact him at a later date. I didn't ring back sooner, because people who get pestered invariably say no. I left it for six weeks, despite my keenness to get on the water. I find it easier to put my case face to face, and it's harder for someone to turn you down when you're standing next to them than when you're on the phone, so I drove over and knocked on his door.

Again I explained how keen I was to fish, but he said he hadn't made up his mind and had to consult his wife. I found out in talking to him that we had a common interest in birds, and I think it was this shared love of nature that made him trust me and give me permission to fish.

Walking on to that water with my tackle felt like a victory already. I was being allowed on to a very special place that no one else had been near for decades. I plumbed the depth in various places and found nowhere of greater depth than eight feet, and the majority about five feet. The water was extremely clear, with a feeder stream at one end and an outlet at the other, and I could see a lot of coarse fish of a whole range of different sizes that hadn't been fished for in thirty years.

I got out my compass and headed for the north-east bank. The water was shallow there, no more than three feet deep. On my third cast with a sink-and-draw wobbled trout, this incredible pike came after the bait, broke the water as it took it and tore off with it. The fight was short and dogged. One of my most memorable moments is when it rolled over in the net and I got my first glimpse of its size. It pulled the scales down to an incredible 35 lb.

I'm sure there were other big fish in there, but that experience had been close to perfection, and I walked away and haven't fished the water since. I did consider it once, but the more often you go back the more likely that other anglers will find out where the water is.

Special occasions

If you get a chance to fish a water that is only open for a couple of days each year it is worth taking the one-off opportunity. Thorpe Park was like that once, allowing people on for lure championships or special occasions, but being closed to angling for the rest of the time. There's a water near Reading that opens its doors just once a year, and it produces 20 lb fish every time, weather permitting.

If you get a chance to visit a protected water, grab it with both hands. The pike are likely to be plentiful and in excellent condition, and not too difficult to catch. At other times, finding new waters can mean watching them being dug and earmarking them for attention once they have become fisheries. It takes two

A 24-pounder taken on a mackerel head.

A 16 lb 4 oz pike taken on a half mackerel fished at close range.

years for fish to become firmly established naturally in a new water. From then on, whether it breeds a monster is down to the shape of the pit and the balance between pike and food fish. I've watched a water near Stanton Harcourt for the whole of its 25-year history, and caught fish to 28 lb from it.

The size and shape of the water depends on the size and shape of the original gravel seam. The biggest pit I have come across was a mile and a half long, but others are only an acre. And while a big water is likely to be the better bet, there is no reason why a small one should not produce a monster. It is all down to food and pressure.

Some are five feet deep almost all over, and others are 20 feet deep in places. You need to know how each one measures up. Some seem ideal until you find they have roosting points for cormorants, and the food fish have been all but wiped out, while others have big populations of bite-size food fish that provide pike with a well-stocked larder.

Some are coloured, where gravel extraction is still being carried out. These often have big populations of bream, and you can be sure that where there are a lot of bream of edible size, there are going to be a lot of pike. And others, particularly Oxford pits, are renowned for their still-water chub, dace and roach, which breed successfully in them and so are present in all sizes. They form an important food source for pike and should be considered as a choice of bait.

Learning to read a water by what you can see above the waterline is a valuable skill, for it enables you to at least estimate the potential of somewhere you are considering fishing while doing nothing more suspicious than strolling round the bank.

Assessing pike fishing potential

So you're standing on the banks of a likely-looking water on a warm, sunny day. What do you look for to assess its pike fishing potential?

Start by peering into the margins as you walk round. As we have said, any water that holds fair-sized pike needs a good supply of food fish of various sizes, so that pike of different sizes can find plenty to eat, and some of these will be visible in the margins or the shallows, especially if it is a warm day. Some pits have a lot of big pike but nothing else, because the only food fish are big, old coarse fish that have ceased to spawn, and with nothing smaller in the water, pike have nothing to eat apart from the jacks.

If it's a silt-bottomed water, it may have tench and carp in it, and if it's a weedy water it should have roach, rudd, tench and perch – worth bearing in mind when choosing baits.

Others are surrounded by farmland and get large quantities of nitrates washed in from the soil during rainfall, which will promote weed growth, perhaps to the extent that the water won't be fishable other than on the surface until October.

The size of the water is a factor to consider, but don't be misled into thinking that a big water means big numbers of pike. I believe that a 120-acre water I fished had just twelve pike of over 20 lb in it. If a water such as this gets a lot of angling attention, and the fish are caught regularly, perhaps without people realising that they are the same ones, the brief burst of good sport won't last. The fish will find some way of eluding anglers, by changing their feeding times and habits and by moving into areas where anglers cannot reach them.

Built on chalk

Some pits aren't gravel pits at all but are formed when extracting chalk, which brings another set of circumstances into play. These tend to be very clear, like the famous southern trout streams, the Test and the Itchen, which run over chalk. Weed growth can be phenomenal, creating presentation problems.

Weed can grow to within feet of the surface, so a sunken-float paternostered or buoyant bait will be more visible. I have cast deadbaits into weed on such waters and caught fish, scaling up from 15 lb line to 18 lb to pull them clear. An air-injected bait fished on top of weed, a pop-up rig with the bait allowed to rise to near the surface or a shallow, float-fished bait are other ways around the problem.

I like to tackle these waters early in the year, in February and March, before the weed has started to grow, or in October, when pike are still high in the water and the weed is beginning to die back. But whenever I fish, I will always go for a very visible bait, like a roach or a dace.

At the other extreme, waters that are very coloured present no weed problems but may have a thick layer of silt that can hide baits when presented near to the bottom. In the water we named the Big Coloured Pit, the fish were very pale, as they often are in murky water. Whenever you get a cloudy water there is always a bream shoal thriving in that environment, and this pit was no exception.

We found out by accident that this water had a deep layer of silt on the bottom. We were fishing there unsuccessfully when Jurassic Phil's tatty old umbrella was picked up by a strong gust of wind and hurled into the water. Most people would have given it up for lost but, being someone with deep pockets and short arms when it comes to paying for new tackle, Phil had to have it back. He tied a 3 oz bomb and two trebles to the end of his line and cast over it to drag it back. Only when he got the brolly, thick with silt, did we realise what the bottom was like and that our baits had been sinking deep into the stuff, out of sight of the pike. Pop-ups were the answer, and still are. Sometimes the solution can be found completely by accident, and the key to cracking a water can lie in one small discovery.

Where do you head for?

The Poplar Pit, with fish holding features marked.

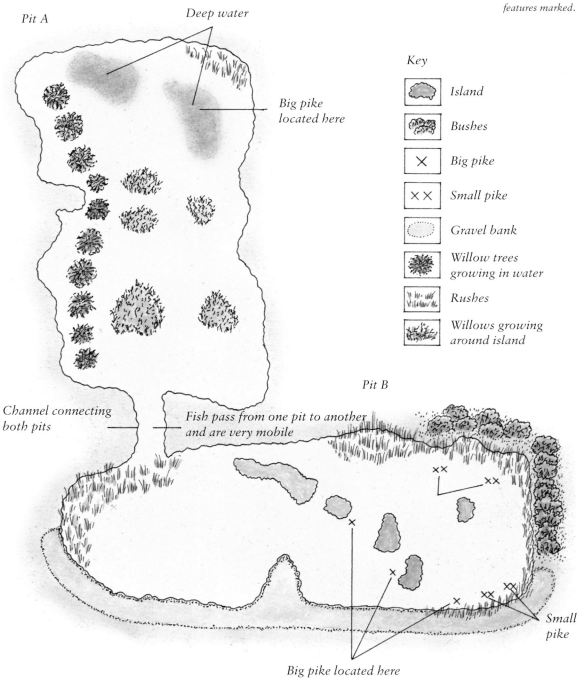

Pit A

Deep water

Big pike located here

Key

Island

Bushes

Big pike

Small pike

Gravel bank

Willow trees growing in water

Rushes

Willows growing around island

Pit B

Channel connecting both pits

Fish pass from one pit to another and are very mobile

Small pike

Big pike located here

On a new water I always start in the north-east corner, because that's where the warmest south-westerly wind will have been blowing. It's also where any dead or dying coarse fish that float up in the water will be carried, and pike there will be on the look out for a free meal.

If that fails to produce, though it usually yields something, I head for the north bank, and then work my way down into the corner again and along the east bank, which will be sheltered from cold easterly winds and their raw chill factor. The east bank can hold a deep gully that is home to large shoals of bream and roach, though this is by no means always the case.

The only time I will fish one of the other banks is when there is a fish-holding feature, like a series of islands, that may have drawn pike away from the usual holding areas, or if the water in the favoured corner is very shallow or extremely deep and unsuitable for pike to live in.

On the Big Coloured Pit, which is 120 acres and 22 feet deep, there were only four swims that produced fish. As an experiment, we tied baits to cotton and put them out in different areas. Many of these rotted away without being taken, which gives you an indication of how few swims are worth fishing, even on a big water.

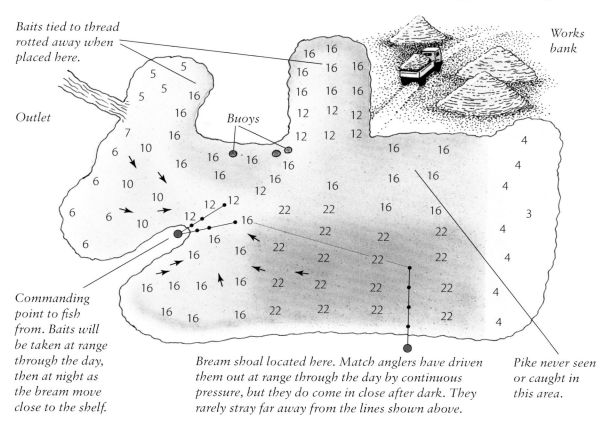

Baits tied to thread rotted away when placed here.

Outlet

Buoys

Works bank

Commanding point to fish from. Baits will be taken at range through the day, then at night as the bream move close to the shelf.

Bream shoal located here. Match anglers have driven them out at range through the day by continuous pressure, but they do come in close after dark. They rarely stray far away from the lines shown above.

Pike never seen or caught in this area.

Wooded banks and islands harbour insects, which drop into the water attracting prey fish, which in turn attract pike.

If the water you are fishing is popular, there's always a chance that fish have been pushed into unlikely areas by angling pressure. That complicates matters, because the fish are no longer behaving naturally, and when working out their likely location you have to consider their need to escape anglers as well as their need to feed and find shelter.

My first line of attack would be to tackle areas rarely fished, at longer range and closer in than the norm, using the least common baits at the least popular times, possibly at night. And on a new water I would try to fish as many different swims as possible to get a broad picture of which areas are most productive.

Whatever the situation on a new water, start by breaking it down into several, smaller parts, to make it more manageable, and look at one area at a time, examining the features. The following places are likely to attract food fish and pike:

Ledges are used by coarse fish like bream and roach, which will follow them, coming in to them at night, searching for food and feeding at the bottom of the shelf, where they feel secure. Baits have to be placed right against the ledge with pinpoint accuracy, not just fairly near, as that is where pike will feed.

Drop-offs likewise. The smaller the water, the less pronounced a contour needs to be to attract fish. In a shallow water a drop-off of a foot is a major feature, whereas in a deeper one it wouldn't necessarily be a spot to head for.

Buoys placed by sailing clubs are attached to their anchors by ropes, and ropes collect algae, which attracts food fish, which in turn attracts pike. On the Big Coloured Pit, if we could hit a buoy with half a mackerel we would catch fish.

Landing stages require a very stealthy approach. We used to creep to the end of one on the Education Pit and lower the bait straight down from the rod top and then stand well back.

When **islands** are created artificially on gravel pits they're often made by digging a deep trough alongside. These can be anything up to twenty feet deep and home to bream and roach, with the pike holding a little way off them, keeping in contact with the shoal.

I like to put a boat with an echo sounder on a new water if the rules allow, and look for contours that could attract fish. However, I won't fish from it, because I don't believe boat fishing on gravel pits is in anyone's long-term interests. Pike need to have some sanctuary where they can escape from the attentions of anglers, and on many waters the only way they can find peace is by getting out of casting range of the bank.

Feeder streams attract large shoals of fry and have large numbers of pike crashing into them. Water piped from another pit will often have the same oxygenating, fish-attracting effect, stirring up food on the bottom and cutting a hollow in the lake bed. Chub in particular seem to like these.

Sticks, dead trees and saplings growing in the water offer refuge and cover from open water. Perch in particular like them. Pike will often get right in among beds of sticks, and heavy tackle will be needed to get them out.

Small pike are fond of **rushes** as they suit their camouflage colouring, and this in turn attracts very big, jack-feeding pike. The best kind of rushes are the ones that have spaces between them so that pike can get in. If they're too densely packed, pike can't penetrate them.

Pike can get so far into them that they can't detect your bait, fished up against the edge. When you have tried putting a bait against the weeds, without success, you can then sometimes flush a fish out by disturbing it, and it is still likely to take a bait. As Fred Buller explained in his book, *Pike and Pike Angers*, Tom Morgan's experiences of flushing pike out of dense weed beds by weed-thrashing with an oar from a boat and then catching them on livebaits has been proven to work on other waters. John Bailey and Barrie Rickards know the same happens among the Norfolk reed beds in East Anglia, and no doubt this would work elsewhere.

Gravel bars are sometimes interlinked throughout a pit, and pike, which know its layout intimately, will follow the contours. They will wait alongside a bar or at the bottom for the chance to attack their prey from below and ambush them without being seen. Gravel bars are a welcome sight as they break up the monotony of large strips of water and offer shelter and food for fish of all species.

Wooded banks and **islands** harbour insects, which drop into the water, and they in turn attract roach and so pike. The best place to put a bait near an island is where the warmest winds hit its shores, which means the southern tip or western side. It's also worth a look at the steepest shore in wet weather, as land-based creatures like worms and slugs may fall into the water.

Fish hooked at close quarters can whip the water into a foam. When fishing the margins, be ready for a surprise.

A fish of 21 lb 8 oz on a sardine freelined against a submerged island.

In raw, easterly winds, **bays** can offer welcome shelter from the cold, for you and the fish, and when the sun is on the water it is these that usually warm up first. If they're on the north bank, receiving warm winds, even better.

Whenever I fish a bay I cover the exit and entrance, so that a pike entering it from anywhere on the water has to come across one or both of my baits. Normally it will follow the contour of the bank and not just swim into the bay from open water, so you should cast on either side of the mouth.

Points and headlands are very important features from an angler's point of view, as pike moving from one area to another can be intercepted by a bait cast from a point. A great deal of water can be covered from a peninsula – far more than when fishing from a straight bank, with a commanding view of the water. And if you have an island close by, even better. You can cast a bait between the two features where it forms a funnel through which food fish swim, and an ideal ambush site for pike to lie in wait. A channel that connects two pits is another good ambush point because it is narrower still.

But the biggest single feature on any gravel pit is **the bank**. Small fish take refuge in the margins, wave action disturbs the margins, dead fish get swept into the margins, and so on. And if a water doesn't have any islands or bars, like the Thames Conservancy pit, for instance, the margins are even more likely to produce pike.

Walk along an undisturbed bank early in the morning and you will see small fish swimming out from the edge as you approach. Even in midwinter you can

WHY PIKE ARE EASIER IN WINTER

A lot depends on the time of year that you are tackling a water. Locating pike is a great deal easier in winter than in summer. Throughout the summer, coarse fish can be seen dimpling on the surface, spread evenly around the lake. The pike are distributed likewise. If they want food it's right in front of them, and there's no competition for it from other pike.

In summer pike can satisfy their hunger easily. But come September and October and the first frosts, food fish begin to shoal in different areas, where the temperature is even and they can shelter in safety. Don't waste time locating pike in autumn, ready for their winter campaign – the fish will be somewhere else entirely come the harsh weather.

Wherever the food fish are, pike will be close behind, made hungry by the cold, and in the process of changing their feeding times from flight to day. Some anglers struggle to catch fish until the first frost of winter, not realising that they are fishing by day for a creature that could be feeding at night until October and November.

When the weather is warm, pike become nocturnal feeders because it is cooler and quieter at night. The darkness provides cover for pike to stalk their prey successfully. But in winter the nights are too cold for feeding, so the warmest time of day becomes the time for feeding. And as food fish are tightly shoaled, pike can pick them off without the aid of darkness.

often see roach topping in shallow water close to the bank, making the most of a warm winter sun. Pike will be close by, and not in the deepest water – where you might expect them, given the time of year.

I once noticed that a mackerel head I had discarded in the margins had disappeared. I threw another in the same place and soon that had disappeared as well. I didn't need any more hints. I reeled in one of the rods and dropped a bait in the same spot. Within five minutes it was taken and I landed a pike of 19 lb 7 oz. The moral of the story is, don't neglect the margins. They are, perhaps, the most under-rated feature.

Psyching out pike

When you've spent time fishing for pike and watching them in clear water you start to understand why they behave in the way they do, and even learn to predict their movements and response to a bait. After a while you can categorise pike according to their behaviour, and this way it's possible to capitalise on favourable

Don't neglect the margins. This 22 lb pike picked up a half mackerel head dropped just beyond the rod tops from a point on the east bank of the Poplar Pit.

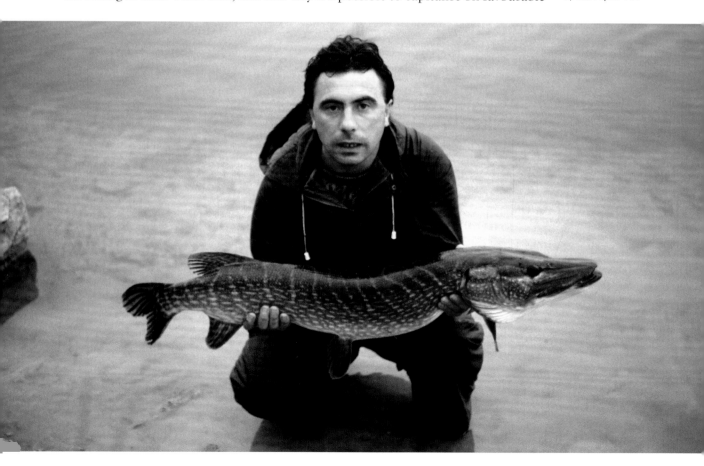

situations, and read the signs when a fish or group of fish are behaving in a way that makes them more catchable.

Here are the main categories I have come across among pike I have observed:

Rovers are nomadic pike that travel great distances and turn up almost anywhere. They are opportunist feeders, fond of scavenging and likely to pick up anything edible, dead or alive, in their path. This makes them among the first fish to be caught in a swim, but they are rarely the biggest because of the inconsistency of their food supply.

Shoal followers stay in touch with fodder fish at certain times of year, following their mobile larder and dipping into it when they need to. They stay at the same depth as the shoal, keeping just a short distance behind it.

Stayers are pike that have found a lie that suits them well, providing cover to spring ambushes and comfort out of any current, but with a ready food supply near at hand. These pike tend to be the biggest, and when one dies, its lie will be taken almost immediately by another, slightly smaller fish. If the lie is big enough, two or more pike may occupy one niche.

A **fierce** pike is one feeding aggressively and taking anything available – usually a small fish. Very big pike don't often feed as voraciously as small ones, because they are not growing at anything like the same rate, but maintaining body weight and replacing energy loss.

An **interested feeder** is the kind of pike we are fishing for most of the time, because it is hungry enough to be tempted by a fresh, well-presented bait, though not ravenous and searching for food.

And the **satisfied** pike is one that has just fed well and is not interested in another meal. This sort will, however, reflex-feed, and grab a livebait to kill it if it finds it annoying. Often, when anglers catch these fish they find the remains of the previous meal still in the pike's throat. If your hooks are positioned correctly you can strike immediately, and you will have a fair chance of hooking the pike before it lets go of your bait.

Feeding patterns can change each day, each week, each month and each year. That is why an angler who catches fish one week may not do so the next.

Choosing the method

You can save a lot of time when investigating a new water by choosing the right method to tackle it. By far the most successful method on gravel pits is the freelined or legered deadbait, normally a half mackerel or a whole sardine.

I would urge you to stick to sardines, but they don't lend themselves to long casting. Use them for close- to medium-range work or for boat fishing. Sandeels also have their day, and don't forget jack pike. You can use a free-roving livebait to locate pike on an open expanse of water, but a deadbait cast to a feature is just as likely to be successful. It all depends which bait you have greatest faith in, and whether you are prepared to try different baits and depths until you get it right.

However, you need to respond to what you see happening. If the fish are up in the water, because it is warm or there is a bar or a shallow area where they can bask, fish your bait up in the water, too. A paternostered livebait just under the surface works well in summer. If you are legering and a fish follows your bait in to the edge as you reel in, that fish may have been up in the water when your bait came past, and it could be worth changing over to see if that is true.

Novices armed with half a dozen mackerel and a pike bung often tether a bait three feet under the float on a nice warm day, cast it out and catch the biggest fish in the lake.

Small pike often take refuge in the margins and bigger pike will never be far away, waiting for a chance to strike.

The lesson is that the bait has to be where the fish can see it, so if there's evidence of fish high in the water, put the bait there. I've caught pike five feet down in thirty-five feet of water in summer, and from the number of times I've seen dorsal fins break the surface, I know they like it up there in the sunshine.

One of the reasons I use bite alarms rather than just silent drop-off indicators is because I like to keep my eyes on the water for signs of fish. I remember seeing a circle of oil-calm water appear in a ripple, where something had struck, and when I cast to it, my bait was taken on the drop by a pike of 23 lb 8 oz. I'm sure that if I hadn't been watching, I wouldn't have caught that fish.

The 23 lb 8 oz fish that created a calm patch and took the half mackerel I cast to the spot, on the drop. Bite alarms give you time to watch the water.

And I always make a mental note of where I have just cast, lining the spot up with a tree or a telegraph pole on the horizon, so I can put the bait in the same place again if this proves to be a hotspot.

At the mercy of the weather

The weather plays a big part in determining whether fish on the gravel pit you've chosen will feed. Frosts, for instance, are the kiss of death, because gravel pits don't have sufficient depth to weather them without being badly affected.

I always wondered why the myth existed that a frosty morning – the classic piker's dawn, when the fields are white and the grass is crunchy under foot – was thought to be good for pike fishing. It certainly isn't good news on gravel pits. The only explanation I can offer is that the idea that frost means good pike fishing is a throwback to the days when still-water fishing was done on estate lakes, which are very silty and perhaps less susceptible to sudden changes in temperature. It could be that some warmth is created in the lake by the thick layer of decaying leaves on the bottom, or it could be that the fish are used to the low temperatures because most of the water is fairly shallow. But whatever the reason, it is certainly true that, of the few still waters worth fishing after a very hard frost, the old English estate lakes are worth trying.

Not all gravel pits are typical, however. The Poplar Pit, which I mentioned earlier, produced fish irrespective of the weather, and in conditions when a session on another similar water would have been a waste of time. I don't know why this should be.

The Poplar Pit produced pike irrespective of the weather, in conditions when fishing should have been a waste of time.

Estate lakes like Blenheim, near Woodstock, may hold the key to the popular myth of the frosty piker's dawn.

If frosts are bad news, then surely mild weather must be perfect for catching pike? Not necessarily so. I believe if the air temperature is 55 degrees Fahrenheit for too long, pike can feed when they feel like it, and they become so well spread out that they are difficult to tempt or find.

The answer, I'm now convinced, is to be on the water the day before a cold snap. The fish know that cold weather is on its way, and that stimulates them to feed. They must feel the need to stock up in readiness for the lean spell about to descend, and feed very hard indeed for that one or two days prior to the change. The cold snap may last for three weeks, especially when there is a full moon in winter – often accompanied by high pressure and sunny days, followed by frosty, clear nights. At this time pike will remain torpid and take little or nothing in the way of food. But as soon as the weather breaks and a short spell of mild, wet weather takes its place they will go on a binge and feed hungrily again. If you can anticipate the weather and be on the water just before or just after that cold snap, you may find pike queuing up to take your baits. My tackle is at the ready throughout the winter, and when the weather man says we're in for a change, I'm out on the water like a shot.

Three twenties caught in twenty-five minutes as the first rays of light broke through at dawn, during a spell of mild weather in winter, followed by fish of 18 lb and 16 lb.

This happened once in November. I just knew that the fish were going to feed. I arrived with a friend at a gravel pit at about tea-time. I kept looking at my watch: 6.30 p.m. ... 7.30 p.m. ... 8.45 p.m ... 10.50 p.m. Nothing had happened.

We were just thinking of going home when the fish switched on. The trip was transformed from a blank to an unforgettable evening. We had thirteen doubles that night. When you put a theory to the test and it comes up trumps it's particularly pleasing, especially if you were about to give up!

Warm spells in winter

Some waters respond to a change in the weather faster than others. It depends on the size and depth of the gravel pit. If the water is deep it can take three to four days for the temperature to rise in a warm spell in winter, and some waters, particularly big concrete bowls, are just too deep for even a prolonged warm spell to bring pike out of their winter torpor.

On the Big Coloured Pit, fishing in winter was a dead loss because it was so deep. The temperature didn't get high enough to make pike respond. But one winter we had such a prolonged spell of very warm weather that there was just a chance the pike had been encouraged to feed. The longer the warm weather went on, the more we fancied our chances at the water, and when we went there, the fish were feeding, though only for the final day or two that the good weather lasted. If you know why the fish in your chosen water respond in the way they do, you're in a much better position to anticipate good sport, and do so with surprising accuracy, and be in the right place to make the most of it when it happens.

Dawn and dusk

Pike feed early in the morning and late in the evening because these times offer a lot of advantages. Shoal fish are grouped together, grazing among the weed, and their preoccupation with feeding makes them vulnerable to being picked off by predators. As the light begins to fade and objects become silhouettes, pike can use this reduced visibility to press home their attack with least chance of being detected.

Flat as a pancake

I've never liked fishing in flat calms. Given a choice between windy weather and still, I would go for windy every time. A gentle breeze will push the surface water down to one end of a lake, which shunts the water on the bottom back to the top end to take its place. This causes top and bottom layers to intermingle, and if the sun has been on the water, this will have the effect of warming up the whole lake. I have found four or five degrees difference between top and bottom temperatures on a very deep water. Perhaps this is why a good breeze improves fishing so much in winter.

Wind in itself is a stimulus to fish to start feeding. It adds oxygen to the water and stirs up food. Pike in clear water respond to it well because it sets up a ripple, which refracts the light, breaking it into uneven patterns, and camouflages them with their gold bars and dappled markings, allowing them to creep up on their prey. On the Norfolk Broads, though, it doesn't seem to be essential for there to be a ripple on the water because many of those waters have a tinge of colour to them. I've discussed this point with Bill Giles, and he is adamant that on the Broads a flat calm is not necessarily a bad thing. But on clear waters, like many of those found around Oxford, a ripple is a distinct advantage.

Fishing in the rain

I've hardly caught any pike while fishing in the rain. In fact, now I come to think of it, I can't remember catching a single fish when it's been pouring. I've done well after rain, or before it, and before and after thunder, but not during rain. It's not for want of trying. For the sake of experimentation I've sat it out, getting cold and wet, and still caught nothing. I find it depressing watching rain pouring down, especially if it's windy, and if that grey, drizzly rain descends that I know isn't going to go away, I'll pack up and come home. Confidence is all, and if I haven't got enough enthusiasm to sit it out, there's no point in staying.

There is an exception, though, and that is in Scotland, when it can do very little else but rain for long periods, so the stuff often can't be avoided. But even then it's not a highly productive time, and from the angler's point of view, it can be downright miserable.

Fishy preoccupations

If conditions are in your favour, and you know the water holds pike, and you've fished around features and things still aren't going your way, you could be dealing with a preoccupation. Pike can become very selective feeders, and sometimes unless you present them with the exact size and species of bait they favour, nothing will happen.

I've known pike to become totally preoccupied with small tench, to the exclusion of all else, or tiny roach fry, and on other waters only jack pike used as bait will tempt a sizeable fish, so preoccupied are they with eating their own kind. Finding out what's on the menu is extremely difficult, and getting them off that food impossible. Preoccupation occurs more often than we realise. When we fail we usually put that down to other factors rather than the choice of bait.

At Theale Lagoon, the big pike preoccupied on fry wouldn't look at anything bigger, and at Blenheim pike were crashing into shoals of fry, stunning them with sweeps of their tails and coming back to mop up their victims. The frustrating thing is that preoccupations can change within days. No sooner

IMMOBILE PIKE

Other influences on a pike's feeding habits include wind direction, barometric pressure, light intensity and water clarity, and all have a direct influence on the feeding habits and moods of fish. On some days, particularly when the temperature is well down, pike will not move to a bait, even though they are hungry, and want the bait placed almost on their nose.

If I'm on a water at a time of day when they usually respond and I haven't had a run for half an hour I will move my bait, sometimes putting it just five or six feet to one side. Whether it's the movement of the fish through the water, or just that pike are rendered almost completely immobile, I don't know, but sometimes pike just have to be spoon-fed.

You can tell when you have caught an immobile pike because the flanks often have two or three leeches attached where they have been lying still in weed, conserving energy.

A fish of 19 lb 8 oz that fell for a tench.

have you found out what they are taking, and found a bait to match, than they're on to something else.

But sometimes preoccupations can last for years, perhaps only affecting one or two fish, often big ones, and these pike don't get caught. If they haven't been seen or caught for years, everyone has assumed they've died or been stolen. Then, after years of avoiding capture, their preoccupation ends and they start picking up anglers' baits and get caught, and everyone wonders where they've come from.

Blenheim Palace lake, where preoccupied pike crashed into shoals of small roach.

It takes only one or two years when the main food fish fail to spawn, or for predators to have made heavy inroads into their numbers, for pike to have to look elsewhere for their staple food. There's also a possibility that old pike can no longer catch fast-swimming roach and dace, and turn to slower species. They don't need to feed so often as they are not growing, so they may become scavengers, restricting their feeding to dead and dying fish. Whatever the reason, preoccupations can strike at any time and should always be considered as a reason for lack of success.

Jack feeders

On one water we discovered, there was a surprising lack of small coarse fish dimpling on the surface in the evenings, and no fry in the margins. When we explored with spinners, we caught three or four jacks, and it was only when we put one of these 3 lb fish on a hook that we found something bigger – a 26 lb 12 oz pike, which had a 4 lb jack in the back of its throat. In all we had nine fish of over 20 lb, every one on a jack deadbait. The water held some very big tench, but I never saw a roach or a perch or any other coarse fish. Pike have got the ability to grow

Remote estate lakes can yield some very big pike, as many are free from angling attention. Get permission to fish one that has been left alone and it could spring a surprise.

big on their own kind if they are left alone, and this was what had happened. I remember seeing a little pike lying just off some rushes and looking very agitated. When he saw me, he spooked into deep water but came back almost straight away. I knew instinctively that there must be a very big fish about. I put a jack bait out, and within ten minutes it was taken by a fish of 25 lb 3 oz. When pike of that size are hungry and actively seeking out jacks, they know the small fish will be in the margins, near the cover of rushes, and they come looking for them.

But ultimately this type of water is living on borrowed time, because there are so few food fish. When the last small pike has been eaten, the big fish will lose weight fast. There were no doubles – nothing below 24 lb. When we first found the water, we could catch jacks on spinners, but towards the end there weren't even those.

If you look at the shape of the pike you catch it will tell you a lot about the water's food supply. Ideally you want pike with deep bodies and heads that look small in comparison with their girth. If the pike have slim bodies and big heads then the chances are there isn't enough food to enable them to grow to their full potential, and some of them won't survive.

The pyramid of pike

To understand the balance of power of pike in your water, you need to know whether you have a pyramid of pike, with only a few big fish and lots of small ones, or an inverted pyramid, with the balance the other way around.

The normal balance is for there to be only one or two really big pike in a water, and then for numbers to increase in each size class. If you have one or two fish of over 30 lb in a water, the size of these fish will have an inhibiting effect on the growth of the 20 lb fish, which can't or won't reach that weight. I've even seen big pike push smaller ones out of the way before taking a bait themselves.

But if one or other of the biggest pike should die or be removed, there will be a surge in the size of some of those upper twenties, and the strongest and most aggressive will grow to take that big fish's place. It will even move into the prime lies that the big fish used to occupy. The queen is dead; long live the queen. And the size that the new ruler attains will be more or less the same as her predecessor, as this is governed by the size of the water and the amount of food available. If the food fish suffer a disease and a drop in numbers, then the pike's weight potential will be reduced, or if it is a particularly remarkable fish with a genetic capacity to grow very big, it may reach a greater weight.

But in other waters there is an inverted pyramid, with lots of pike of the same stunted size, nothing bigger, and only a few smaller. In this case the number of these single-figure pike of the same year class will have an inhibiting effect on each other's progress. Often there will not be enough food to enable one or two fish to grow bigger and faster than the others and dominate the population.

But sometimes one or two will find the character and the aggression to begin feeding on their similar-sized brothers and sisters, and if they are successful, they will surge ahead in size. If they manage this leap they will have a vast larder of pike now smaller than them on which to feed, and the size they can reach can be awesome. If you come across a water like that, where normal baits produce lots of single-figure fish but nothing bigger, and you suspect a few fish have become exclusively cannibalistic, waste no time in trying a jack pike as bait. You could be in for a big surprise.

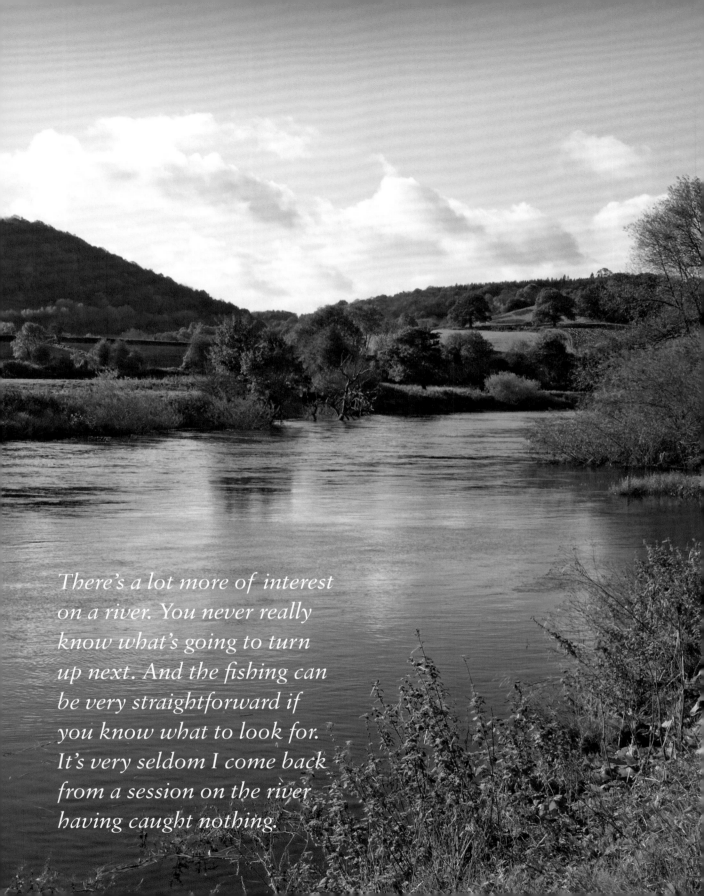

There's a lot more of interest on a river. You never really know what's going to turn up next. And the fishing can be very straightforward if you know what to look for. It's very seldom I come back from a session on the river having caught nothing.

CHAPTER 8

RIVERS

R IVERS ARE THE LAST, UNEXPLORED FRONTIER as far as pike fishing is concerned. Many stretches haven't been pike-fished for years. Some are privately owned, but some are just very inaccessible. You may only be able to get to them by boat, or they may run into wide open country that requires a lot of hard bank walking. So many pike anglers are just not prepared to walk for miles to find their quarry. There's all that untapped potential, yet so many anglers huddle around gravel pits trying to catch fish that have been caught many times before.

Pike fishing on rivers is totally different from gravel pit fishing. Indeed, on the big rivers like the Thames, the Severn and the Trent, pike fishing is more akin to that of the big Scottish lochs. There's hundreds of miles of water offering endless

Colin House holding the Thames record pike weighing 34 lb 2 oz, caught from Hampton Court Weir near London in December 2011, on a roach dead bait.

opportunities and, as with lochs, they are an unrestricted environment, with the pike free to move miles.

There's a lot more of interest on a river. You never really know what's going to turn up next. And the fishing can be very straightforward if you know what to look for. It's very seldom I come back from a session on the river having caught nothing.

Pike in rivers are more opportunistic feeders – they have to be, because if they don't make up their mind quickly, the meal is swept away in seconds. They need to feed more frequently than pike in still waters, to replace energy used up maintaining their position in the current, and searching for food that the flow tries to hide or take from them.

Rivers, especially the big ones, can be a daunting prospect to fish, but break them down into manageable sections and look for fish-holding features, and you'll get along fine. Rivers aren't easy to fish, that's for sure, but the fish are hard-fighting, athletic and a large proportion haven't been caught before.

There's no doubt that river fish fight much harder than still water fish. There's no comparison between the two – a pike of 15 lb from a river will fight harder than, and in a different way from, one of 25 lb from a gravel pit.

The best fight I ever had from a pike lasted 15 minutes. This was a fish of 26 lb 12 oz that I caught in February, as the river was fining down. It tail-walked across to the other side and made one deep, boring run after another, taking 30 yards of line, and just wouldn't come in. When I looked at it on the bank, it was the muscle tone of the fish and the size of its fins that astonished me. English river pike don't quite match pike from the Scottish lochs and Irish loughs for fighting qualities, but they're the closest you're likely to get. Catch one in the peak of condition and you will have a fight on your hands.

Advantages of being on the spot

Living on the spot helps enormously because you can keep an eye on the condition of the river and get to know its moods. Living in Oxford, I can be on the Hampshire Avon or the Severn in an hour, and I can be fishing the Thames within five minutes of leaving my house, picking the tackle up from where it stands ready, with the rods already set up. The short sessions this allows can produce big fish, often within the first few casts.

It's also handy for night sessions, fishing on into the evening and still being in bed at a reasonable hour so that I can get up for work the next morning. Regular sessions on a river just around the corner are an excellent way to get to know it.

But living on the doorstep is not absolutely essential. If you have contacts in the right parts of the country who can give you an insight into what the river is doing, you can keep in touch through them. You need that kind of contact if you are to know where the fish will be, because river pike are nomadic creatures

FRIGHTENED OF FLOODS

Perhaps one of the reasons why rivers are neglected by pike anglers is the way they can change from one week to the next. A few days of heavy rain can transform a steady glide into a swirling mass of chocolate-brown water sweeping towards the sea with its cargo of fallen trees, household refuse and the odd dead sheep.

You need determination to get to grips with them. I've driven all of the way to the Wye in September only to find it an unfishable torrent that had come up overnight, and had to turn round and come straight back.

But if anglers could fish a river as it is rising or as it is fining down, with a tinge of colour still in the water, they would find the pike in feeding mood and sport second to none. A rising river stimulates the fish to feed in preparation for the lean pickings when the water course is in full flood. When the period of

fasting is over, as the river runs off, the biggest pike go on the feed, making up for lost time. There's a hunger there that gives them the same sense of urgency they have just after spawning, and as the water clears so the pike can see their prey. The joy must be like a blind man slowly getting his sight back.

When the river is clear, and pike are able to hunt by sight, pleasure anglers and matchmen get plagued by them snatching roach and skimmer bream on the way to the net. A walk along the bank during a match will give you a good idea of which swims hold numbers of pike.

The problem is at its worst in mid-autumn and winter, when pike are feeding by day. The clarity of the water makes hunting difficult, so pike are more likely to be hungry. In summer, the need doesn't arise because pike are feeding more at night.

Heavy rain can turn a sedate river into a swirling mass.

A rising river stimulates fish to feed in preparation for lean pickings when it's in flood.

and can travel great distances and follow food fish shoals for miles. They live in a totally wild environment with an enormous number of options open to them. I have caught the same fish two days running in spots a mile apart.

So location is the most crucial part of being successful on rivers. The swim that held fish yesterday could be empty today, and it could take hours of searching along miles of bank, fishing lots of swims, a livebait on one rod and a deadbait on the other, before you find them again. I've covered five or six miles in a day, and you can lose up to a stone in weight in one winter. There's no place for moon boots, one-piece suits and rod pods – it's walking boots, bib-and-brace and bank sticks.

Don't get me wrong, when the river has burst its banks and flooded the fields you won't find me fishing it. When this happens I turn to a gravel pit like everyone else. In the depths of winter, when some gravel pits freeze over, I go back to the river.

THE BENEFITS OF BOATS

Having a boat is a huge bonus on a big river like the Thames. In summer, I head for the weir pools, which can only be fished properly by getting out on the water. And in winter, when the weir pools are often too fast to be fished, I use the boat to get to inaccessible places, mooring up and getting out to fish from the bank without disturbing the water.

But it's a great help having a boat when searching for features, or tracking down big bream shoals, using the fish finder to locate underwater contours. I've covered miles of river devoid of fish and then hit a feature that's been black with them. There aren't as many hotspots as you might imagine.

I know of three miles of river and only two really hot areas in the whole of that. There are ways of cutting corners, like finding out where matches are being won, but many areas don't have matches, and then it's down to hard work.

Having spent a lot of time in my younger days fishing for other species on the river I have learned a lot about their movements, and this gives me a good idea of where they, and thus the pike, are going to be. And I'm lucky that many of my friends are match anglers and pleasure anglers, and they can provide me with extra information that helps with location, and will do the same for anyone who bothers to ask.

Weir pools are always best tackled from a boat.

Rivers are much less vulnerable to rises and falls in temperature, and the fishing suffers far less in really cold spells. The water is constantly changing, coming from small feeder streams, from springs deep in the ground and draining from neighbouring hills and fields. I've caught fish in minus eight degrees Fahrenheit – a temperature that would be the kiss of death on every gravel pit I know.

There are times when fish really won't feed, because they are in a torpid state, and then it takes something with a bit of movement to get them to respond. I turn to legered livebaits, and there are days when these can be deadly.

Floodwater fishing

Covering several miles of river in a day helps you build up an intimate knowledge of the river that will pay dividends, as you will know where to find the bays and slack water.

Dennis Fogden holding a 30 lb pike caught from the River Thames at Wolvercote, Oxford, on a half mackerel.

Many anglers will not fish chocolate-coloured, fast water, but this is a mistake because location has been made easy for them – the pike have been forced into small areas. They will be feeding mainly by smell, so legered deadbaits are the order of the day. You will be surprised just how good your results will be if you approach rivers in this way.

Keeping on the move, I like to give each swim about twenty or thirty minutes before moving on, dropping back in the same places later in the day. There may not have been a pike in them earlier, but as river pike are highly mobile, they may move in there later. The mobility of pike is not random, though. They have a clear idea of where they need to be to intercept food, and by their movements they are taking advantage of all the opportunities the river offers. They will visit various potential food sources during the course of a day in their search for sustenance.

Several sorts of river

Rivers can loosely be divided into four types: big and slow, medium-paced, fast, and small tributaries. An example of a big, slow river is the Thames; a medium river is one like the Trent; fast is like the Wye, Hampshire Avon and Dorset Stour; and a tributary, the Evenlode.

The Wye is turned a deep red colour by the silty soil when it is in flood, while the Avon and Stour run over chalk and are supposedly clear, though trout farm effluent and pesticides and fertilisers from the land have banished any claim to true clarity.

The River Wye at Symonds Yat, a rich waterway quite capable of producing a pike in the upper thirties and maybe even a 40 lb fish.

The Trent is also subject to tainting by any number of substances, from treated sewage and the by-products of industry to oil washing off neighbouring dual carriageways, yet still produces excellent sport. The Thames, however, is clear a lot of the time, even after rain, because the amount of water in it is strictly controlled according to the amount being held in reserve by sluices, and its level may bear no relation to the weather.

The Hampshire Avon is the richest of all of these rivers, as pike that live in its lower reaches have access to extra food from the sea, as well as a substantial run of game fish. Mullet and mackerel, sea trout and grayling, and a big run of eels are all available. Couple that with the high-quality water and you have a river capable of growing a pike to 40 lb.

Large areas of the Hampshire Avon flow through private estates where all anglers are excluded, or through salmon beats where anything other than game fishing is forbidden. The Wye has too many rapids and boulders to be navigable, and the Stour and the Avon have strict controls on the amount of boat traffic, all of which benefits pike and anyone fishing for them.

The Wye is also a rich river, with its run of migratory fish, and quite capable of producing a pike in the upper thirties. It wouldn't surprise me if it produced a 40 lb fish. In addition to the salmon there are plenty of roach, chub, trout and eels for food, and much of the river doesn't get fished for pike, so they are left alone to pack on weight.

The Symonds Yat area has produced good fish, but so many of the stretches look attractive that almost anywhere you can get permission to fish and have the time to experiment and observe would be worth a try.

The potential of the Thames

The Thames isn't as rich a river as the Hampshire Avon or the Dorset Stour – no big runs of game fish or escapees from trout farms. There used to be dace shoals for which the Thames was famous, but cormorants have made huge inroads into them. Anglers on the lower Thames have counted as many as eighty cormorants in one spot, all looking very well fed. As a result there are fewer double-figure pike on the tidal Thames than there used to be, most being either jacks or fish of over 20 lb, with little in between. This points at a gap in the food fish stocks, for you need progressive sizes of food to feed a full range of pike, and if you miss out a food fish size then you get gaps in the ranks of the pike.

A fish of 24 lb 7 oz caught in the Thames at Medley. The middle reaches of the Thames hold shoals of bite-sized bream that enable pike to put on weight quickly.

But on the middle Thames the picture is very different. The shoals of bream that led to a pike-fishing bonanza more than a decade ago are back, and pike are getting bigger. Everything moves in cycles, and sport was excellent the last time bream were around in large numbers, until stocks dwindled or bream outgrew the size at which pike could eat them. Then roach took over as the dominant species, and the piking peak was over. Now, once again, we have bite-sized bream in places like Medley and Northmoor, and lots of double-figure pike, a good number of twenties and a sprinkling of low thirties, helped by a balanced spread of age classes among the bream, roach and perch.

The way river flows are being managed is in the bream's favour. These days, the Thames is often turned into a spate river, even when there is no rain, because the Environment Agency is afraid that rain is on its way and needs to prepare. So they let the water out, running it off very quickly, flooding the river and causing it to colour, instead of letting it go evenly, which does a lot less harm. However, the slower flows that follow these artificial floods, and the silt they deposit, produce

As long as the river remains sluggish, big pike will be caught at Medley.

A mid-Thames twenty caught in sixteen feet of water on the outside of a bend.

Steve Kilbee holding a beautiful 19 lb River Thames pike caught near Oxford. River pike feed quite happily even in arctic conditions.

an ideal habitat for fish like bream to root around in. It's back to the days of the sixties, when big bream shoals were everywhere, and I don't think it will be long before the river produces a real monster pike.

What price a monster?

If these conditions persist, a very big pike could soon grace someone's net. The current Thames record is held by Colin House with a fish of 34 lb 20 oz, caught from Hampton Court Weir on a dead roach in 2011. Before this the record was a fish of 33 lb 6 oz caught by my old friend Bill Rushmer, from a boat at Teddington. Other Thames monsters discovered include a pike trapped in the stanchions of Teddington Weir which weighed 35 lb, and the body of a fish that weighed in the mid-thirties, found at Wallingford. I think the upper limit for pike in the river at present would be about 36 lb, without spawn, and at the right stage of the year, say late January or February, one could weigh 38 lb or 39 lb.

The upper Thames is a different river again – faster-flowing, with chub as the main food fish. There is much less food in the upper reaches than middle and lower-middle. Lower down, around Medley and Mapledurham, a big fish is most likely to be found.

TREES

Usually these are very visible features, but sometimes a tree gets snapped off beneath the water line. The stump forms a barrier to the flow, and a slack area that will hold fish. A bait lowered into the slack, while standing well back out of sight, can often produce a sizeable pike.

Branches of overhanging trees trail in the water; and debris such as leaves and rubbish carried down in the current can get trapped, forming a raft of floating material that provides food fish with shelter from the sun and protection from attack. If there are grass and plants growing from this debris then so much the better, as this will attract insects, which will attract small fish, which will in turn attract pike. Pike love these natural rafts, as they offer cover in winter and shade in summer. Any fish that die and float to the surface will get buoyed up by the raft, and flies will lay their eggs on the fish-producing maggots that will fall into the water to be eaten by fish. However, you must present your bait dangerously close to the raft. It's no use being three or four feet away, as pike will not always move to the bait. I like to trot a livebait tight to the branches, and will often allow my float to be

trapped momentarily at the front of the raft, allowing the bait to explore the darkness beneath. You can also float-leger a deadbait, keeping as much line off bottom and out of snags as possible.

Willow roots often reach underwater to form a canopy, and pike like to hide among them. I know this from people who go scuba diving and have seen pike tucked in there, right under the bank.

Fallen tree branches have great pike-fishing potential. I like to trot a livebait tight to the branches and let my float stop, allowing the bait to explore the darkness beneath.

The skull of a near 40 lb River Cherwell pike held by the author.

Both stretches are rich enough for coarse fish to thrive and grow in huge numbers, and the introduction of salmon smolts by the Environment Agency has boosted the larder. It wouldn't surprise me if a really big fish came from Molesey weir or the River Mole, where the salmon smolts are being introduced, but realistically, anywhere from Oxford to Molesey weir could produce a river record. Most likely of all it will be caught in an area that rarely gets fished, and be a pike that has never been caught before.

The livebait/deadbait river theory

There's something about the speed of current that seems to govern whether rivers respond best to livebaits or deads. The faster and clearer the river, it seems, the more it lends itself to livebaiting. The Trent and the Hampshire Avon and Dorset Stour are all livebait rivers, and don't seem to respond so well to deadbaits. The slower-moving Thames, on the other hand, responds as well to deads as to livebaits.

I have a theory that if a river is fast-flowing, a pike has less chance of picking up a fish from the bottom than on a slow river like the Thames. On the Thames, a fish that has died is around for longer, and has time to rot and sink to the bottom, but on a fast river it will float to the top and get carried away before it has time to decay.

The main feature …

Location is the single most important factor on any water, because if you can't find the fish you certainly won't catch them. So, where do you start if you want to find quality river pike? The following is a list of some of the places from which I have caught pike consistently.

Deceptive bends

Bends can be deceptive. Some ought to hold big pike but hold only jacks, while others always have a good double and a chance of a 20. I've often wondered why this is.

In my experience, a long meandering bend doesn't produce as good a stamp of fish as a tight elbow bend. In the latter, there's enough of an area scoured out by the current for pike to get under the bank. However, when a long bend does hold fish, there are generally more of them because there is more room for food fish.

Pike like deep water, and so do other big coarse fish, particularly bream and chub, which will tuck in tight under cover of the bank. On the inside of the bend, you will find small fish in the shallow water, out of the main flow.

Bends are two swims in one – deep water, and undercut banks. If there is a very strong flow hitting an elbow bend, the fish may move out from the bank to where the shallows begin to drop into deeper water. A legered livebait can prove deadly. If the flow is less strong, the fish may be right across, and if I can't get

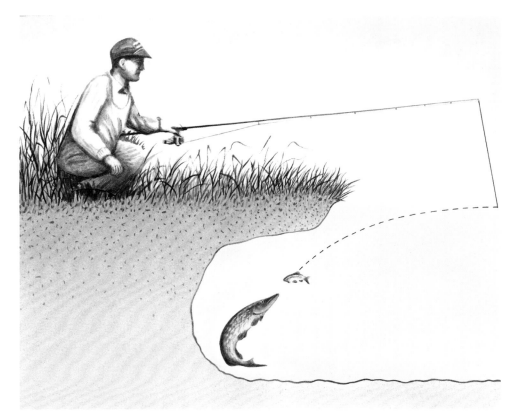

Tight elbow bends scour out an area under the bank. A bait allowed to be pulled under the bank by the current will find pike lying in wait, and a slow retrieve will give a big fish time to make up its mind whether or not it wants the bait.

access to fish the far bank I will point my rod high after casting out and keep as much of the line out of the water as possible, to stop the bait being dragged out of position.

If the river isn't too wide or fast, I like to cast a fluted float in at the top of the bend and use this to take my bait down to the pike. However, this type of swim could be too difficult to fish if there is debris like leaves and dead weed coming down, as this will give false indications.

If you can reach the bank on the outside of the bend you are in a perfect position to work a wobbled deadbait, sink-and-draw style, almost anywhere. This will often outscore any other method. Start at the top of the bend and systematically search the whole of it. Cast well out from the bank and let it swing in an arc downstream to cover the deep water, which should hold fish, and bounce the bait across the river bed before letting the current pull it right under the bank to where a pike should be lying. Reel it in slowly, occasionally drawing it up. Allow it to bounce on the bottom or trip back, covering the whole swim. The rate of retrieve is crucial. Bring the bait as slowly as you can through the pike's striking zone, allowing a really big fish enough time to make up its mind.

REED BEDS

There's a certain type of tight, green reed with a round nodule on the top that always seems to attract pike. It acts as camouflage and allows them to strike from cover. Find a bed of these leading into deep water; with gaps between the reeds for the pike to get in and out, and you will have found a favourite haunt of pike.

Tight beds of reeds allow pike to strike from cover.

Big fish don't move quickly unless they have to, and for one of any size to accept the challenge of chasing a meal, it needs to get a good look at what's on offer.

Bays

When viewed from the bank all bays look alike, but some produce quality and quantity of pike, whereas others yield little or nothing. It is only when you examine them with an echo sounder and can see the big difference in the bottom contours, or topography, of each bay that you realise why they differ greatly in what they hold.

Deep bays usually contain a good head of bream, while other bays have gravel beds and weed, which attracts roach. There are nursery swims that hold only very small fish, and others that have quantities of good-sized food fish. Generally, it is the bays between two and five feet deep that hold the small fish.

However, on the Hampshire Avon the slacks of between two feet and nine feet produce the better fish, whereas on the Thames I prefer slacks of between nine and thirteen feet.

Islands

Islands make perfect ambush points for hungry pike. The eddies at the back of them create havens of slack water for shoal fish, and pike can pin these fish against the island, or funnel them in between picking off their prey.

I know of one swim on the Thames that could produce the next river record. It has two islands through which pike come to ambush the fish moving upstream towards the shallows at the head of the run. This is the only feature for hundreds of yards, and acts like a magnet for the coarse fish in this stretch, luring them into the lair of the pike. It has the perfect features to produce big pike, and will continue to do so as long as the islands remain.

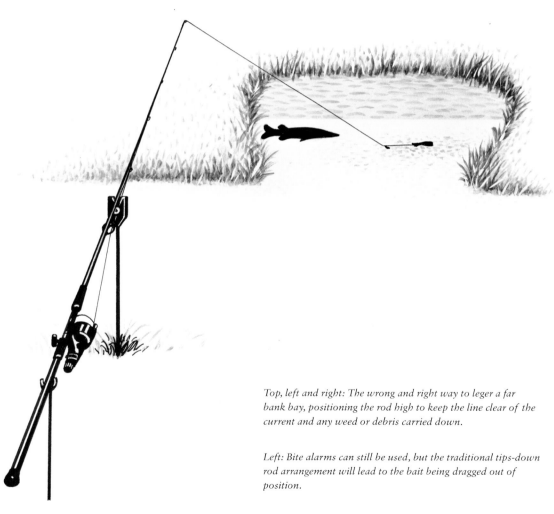

Top, left and right: The wrong and right way to leger a far bank bay, positioning the rod high to keep the line clear of the current and any weed or debris carried down.

Left: Bite alarms can still be used, but the traditional tips-down rod arrangement will lead to the bait being dragged out of position.

Slacks

When a river is in flood, all the fish will have been driven into slacks areas, out of the current, and any obstruction that holds up the main flow should hold fish. The best way to find these spots is to walk the bank when the river is at normal or below-normal level, and you will see the areas with little or no flow. These are where you want to be when the river is high, with a strong-smelling deadbait like a sardine.

Marinas

Take an athletic river pike with a healthy appetite and put it in a backwater such as a marina, where coarse fish stocks are high and there is no current to fight against, and you have the potential for producing a very large fish.

River pike use up a lot of energy maintaining their position in the current, but put them in with populations of big bream like the ones you find in places like Abingdon marina, at Dean's Farm, Bray, at Windsor, and on the River Kennet, and 30 lb plus is easily achievable. I have had big twenties and seen a fish of 32 lb 8 oz caught.

The problem with marinas is getting permission to fish. The banks are often private, so you have to fish from a boat, and the summer is a waste of time because of the amount of traffic on the river. But get permission to fish in winter, and get there early before the boat owners have got out of bed, and you can have some excellent sport.

Multiple double-figure pike, part of a 365 lb haul caught from Abingdon Marina near Oxford.

Some of the pike in marinas are ones that have learned to avoid the bits of river anglers are allowed to fish, and have moved into these areas to get away from them. I've had a haul of 300 lb-plus from a marina, including fish of up to 21 lb 9 oz and 13 mid- to upper-doubles, all on sardines float-fished from a boat when the river was in flood. Pike move in there to get out of the flow, up the man-made channels that run at right angles to the river, and when the main flow is high and the fish are hungry they are queuing up to take a bait. But if they find it to their liking they may stay there permanently, and forget that some meals come with treble hooks attached.

Moored boats

On parts of the Thames, the Environment Agency moor their dredger boats for the winter, and these provide cover for food fish like chub and roach, and a dark place for pike to stalk their prey.

House boats on the tidal Thames provide havens for roach and dace shoals, offer shelter from the sun and frosts, and from cormorants, as well as scraps of food thrown over the side to enjoy.

Lock gates

One of the best places to find pike is just below lock gates, which are very slack areas in winter. The main flow goes over the weir, while the water below the gates is only disturbed when a boat comes through, which is seldom in winter. The action of the gates being opened frequently in summer for boat traffic scours out a deep channel, creating slack water that attracts shoals of food fish. When the boat traffic eases in winter, fish will head for this deep hollow, and can often be seen rising when the sun is strongest, at midday.

Below left: Lock gates on the Thames at Iffley, where vast numbers of pike congregate at the end of the season to spawn.

Below: Lock gates attract food fish to their slacks and hollows, particularly in winter when boats are infrequent, and pike are never far away.

The sides of the channel become silted, are shallower, and come into their own early in spring when the pike move on to them to spawn.

You'll need special permission from the lock keeper, as fishing is not normally allowed within thirty or forty yards of the gates. I like to tackle these spots from a boat, tying up to the wooden mooring poles from which I can cover all the water.

Weir pools

These are wonderful gathering places for fish of all species, which live side by side in the areas that suit them best, benefiting from the extra oxygen in the water and foraging for food items that swirl round in a giant eddy on the edge of the current.

In summer and winter, weir pools hold food fish and pike of various sizes, and the angler who can read the pattern of flows will catch fish in most conditions. Big pike will have taken up the prime lies, where they are in the best possible position to intercept food fish as it passes or is brought to them on the back eddy or over the top of the weir.

Finding the bars, the submerged banks, the snags and the hollows has to be done by sight and 'feel' through the rod, as a fish finder won't work due to the

A Hampshire Avon weir pool showing the flow of water and fish-holding areas. The angler who can read the pattern of flows will be the one who catches the most fish in any given condition.

clusters of bubbles rising from the bottom in the white water. Where the main line of foam forms on the surface is where the fast water meets the slow, and this will be home to food fish, with pike on guard nearby.

At Mapledurham weir on the Thames, the water travels round in a big eddy, and pike like to lie on the crease between fast and slack water. Pike also lie under the stanchions of the weir, out of the main flow, and over the shallow silted areas on the sides, where food fish gather to spawn. If there are obstructions, like mounds of rocks and debris, they also like to lie behind these, where they can lie tucked in out of the current and strike from cover.

In summer many of the really big pike can be seen in the reedy bays on either side of the weir. I have seen two or three 20 lb fish basking there in warm sunshine in no more than three feet of water. These fish will move off to feed elsewhere and come back at night.

In summer they may be right under the main part of the weir, which carries too much water for them in winter but is slack enough for comfort when the flow is a little less. It's a mistake to think that big pike will not be found in the main flow of a weir, as they like to feel the push of the water on their backs and are streamlined and athletic enough to cope with surprisingly fast flows.

Getting to grips with weirs is an apprenticeship, because each one has its own unique contours and obstructions. The first time you fish there you will hit snags, and if you are fishing from a boat – the only way to do a weir pool justice – that means moving the boat to free your tackle, which disturbs the swim.

Weir pools have their own features. Some have salmon ladders to help migratory fish running the river pass the weir on their way upstream to spawn. Small fish can't get up these ladders and food gets washed down them, so pike lurk at the bottom waiting for something of an edible size to have a momentary lapse of concentration.

Food fish gather in weir pools, and pike like to lie behind mounds of rocks and debris, where they can tuck in out of the current and strike at prey from cover.

Some weirs are prone to silting, and have reed beds encroaching on the main pool and red buoys positioned to warn boat users of shallow water. Both are worth investigating. Pike enjoy basking in the sun, and the shallow edges of the main weir can be real hotspots, especially in summer, when weir pool fishing is at its best.

Look along the ledge of a weir, which can get choked with weed in low flows, and if there is a gap in the weed somewhere in the middle, there will be fish waiting below this spot for whatever the current may bring. Look at the debris on the surface: if this has been carried to one place, the same may have happened below the surface.

My favourite tactic for weir pools is a sink-and-draw wobbled trout, freshly killed, or if the pike are in a choosy mood and not looking at deadbaits, a 12 oz roach or chub livebait under a

Above: Pike will live happily in really fast water. Anglers must be brave enough to fish it and adapt their methods accordingly.

Right: Bringing a mid-double caught on a sink-and-draw bait to the boat while anchored in a Thames weir pool. A multiplier forces you to retrieve the bait at just the right speed.

float. I wouldn't choose to use baits of this size, but sometimes, in certain weir pools, pike won't look at anything else, and even reject only slightly smaller livebaits.

There's no need to cast; just send the bait down one line in the current and, after a pause, pull it back up on another, against the flow, which is easy from a boat. I like to hold the float back, so that the bait rises up in the water almost to the surface, before letting it go again. Sometimes you can't control a float in the flow, and then a big legered deadbait is the answer.

But when a wobbled bait works it is a dream to use, cast out underarm and brought back on the crease of the flow, fished deep or allowed to flutter up near the surface, covering lots of water at a complete range of depths. A multiplier is the tool for the job, as it forces you to retrieve slowly, and this is crucial. A big pike is a sluggish fish, and it needs time to make up its mind as to whether it wants that bait. The longer it takes to bring that bait through the pike's striking zone, the better. On some days pike will take the bait gently, just plucking at its tail, but on other days they will lunge at it, scattering scales like confetti. With a multiplier you are in touch with what is going on, and feel every tap and twitch through the line.

There are exceptions to the success of wobbled deadbaits on weirs. The weirs on the Thames at Marlow, Temple and Hambledon do not respond as well to moving baits. I have tried to catch pike on livebaits, wobbled baits and spinners, but they respond far better to deadbaits.

It just goes to show that you shouldn't let appearances deceive you. While the surface may look very fast, all white water and spray, things will be a good deal slower beneath the surface.

Getting to grips with weirs is an apprenticeship, but they will yield rich rewards for the anglers who persevere. Each one has its own unique contours, character and obstructions to be discovered.

Above: A 21 lb weirpool pike caught on sink and draw in June.

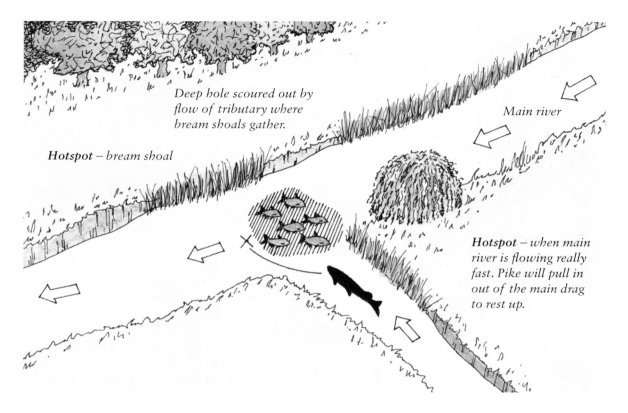

Deep hole scoured out by flow of tributary where bream shoals gather.

Main river

Hotspot – *bream shoal*

Hotspot – *when main river is flowing really fast. Pike will pull in out of the main drag to rest up.*

A bream shoal is usually in residence where a tributary hits the main river, holed up where the current has eroded the bottom.

Trout farms

Anywhere with a trout farm above has the potential to produce big pike, because escapees from the farm will enrich the food source just downstream. Trout farms on tributaries of our major rivers reduce water levels and cause pollution through waste products, but bite-sized escapee rainbow trout are one of the benefits.

Above weir pools

Most anglers never consider fishing directly above weir pools, and are missing out on fantastic sport. The water above them funnels food towards roach, bream and perch, and the pike are never far away. Many lock keepers keep two or more bucks closed almost permanently, and the pike simply sit in the slack water above them.

Warm-water outlets

Temperature plays a huge part in dictating the movements of coarse fish, especially when the weather is extreme. When it's very hot, fish will head for well-oxygenated water just below a weir, and in extreme cold, fish will find somewhere deep enough not to be affected by frosts and sudden drops on the thermometer. If a river has a warm-water outlet from a power station, it will attract fish of all sorts in winter. The temperature difference may be no more than a degree or two, but that's enough to attract food fish, which attract pike, and keep all of them feeding when fish in neighbouring stretches have stopped.

Tributaries

February and March are the months to take a look at the places where tributary streams enter the main river. Bumper catches of big fish are possible from them at the back end of the season, as specimen pike in the mid-twenties gather prior to spawning in the shallow water, or come on the feed straight after. The ethics of catching fish just before or just after spawning are another matter.

In the past on the Thames I have had several 200 lb-plus bags from where a tributary joins the main flow, made up of fish of up to 25 lb, all taken on trotted livebaits.

Usually there's a bream shoal at the point where the tributary hits the main river, holed up where the current from the feeder has scoured out a small depression in the river bed, which will have partly filled with silt. Bream will use this to rest out of the main flow and to feed, and even if there are several side streams in a row, they may all hold bream and have pike waiting nearby to move out of the main river.

If you fish a swim that usually produces lots of moderate pike, and yet find there's no response on one visit, that's often a sign that there's one very big fish about. It's well worth persevering.

Try fishing in the mouth of the tributary. Also try a little way up the tributary, especially if the main river's flow is strong. Pike wait there before spawning, while others may be leaving after spawning. Whichever way they are going, there's bound to be a lot of pike in one small area.

Gravel pit pike can be tracked down to their spawning haunts just like river pike, but river pike are opportunists and more likely to be tempted with a bait, particularly a livebait.

When fishing in the tributary, there may be so many pike in one area that they have to compete for any food that comes their way, like a flock of birds chasing a few morsels of bread. Each one that picks up the bait will run off upstream with it before another fish can take it away. But, contrary to popular belief, that kind of competition will make pike grow bigger instead of putting a ceiling on their weight. Experiments with trout in a pond showed that a shoal of 20 or 30 pike grew bigger than one on its own, because they competed for food rather than living aimlessly.

Shrunken side streams

Some small side streams become shrunken through abstraction, yet they are still very attractive to pike at spawning time. Reeds may have encroached and mud and silt built up, like on the Pot Stream near Oxford, which Dick Walker used to fish, but if you can overcome the difficulties of soft mud banks extending into

The next Thames record could go from any of the of the following weir pools: Teddington, Molesey, Penton, Hook, Sonning, Culham, Chertsey. The tidal Thames receives extra riches coming in from the ocean, which in turn enable the pike to grow just that little bit bigger. The Thames in my opinion could produce a fish in the region of 38lb.

the margins you can get among a lot of fish. You need to stand well back from the reeds and use a bait that gives out plenty of vibrations; draw the pike to you, and stimulate them into feeding. Failing that, if you can waft a freelined deadbait under the reed encroachment and let the bait settle right in under the near bank, this can work well. You can do this with or without extra weight, depending on the flow, and you should have the rod facing straight towards the bait so you get an immediate indication of a fish picking it up.

I use very light bobbins as bite indicators, so the bait isn't dragged along the slippery silt bottom after being cast. Long bank sticks are needed to get through all the mud to the firmer ground that will give you a grip, yet with enough bank stick above the surface to keep the line above the reed stems.

But the most important thing to remember on these side rivers with unpronounced banks is not to walk on the floating rafts of reed and mud in the edge. When trodden on they shudder, and this vibration will put pike down.

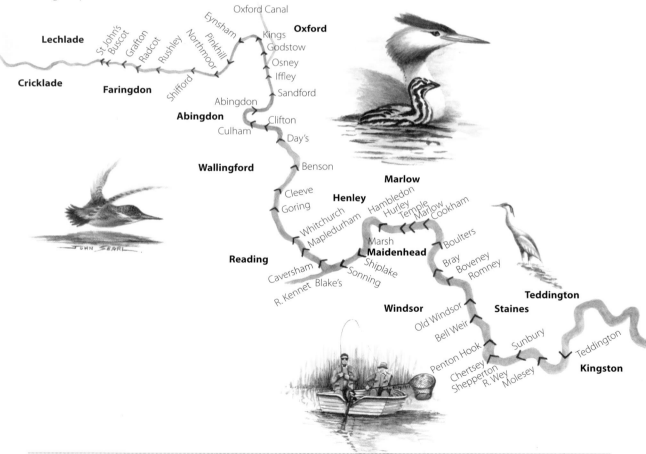

Estuaries

On the estuaries of rivers like the Hampshire Avon, pike have an incredible larder of back-up food in the form of mullet from the harbour. Stamp your feet on the estuary shore, and the surface of the water will erupt with the bow waves of alarmed mullet.

Some of the biggest pike in the river live in the mouths of these estuaries, only moving upstream once a year to spawn, in February or March. This is the one time they are vulnerable, and it is this life cycle that is likely to produce a real leviathan.

History repeats itself

As I stated in the previous chapter on gravel pits, if big pike die or are removed from a swim, the few that are the next biggest will compete to take over the old queen's status and prime position. The one that inherits the throne will be found in the same location as its predecessor, so any location that has produced a big pike will, provided things don't change, produce another within a few years. I know of a swim on the Thames that produced a fish of 34 lb 3 oz many years ago, and then five years ago, a 34 lb pike was found dead in the same place, a sharp bend on a long, straight section.

If pike are left alone, history will repeat itself, and in this case it's a good couple of miles walk from the nearest main road. Even in a boat you have got to pass through several locks to get there. I've had fish to 25 lb and another of 24 lb from this swim since and, given time, I know it will produce another pike nudging the 35 lb mark. The locations mentioned in pike fishing books published as much as eighty years ago and said to hold big pike are the ones likely to produce big fish now, because many of them have not changed, and still offer the same unique advantages.

The strength of the rig lies in its simplicity – a straightforward solution to a common problem – for, the more simple a rig, the better it works.

CHAPTER 9

RIGS

T HE BEST RIGS ARE SOLUTIONS TO PROBLEMS. Perhaps you want to put a bait in a certain place and present it in a certain way, but you can't achieve this with any of the methods at your disposal. So you find some way of overcoming the problems, by experimenting with terminal tackle until it does what you want, doesn't tangle and, above all, catches you fish. Eventually you refine the rig to the extent that it probably can't be improved upon and, if it includes items not commercially available, as in the case of my Deadbait Support Links and Wobble Bars, you find a firm prepared to produce them. But the strength of the rig lies in its simplicity – a straightforward solution to a common problem – for, the more simple a rig, the better it works.

The rigs shown here are open to interpretation. Make of them what you will, and experiment with them by adding to or subtracting from them according to your preferences. I offer them simply as working examples of ways of presenting a bait, live or a dead, in a certain way to suit a certain type of swim.

Armed with these you will have a few solutions to potential problems, and a trick or two up your sleeve for when the need arises.

The following is a rough guide to when and where to use the rigs described:

The bottom trace is my preferred rig for dead baiting in gravel pits. The top treble is fixed and is tubed. The top trace has problems as the treble upends itself, which in turn gets stuck into dead baits and cannot be pulled clear. This leads to the loss of pike on the strike.

Gravel pits and lakes
Deadbait support rig/Legered deadbait/
Wobbled deadbait/Pop-up deadbait/Floatfished
deadbait/Float-paternostered deadbait/Free-
roving livebait/Float paternostered livebait/
Trailing and trolling

Rivers
Legered deadbait/Wobbled deadbait/Trotted
deadbait/Float-paternostered deadbait/Float
legered deadbait/Trotted livebait/Legered
livebait/Float-paternostered livebait

Lochs and loughs

Legered deadbait/Wobbled deadbait/Float-fished deadbait/Float-paternostered deadbait/Float legered deadbait/Free-roving livebait/Float paternostered livebait/ Trailing and trolling

Legered deadbait

A legered deadbait is the best method when you want to anchor a bait in one spot. It is useful when you are fishing the far side of a river and your float keeps getting dragged out of position, or if the far bank is too far to reach with float tackle. You want a heavier, more streamlined rig to get the extra distance.

On gravel pits a legered deadbait is the first choice for distance casting, especially when presenting a small bait like a sandeel or smelt as an alternative to a mackerel. The added advantage of legering a small bait rather than freelining one is that you can tighten up harder to the bait and so spot runs earlier.

The lead is attached to a Cox & Rawle boom, and this slides on the main line stopped by a bead above the trace swivel. The top treble or Parrot Beak single goes through the root of the tail, with fuse wire or freeze spray to hold it if it is a sardine, and the end treble is pinned loosely into the flank of the bait.

Wobbled deadbait

This is a deadly way of finding fish and covering a large amount of water. The deadbait, usually a rainbow trout of about 6 oz, is hooked through top and bottom lips with one point of the top treble, and very lightly nicked in the flank with the end treble. Alternatively a Parrot Beak single can be used to seal the lips. The stainless-steel wobble bar is attached to the eye of the top treble or Parrot Beak by an inch and a half of crimped wire. Carbon Kevlar braid can be used as an alternative, knotted instead of crimped. The wobble bar is pushed into the back of the throat of the bait so that only the top is visible. If it isn't pushed down far enough, it may come out through the gills and the bait won't come back in a lifelike manner. Similarly, if the bar is pushed too far down into the fish it will inhibit the action of the rear half of the body as it moves through the water. Where the bait is only hooked through one lip instead of both, it will spin awkwardly as it comes back on the retrieve, whereas in an ideal world I want it to wobble enticingly.

Deadbait support rig (or instant strike rig)

I've explained the background to this rig in previous chapters. It is simply an excellent deadbait rig for freelining.

A plastic bait support link attaches to the bottom eye of the trace swivel by an oval split ring. A loop of 8 lb or 9 lb line sits on the flat ridge of the link, and the other end of it is lassoed around the tail root of a deadbait with two half hitches.

The loop should be about 17 inches long, roughly three inches shorter than the wire trace. If I use a longer trace, because I'm fishing over gravel bars or snags, the loop will be longer, too. The loop falls off the ridge of the bait support link as soon as the bait hits the water, because it is only held in place by the tension provided by the weight of the bait. If you pass your wire trace through the loop of line before the cast is made, the loop catches on the trace on the retrieve, and the bait comes back even if it's worked its way off the hooks.

A typical deadbait support rig. Note the wire trace is threaded through the loop of the line attached to the mackerel's tail: thus the angler gets his bait back, and deadbaits are not left on the lake bed during a fishing session.

Pop-up deadbait

On waters that are particularly silty or weedy, a bait that falls slowly and settles gently, or sways in the current at a predetermined height off the bottom, is an advantage. Injecting air into the side of a deadbait will lift it off the bottom, making it more visible to pike and keeping it clear of debris. I always go for a bright bait like a roach or a dace. I aim the needle at a spot close to the lateral line. Don't go for the gut cavity underneath, because air will escape through the mouth, and you risk puncturing the swim bladder, which will make the bait less buoyant.

I like to test my baits in the margins prior to casting to see if they are doing what I want them to do. An air-injected bait can be fished anywhere between bottom and surface, anchored in place with a lead sliding on a Cox & Rawle boom and a back-stop of pole elastic and bead. Tighten to the bait gently when it is in position to avoid reeling it down to the bottom. Some anglers favour putting lead shot on the trace, because that takes the bait a little further away from the main line and lessens the chance of a bite-off. The treble hooks can be positioned in the bait to make it face head-up or head-down, and the direction doesn't seem to make any difference to the number of takes.

Despite the dangers of sharp needles, I prefer to inject deadbaits with air rather than stuff polystyrene down them. If a bait is lost, any polystyrene will end up in the stomach of a pike, which can't be good for it.

Floatfished deadbait

Floatfishing a deadbait allows you to present the bait at any depth. If you want a bait close to the surface, to lie on top of tall weed for instance, it's easier to suspend it below a float than try to pop it up.

The rig I use is a straightforward one with a float running on the main line above the trace. Various hooking arrangements can be used, depending on the size and type of deadbait chosen. The top treble through the root of the tail and the end treble in the flank will make it sit tail-up, and top treble through root of dorsal and end treble through flank will make it sit upright in a natural manner.

There doesn't have to be tall weed for the method to work. Sometimes a bait fished a couple of feet below the surface over deep water will take pike cruising in the upper layers. A good way of searching a big open still water for near-surface cruisers is to go to the upwind shore and drift a bait, set shallow, out under a balloon attached to the line with a paper clip. The balloon will come off on the strike and can be retrieved from the down-wind shore at the end of the session.

On lochs and loughs I use big, bright, self-cocking floats that will be visible through waves as much as three feet from peak to trough. A hefty float is needed to get any distance on the cast with a multiplier, and a good cast is often needed to avoid spooking pike or fouling the anchor rope. My floats are four or five inches long, with a stem made of a brass rod inserted in the body. They are attached bottom-end only, with a snap-link swivel that runs on the main line, stopped by a bead and a knot of pole elastic.

Trotted deadbait (rivers only)

Trotted deadbait is a deadly method for finding fish. The kind of swim you are looking for is somewhere with a clear gravel bed, or one that is weed-free. Any obstacles on a stretch make it difficult to fish effectively, but if you can find a length of water about five or six feet deep and of fairly uniform depth, with a bottom that is clear, you will have perfect water for trotting. Ideally you will be able to trip the bait along the bottom and then hold it back so that it rides up in the water before letting it go again. It's often the sight of the bait doing something different that triggers the strike. I like to trip a bait through on the far side and come round in an arc across the river, do the same again on lines closer in, and then retrieve it and work it down the near bank.

Float-legered deadbaits suit loch fishing, where baits need to be anchored despite strong surface drift, and line needs to be lifted clear of those waters' notoriously boulder-strewn bottoms.

You can also trot a deadbait off bottom if you have weed or other obstacles in your way, simply by shallowing up. If you trot a bait down to a weed raft under overhanging branches you can let the float trap itself momentarily on the front of the raft, and the bait will lift up into the darkness beneath. Whatever the deadbait used, the top treble should be hooked in the root of the tail and the end treble in the flank, so it sits head down with the hooks clear of the bottom. This allows the bait to travel through the swim unimpeded.

The float can be a fluted balsa or a cigar shape, depending on the flow, or even a round polyball.

Float-paternostered deadbait

See float-paternostered livebait, page 168. The method is the same, but a deadbait is hooked with the top treble in the dorsal root and the end treble in the tail.

Float-legered deadbait

This is generally used from boats, where alarms can't be used but you need visual bite indication and a static bait. I use it only on lochs, and for fishing marinas and weir pools. The float provides extra casting weight and lifts the line up.

My floats are attached bottom-end only, and the weight is provided by several swan shot pinched on the trace. The top treble goes through the root of the tail, and the end treble is pinned loosely into the flank of the bait.

On a loch, there is a lot of drift to be countered to keep the bait in position on the bottom, and a float-leger rig allows you to anchor the bait firmly, but with all of the advantages float-fishing has over legering. Loch bottoms are strewn with snags, but this rig keeps the line away from them. Even so, I often use traces two to three feet long to prevent damage to the line by jagged rocks and boulders.

Floatfished and trotted livebait (or free-roving livebait)

Float-fishing covers large volumes of water a lot more quickly than legering, keeps the bait away from bottom weed or snags, and makes a welcome change from sitting behind alarms.

When I am float-fishing livebaits in gravel pits, I hook the top treble in the tail root, and the end treble is nicked just under the adipose fin, in the case of a trout, or the dorsal root in the case of coarse fish.

When I am float-fishing a weir pool, I will put the top treble through the upper lip to make the bait face into the current. I will also use the top lip hookhold when I am fishing a very small livebait for which only one treble is needed. But lip-hooked fish are more likely to fly off during the cast, so I locate the hooks elsewhere for long-range styles.

For long-range casting with trout livebaits, for instance, I put the top treble in the adipose fin and the end treble in the flank, which offers a good hookhold and makes the bait much more streamlined.

When fishing a livebait in rivers, everything depends on whether you are letting the bait trot downstream, or making it work upstream against the flow. If you are trotting downstream, a pike will expect a bait to be facing downstream when it is travelling in that direction if it's going to look natural. To do this I put the top treble through the tail root, and the end treble in the adipose fin, in the case of trout, or in the tail root and the dorsal root for coarse fish. But when a bait is being brought upstream it should be facing into the flow, so you will need to place the top treble through the top lip, and the end treble in the flank, to make it look natural and be streamlined when being brought back against the current. It will last longer like this, and can be made to rise up in the water and fish at different depths. Make sure you put the hook through one lip only, though, for if you seal the lips together, the bait will drown. And use the top lip, so that it can open and close its mouth without being impeded by the hook. Use as little lead as you can get away with, to avoid tiring the bait: a couple of swan shot pinched on the line for a small dace, or a streamlined barrel lead for something bigger. The trace should be about 16 inches long.

Free-roving or float-fished livebaits are particularly deadly used up against the beds of potamogeton weed in lochs, and in rivers when pike are moving into the mouths of tributaries ready for spawning.

Float-fished and trotted livebaits cover large volumes of water a lot more quickly than legering, keep baits away from weed and snags, and make a welcome change from sitting behind alarms.

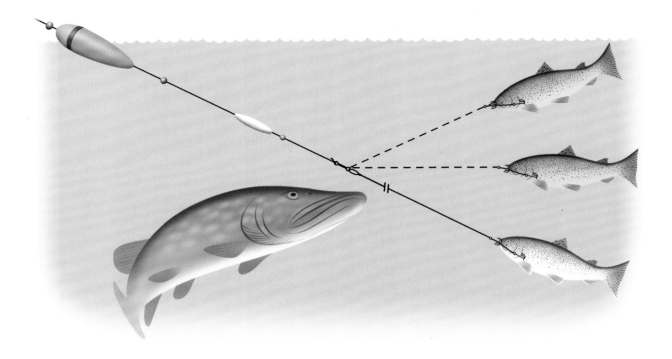

In weir pools I like to explore different depths of water by holding back the bait, and then letting it travel on and ride up and down. A cigar-shaped sliding float and barrel lead have the type of streamlined profile that does not catch in the current and offers little resistance to taking fish.

If pike are only in a mood to reflex-feed, and let go after a second or two, the hook position for an instant strike is top treble through the dorsal root and end treble through pectoral root, to aim the hooks at the centre of the body so that they will find a hold instantly. With this hooking arrangement the strike can be made instantly, as soon as a sign of a take is noticed, and hopefully before the jaws are opened and the bait discarded.

Legered livebait

When pike are on the bottom, in rivers after a heavy frost for example, and are in a torpid state and reluctant to respond, a legered livebait is the best bet. If you know of a deep hole where pike are likely to be, you can use this method to hold a bait in place. There are days when a deadbait won't be looked at, but a livebait creates just enough of a stir to provoke some interest in pike, and then this method will outscore any other. There have been times when a float-fished livebait has been ignored, but a legered livebait has been successful.

Brown trout or rainbows are the first-choice baits, though chub also work quite well. It doesn't matter how they are hooked, but I prefer to put the top treble through the tail, and end treble in the dorsal root for ease of casting.

A float-paternoster is the best way of presenting a livebait off bottom in weedy water, or to hold a bait off bottom in a river or gravel pit hotspot. In snaggy swims the line is kept up in the water away from trouble, which gives it an important edge over straight legering.

Float-paternostered livebait

This is the best way of presenting a livebait off bottom in weedy water, or to hold a bait off bottom in a known hotspot in a river or gravel pit. It is particularly useful if the chosen spot is close to a snag, where the repeated casting necessary with roving float tackle would be a disadvantage. In these spots, leger tackle can't be used, because the line has to be kept up in the water and away from further snags.

A green, sunken float or a standard balsa that shows above the surface goes on the main line, stopped by a knot of pole elastic and a bead. I always use a 13-inch uptrace of wire below the float to prevent bite-offs, as a pike can catch the line in its mouth as it strikes. A John Roberts Pike Paternoster Boom keeps the 10-inch hook trace and bait away from the main line, while the lead is attached to an 8 lb nylon weak link in case it gets snagged. Rudd and dace tend to ride up in the water and can spin around the float, so I don't use them for this, but roach, rainbow trout and brown trout work well.

Two things to remember – always make sure the hook trace is shorter than the uptrace to avoid bite-offs, and always keep a tight line to the bait so that it is working constantly. As soon as you let the line go slack, the bait doesn't have any resistance to pull against and stops moving around, making it less visible and attractive to pike.

Trailing and trolling

Trailing with a float works particularly well on estate lakes and trout waters, and enables you to cover a lot of water. I use the same set-up as for free-roving livebaits, but with the top treble through the upper lip and the end treble in the flank. Trout and roach are the best. To work well, though, trailing must be carried out slowly, using a small electric motor and lines paid out behind the boat. Many anglers trail too fast to cover water effectively, and do not give a big pike enough chance to make up its mind whether it wants the bait.

The float acts as an indicator and a means of controlling the depth at which the bait is fishing, which is usually shallow. A fairly heavy lead is used to hold the bait down. A special float is used, with a length of bent plastic tubing protruding from the top, through which the line is threaded, before going through the centre of the body. The line in this tubing is bent at an acute angle, which stops the float from sliding down to the bait and shallowing the rig.

Trolling, on the other hand, is very different, and involves the use of deadbaits and lures over deep water in large lakes like Scottish lochs. There is no float on the line, but a downrigger takes the bait to the desired depth. The hooking arrangement for trolling is top treble through top and bottom lips, and end treble through flank. I use mackerel, chub, trout or any sizeable fish, but the lips must be sealed to stop it from spinning in the water and allow it to run on an even keel. Trolling is another good method for searching water, and uses the same electric motor and lines paid out behind the boat, but it is carried out at a slightly faster speed.

Traces

My standard trace is 20 inches of titanium wire. Two size-8 trebles are crimped on, two to three inches apart. These are Owner 3X Extra Strong Trebles for either dead or live baits. I always make sure the top treble on the trace is fixed. Some anglers like to leave it sliding, so that they can move it up and down the trace to suit the size of bait, but if it slides when you move it, then it will slide when you strike, and you won't get a proper hookhold. Sliding trebles also have a habit of damaging traces, making them coil like a spring and reducing the breaking strain. If I'm using different sizes of bait, I will take a number of different traces, with trebles firmly attached at different distances apart, and match them up, changing traces if I change bait size.

To attach the top treble so that it won't slip, pass the wire through the eye of the hook and back through again, while allowing a loop of wire to be drawn tight between the three prongs where they separate as they leave the shank. Then wrap the wire three times around the hook shank, go through the loop formed at the shank, and pull the end through. Check that the wire is pulling against the hook when it is drawn tight, not against the wire, which will make it kink or fracture. I find it easier to attach the top treble first and then add the end treble a suitable distance away.

To attach a single Parrot Beak hook, do the following. Slide a crimping sleeve on the wire, and pass the wire through the eye of the hook and back through the crimping sleeve again. Double the end over and bring it back through the sleeve for a third time, making sure not to pull the loop you have just made right back out of the sleeve. Adjust the size of the loop next to the eye of the hook, and then crimp once in the middle. You can then put the end treble on the loose end of wire and the trace is complete.

The average size of the pike that we caught at night was much higher than during the day. There's no doubt that some of the biggest pike on any water feed at night.

CHAPTER 10

NIGHT FISHING
& THE NEUROMAST SYSTEM

I F I'D BEEN WRITING THIS BOOK LITTLE MORE THAN A DECADE AGO, a chapter on night fishing for pike would have been treated with derision. Pike were thought to hunt by sight, and fishing at night for a species that chases fish and flashy plugs would have been laughable. Early manuals on pike fishing wrote off night fishing as a waste of time, but how wrong they were. Slowly we've come to realise that when the sun goes down, pike go on the prowl, and in summer the cool hours of darkness are the ones in which most of the feeding takes place. What better time for a pike to stalk its prey in the underwater alleyways between the weed than when everything is cloaked in darkness?

Peter Shefford holding a 31 lb 6 oz pike caught from an Oxfordshire gravel pit on half mackerel after dark.

How it all began

The first pike I caught at night was by accident, while legering a gudgeon head for eels on the Coca-Cola stretch of the Thames, and I don't know who was more surprised, me or the pike. It came at a time when it seemed that pike stocks in gravel pits around Oxford appeared to be dropping after several years of successful fishing. Initially we had thought the fish were feeding beyond our casting range, but after the Coca-Cola fish we had other ideas. We decided to try close in at night, and sport was amazing. It seemed the pike had learned not to accept food items during the day, but at night they came into the margins to feed and pick up baits discarded by anglers.

In the course of our experiments, we found that pike fed most freely on dark nights when you could hardly see your hand in front of your face, in particular between one and three hours after dark, but often well into the night. As summer turned to winter, the feeding period took place earlier, in the first few hours of darkness, rather than the middle of the night or early morning. And the most productive method by far was a static deadbait.

However, on bright, moonlit nights, the pike responded best to moving baits, twitched or retrieved or on the drop, and we reasoned that if it was a moving bait they wanted, perhaps livebaits would be a better bet than deads. We made some floats for the job, with Betalights glued into the tops, and the results were even better than with deadbaits. This was exciting fishing, watching isotope-topped floats race across the black surface of the dark water and disappear suddenly as they plunged under with an audible plop.

However, while livebaits were three times more effective than deads when there was a big moon, deadbaits still outscored livebaits on the darkest nights. This suggested that the pike's sense of smell played a bigger part in finding food when visibility was poor.

Pike that feed only at night

As we broadened the scope of our experiments we discovered that pike were feeding at night even on waters that had very little angling pressure, so their nocturnal activities weren't just to avoid capture. And we started catching fish no one had seen before, which suggested that they were exclusively night feeders and had been so for a long time.

We also noticed that the average size of the pike that we caught at night was much higher than during the day. There's no doubt that some of the biggest pike on any water feed at night. Most of what we caught were 12 lb and over, and there were none of the jacks that turned up regularly in the day.

The transformation in our fishing was amazing. Fisheries that had produced next to nothing for several seasons now yielded pike up to the upper twenties at night. We were arriving at waters as other pike anglers were packing up fishless, and by staying until 10 p.m. or 11 p.m. we were catching a fair few fish, some of them big. On the Big Coloured Pit, I had three twenties in quick succession one night, yet fishing there was very slow during the day. It wasn't that we were better anglers than the others, just that we were fishing at a time when the pike were feeding.

We were also fishing at night on the river, as it was there that the whole idea had been born, and livebaits presented correctly in flowing water produced a lot of fish for us early in the year.

Mostly in the margins

Stealth is essential at night because often the fish will be almost under your feet. On mild nights, pike come in close on gravel pits to feed on the small fish that take refuge in bankside reeds and tree roots. Other coarse fish move into the shallow margins in late afternoon, when the threat of attack from birds and animals has decreased, and stay there for the night, foraging for food. When the sun rises, both they and the pike will move out into deeper water, where they feel more secure.

But it isn't just food that pike seek when they move in close after dark. They are looking for shelter as well. On one water where scuba divers were studying fish movements at night in winter, they found that over 70 per cent of the big pike spotted were close to the bank, many swimming right under wooden platforms. They watched them cat-nap for ten minutes or so and then move on to patrol the margins.

In Scottish lochs, pike will only move in close to the bank during the day if they have cover from weed. Bays without cover are unlikely to be visited until the sun begins to fade, though once the strength has gone from its rays, these could be as good as the weedy ones.

And if you catch a fish from one swim it's often a good idea to move to another straight after, to let things settle down before trying there again.

Summer and winter

The milder the weather, the more chance there is of action close in at night. In summer the nights can be light and warm and pike will feed because it's cooler than in the heat of the day, and quieter. But in winter, the darkest nights are the best because they are the warmest.

At this time of year the nights are a lot longer. There are no people around to disturb the peace and quiet, and no boats on the river to disturb the calm. It's a perfect time for any secretive angler to catch fish. Big pike are landed, weighed, photographed and returned without another soul knowing what has happened.

This is the magic of night fishing. It is totally unlike anything you will experience by only fishing during the day. The atmosphere is completely different. Every sound

LOCATION IS THE KEY

Going night fishing without deciding in advance where you are going to fish is a shortcut to failure. It's no good adopting a chuck-it-and-chance-it approach, because if your bait ends up yards from the hotspot, it could go unnoticed.

I like to walk the bank in the evening on a river and pick out features on the far bank to mark swims for when I return later. Reconnaissance trips are a must, and information built up by fishing during the day and talking to people who know the water well will lead to success at night.

Tributaries and the points at which they join the main river are ideal places to try, especially if there is a lot of water flowing through and fish have moved a short way up out of the flow. Static deadbaits will outscore livebaits in these conditions, as pike feed more by smell than sight in coloured water.

But all of the usual fish-holding features listed in the rivers and gravel pits chapters will also be well worth a visit, as will any noted swims or known hotspots. Then when you return at flight you will have a good idea of the characteristics of each swim, and where

to cast to avoid snags and get results. It's surprising how different waters look at night, and the degree of technical difficulty is greatly increased. Just knowing your way around the swim without stumbling over tree stumps and scaring fish will be a big advantage. An absolute must is a small headlamp, preferably a Petzl, for mounting the bait on the hooks, for positioning the bait when casting, for unhooking pike and for finding your way around. A torch is not enough, because you need both hands free when casting baits, netting fish and unhooking them. Over-use of lights can have an adverse effect on sport, but so can blundering around because you can't see what you're doing.

Pick two or three swims, so that if your first choice is unproductive you can move on to another. It is easier to fish deadbaits because they pose no problems of transporting them to the water. A dozen or more sardines wrapped in bubble wrap and pushed into a Packaseat with a few odds and ends of tackle and a camera is all that you need. Bank sticks can be wrapped up in your landing net and carried in one hand, and your rods will go in the other.

My son Mathew, with a 21 lb pike caught from the River Thames near Abingdon.

is magnified, and the imagination runs riot at every noise nearby, as unseen creatures rustle through the undergrowth just inches from where you are sitting. When a fish swirls, it sounds like a body being dropped from a bridge; when a fox calls, it sends a chill through the night air; and when you get a take, it makes your heart beat so fast you don't know whether to run towards your rods or away from them. Playing an unseen creature that is wrenching the top of the rod over from somewhere out in the deep, dark water, lunging to the left and to the right, you can't help wondering if you've bitten off more than you can chew. It's fishing in a different world, and as exciting a branch of the sport as any I have experienced.

Tripping the bait through close to the bank while sitting quietly to avoid any potentially fish-scaring vibrations in the swim.

Above: A trotted trout livebait under a luminous float about to be tried on a bitterly cold night on a River Thames backwater.

First cast a 20 lb pike, which took the bait confidently and headed off across the pitch-black river with its prize.

The big chill

In September, when the weather is still mild, I will fish moving baits at night but, come October and November and those first frosts, and it is static baits most of the time.

Runs can be no more than gentle twitches. On a particularly cold night on the Thames, with the mercury in the minus, I saw one of the tips of my rods move slightly and the line between tip and water quiver and twitch. This happened for 10 or 15 minutes without a take developing, so I moved the bait about six inches.

At once there was a steady pull on the rod, and I tightened into a fish. It shot 40 yards down-river and took a lot of landing. It weighed 23 lb 8 oz. I believe it had been guarding the bait but was not hungry enough to eat it, until it thought it was going to lose it. The line twitching may have been caused by the pike's pectoral fins and gills vibrating slightly and displacing water as it held itself steady.

The neuromast system – a pike's secret weapon

The great barrier to night fishing for pike has always been that pike were traditionally believed to hunt entirely by sight, so what was the point of trying to catch them when they wouldn't be able to see the bait?

A very cold night on Dorchester Lagoon, and a heartwarming 22 lb 8 oz fish on a half mackerel.

A quick snap of the two 18 lb, because the low temperature threatened to freeze their fins.

Above: Petzl headlamps are a must when fishing at night.

When my friends and I started to catch pike at night, we began to discuss how they could find a live fish, and take it swiftly and cleanly when they couldn't see further than the end of their noses. When you start pondering this question, you realise that pike also manage to do the same in dirty, flooded rivers, and in gravel pits that are still being worked and remain cloudy. When a scientist in Holland conducted an experiment whereby he blindfolded pike and found them still able to catch their prey, it became obvious that pike possess a secret weapon that we know very little about.

Further research has revealed that the special fish-detection powers pike possess are a remarkable vibration-sensitive perception known as the neuromast system. It is vital to the survival of pike, and one of the prime ways in which they detect food, yet few pike anglers have even heard of it, let alone understand how it works. Since finding out about it, I have changed my approach to livebait presentation radically, as I now know how easily pike can find a bait located in weed or at great distance from them, no matter how dark the night or coloured the water. Furthermore, I know that the livelier the livebait, the better the chance of it being detected by the pike and taken, especially in a flooded river or a silty gravel pit.

The perfect predator

The neuromast system consists of a group of cells running in a row along the lateral line, and others above and below in horizontal columns, like large plus signs. The lateral rows pick up lateral movements, and the horizontal ones horizontal movements, working independently to provide the pike with a complete picture of the source of the activity. Each cell has a structure called a cupola, which is positioned in the epidermis of the pike's skin. Each cupola is linked by a short hair to nerve endings, and as water is displaced from around the pike's body the cupola and the hairs bend, stimulating the nerve endings and telling the pike that something nearby is moving.

There are other sensitive cells along the underside of the jaw that can be seen as a series of shallow pits, called the mandibular pores, and some that run across the top of the head. All of these combine to provide an accurate picture of the location, direction and speed of whatever has caused the disturbance.

The neuromast organs which run across the head, cheek and lateral line, along with the mandibular pits, are superb water displacement detectors. Pike are able to get a fix on any moving object around them.

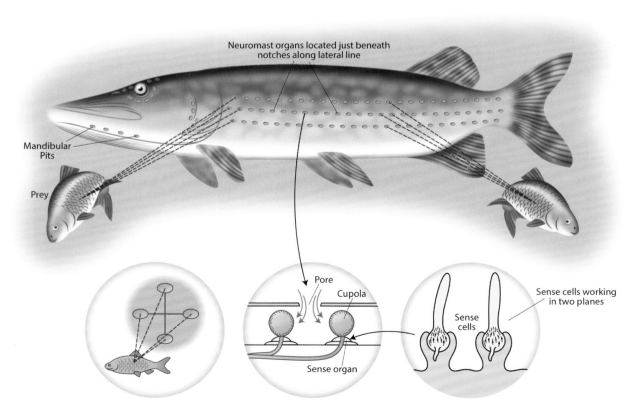

If the cupola bends by as little as a thousandth of a millimetre, the sense cells at the foot of the cupola are stimulated and messages are immediately sent to the pike's brain.

The mandibular pores and neurotransmit organs running across the head and cheeks also help pike locate prey hidden in the densest of weed beds.

The cupolas are so sensitive to water displacement that even the movement of the pike's own fins can prevent it from detecting prey fish. For that reason the neuromast organs are positioned well away from its own pectoral and dorsal fins, so their movements do not 'deafen' the pike's sensory system.

Moving water can also deafen a pike's vibration detection system, forcing it to hunt more by sight and smell than by vibrations. But even when forced back on these two food-finding aids, pike are still deadly fish catchers, as they have very good vision and sensitive olfactory organs in their nasal cavities, which are able to detect scent trails and fear pheromones given out from prey fish. They have remained almost unchanged for millions of years while other creatures, ourselves included, have evolved. Nature got it right first time, and created a design classic and a perfect predator that could be improved upon only slightly over millions of years.

The olfactory chamber is clearly visible, along with the lamellae of the rosette. Pike do not have a great sense of smell, which is the reason that deadbaits should be placed in exactly the right spot.

CHAPTER 11

SENSE OF SMELL,
OR OLFACTION

PIKE DETECT ODOURS OR CHEMICALS IN THE WATER through a pair of nostrils, or nares, which are located between the eyes and the upper part of the jaw or snout. Their nostrils, as in many other fish, have an inlet and an outlet that are separated by a flap of tissue that helps direct the water into the olfactory chamber. At the base of the chamber there are folds of tissue known as lamella, which form a structure called the olfactory rosette. The folds of lamella within the rosette increase the overall surface area, in turn helping to accommodate a greater number of olfactory receptor cells, which detect various chemicals in the water. When these cells are stimulated, they then trigger nervous impulses that travel along the olfactory nerves leading to the olfactory bulbs in the brain. Here all incoming messages are sorted out, and the pike is then able to interpret what it has smelt.

Recent studies on olfaction and responses to biological chemicals in many fish, including pike, have revealed some interesting results. Sharks and eels, for example, have ninety or more folds of lamella in their rosettes, which can contain hundreds of thousands of sensory cells per square millimetre. Pike and sticklebacks, in comparison, have poorly developed sense organs. Pike may have as few as twenty folds of tissue in their rosettes, hence they have fewer sensory cells.

Over the past twenty or so years, scientists both in Canada and Europe have carried out detailed experiments using fish blood and other tissue extracts, in order to identify what pike smelt best of all. These revealed that pike didn't respond that well to fish extracts or blood, but did respond particularly well to fear pheromones given out by minnows. They also responded very well to sexual pheromones (extracted from the gonads). These particular pheromones are excreted during the breeding season, which probably accounts for why so many males and females are found in one particular location.

So how does all of this information help us as pike anglers? Well, I think it clearly shows that sense of smell is not as important as sight and the neuromast organs in detecting food items during their daily routine. I firmly believe that a

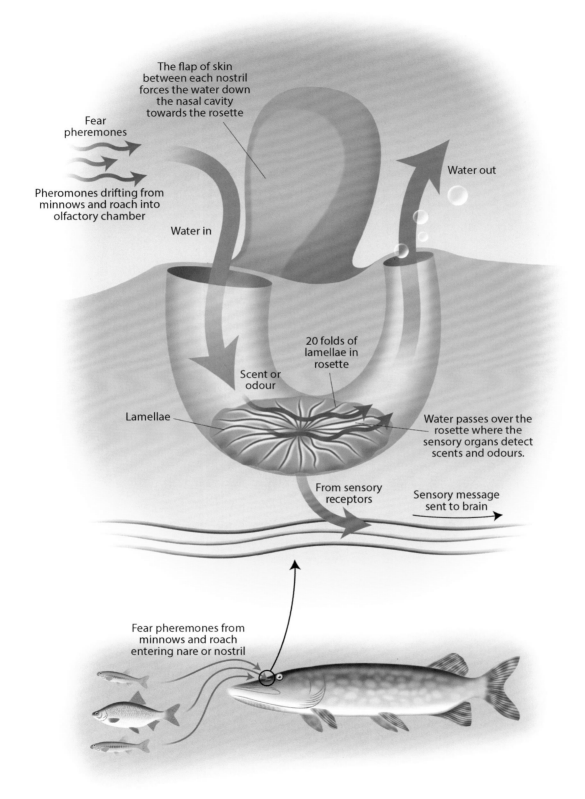

The flap of skin between each nostril forces the water down the nasal cavity towards the rosette

Fear pheremones

Pheromones drifting from minnows and roach into olfactory chamber

Water in

Water out

20 folds of lamellae in rosette

Scent or odour

Lamellae

Water passes over the rosette where the sensory organs detect scents and odours.

From sensory receptors

Sensory message sent to brain

Fear pheremones from minnows and roach entering nare or nostril deadbait must be placed close enough for a pike to smell it or seek it out. My other belief is that pre-baiting is not worth the time, money and effort spent on it, unless you live right on the water and can carry out a long-term pre-baiting regime in order to educate the pike onto specific baits. This is a view shared by Fred Buller, who says that pre-baiting has never worked particularly well for him, either. Maybe one day we will develop a pike groundbait containing fear pheromones to attract pike! Yes, there are nomadic, foraging pike that will pick up a bait as they pass, but on the whole, location on any water is of paramount importance. In which case, hours and hours should be spent concentrating on finding those hidden features, drop-offs and submerged islands, rather than on baiting programmes.

There are several waters I know where, unless your bait is placed within two feet of an underwater channel, you have no hope of getting a run all day, as the big fish have set themselves up in prime locations to intercept food and simply don't have to move. It's this conservation of energy, made possible by not needing to travel from place to place in order to locate food, that enables them to grow big!

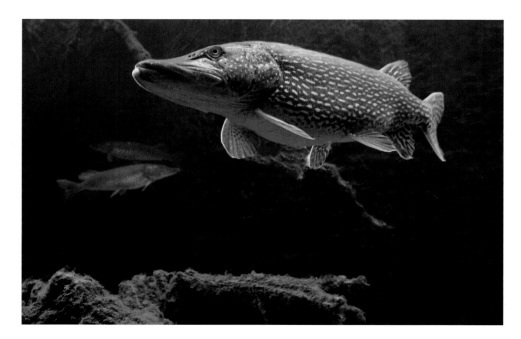

A female pike arriving on the spawning grounds in February.

Fish scientists and physiologists have made great strides over the past 30 years, and now have a better understanding of how pike see things, but more importantly what colours they see best of all.

CHAPTER 12

SIGHT & VISION

THERE IS NO DOUBT THAT PIKE DO SEE COLOUR, and their colour vision is confirmed by their ability to change colour to suit the environment in which they are living. For example, pike that were kept in ponds with a sandy-coloured bottom soon took on a light colour with a darkish underside, whereas pike that were kept in dark, peaty-coloured water adapted backs that were almost black. Blind pike find it almost impossible to do this, so we can conclude that the colour receptors within a pike's eyes are responding to specific colours, and trigger a change in overall body colour. Pike do see many colours in the spectrum, but we humans find it difficult to comprehend, let alone understand, the window of the pike's world, what colours they see and which colours they see best when it comes to choosing natural and artificial baits. Water as a medium transmits sound far better than it does in air. However, it is a poor medium when it comes to transmitting light, as it absorbs it. The deeper the water, the further light has to travel; hence the amount of light available for a pike to see things such as colour decreases markedly. Waters that are 'algefied', muddy or turbulent pose even greater problems for pike anglers who hope to succeed with visual baits, as light and water clarity are impaired even further. However, fish scientists and physiologists have made great strides over the past 30 years, and now have a better understanding of how pike see things, but more importantly what colours they see best of all.

As we know, visible light is composed of a range of wavelengths, violet being the shortest, and red the longest. Fresh water absorbs longer wavelengths of light such as red, green and yellow far better than it does blue. It is not surprising, therefore, that both pike and perch in particular have developed colour vision biased towards the red end of the spectrum. The retina, the light-sensitive layer within a pike's eyes, is where the fish absorbs much of the available light. The inside layer is packed with photoreceptors, which contain rod and cone cells. The cones contain a pigment called porphyropsin, which allow the fish to see various wavelengths of colour, including infra-red, orange, yellow and green, during daylight hours.

Josef Schrank's pike caught on a spoon in Oster Lakes, Bavaria, Germany. Weight 44 lb 4 oz. The pike probably saw the spoon and picked up the vibration too. (Picture courtesy of Jan Eggers.)

There are different types of cones within the retina that are stimulated by different colours of light, and no single cone absorbs just one colour. A red-preferring cone, for example, will absorb colours from its close neighbours in the spectrum, which are orange and yellow. A blue-preferring cone, on the other hand, will absorb indigo and violet, both of which are not absorbed that quickly in fresh water, unlike reds and oranges.

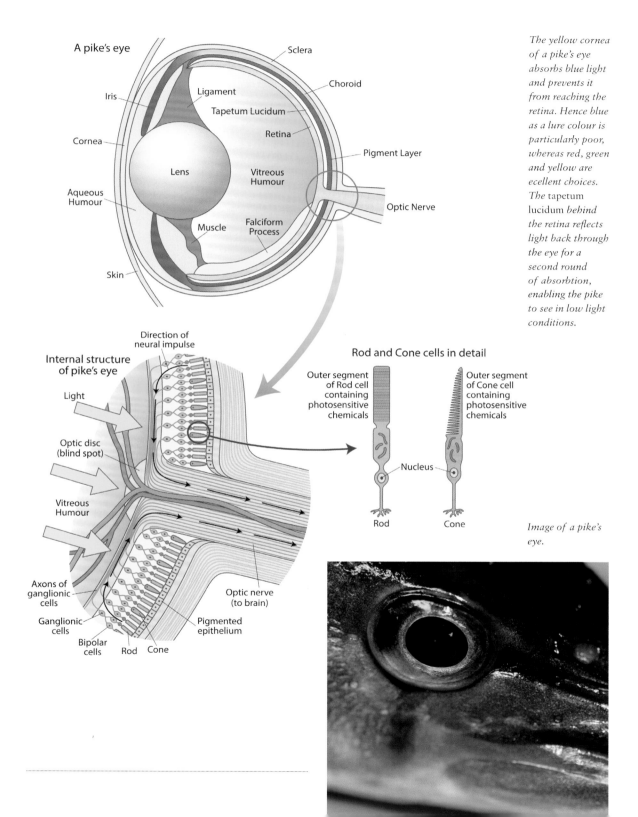

A pike's eye

Sclera

Iris

Ligament

Choroid

Tapetum Lucidum

Cornea

Retina

Lens

Vitreous
Humour

Pigment Layer

Aqueous
Humour

Optic Nerve

Muscle

Falciform
Process

Skin

*The yellow cornea
of a pike's eye
absorbs blue light
and prevents it
from reaching the
retina. Hence blue
as a lure colour is
particularly poor,
whereas red, green
and yellow are
ecellent choices.
The* tapetum
lucidum *behind
the retina reflects
light back through
the eye for a
second round
of absorbtion,
enabling the pike
to see in low light
conditions.*

Direction of
neural impulse

Internal structure
of pike's eye

Rod and Cone cells in detail

Light

Outer segment
of Rod cell
containing
photosensitive
chemicals

Outer segment
of Cone cell
containing
photosensitive
chemicals

Optic disc
(blind spot)

Vitreous
Humour

Nucleus

Rod

Cone

*Image of a pike's
eye.*

Axons of
ganglionic
cells

Optic nerve
(to brain)

Ganglionic
cells

Pigmented
epithelium

Bipolar
cells   Rod   Cone

American muskies, covered more fully in Chapter 13, like many other pike have no blue-cone-sensitive pigments within their retinas, and hence cannot see into the blue end of the spectrum. What is also interesting is that the cornea, the outer transparent part of the eyeball, is yellow, and filters out shorter wavelengths of light such as blue. Consequently, blue as a colour is of little benefit to us pike anglers.

The rods, on the other hand, help the fish to see in low light conditions, and they are highly sensitive to both black and white. They are perfectly adapted for night vision, and capable of picking out silhouettes moving across the surface on moonlit nights.

Pike also have something known as the *tapetum lucidum*, a reflective layer of pigment situated directly behind the retina of the eye. It acts as a retroreflector,

Savage Soft 4Play loose bodied lures with nose cones. Fluorescent orange is particularly deadly.

and bounces light back onto the photoreceptors so that they can absorb any light that was not caught first time around. The *tapetum lucidum* is a vital part of pike vision, as it enhances their sight in low light conditions, at night or when hunting in deeper water.

Pike can also see ultra-violet light, which is short-wavelength, high-frequency light coming from the sun. It is invisible to us, but highly visible to pike, so it makes sense to have a range of lures coated with UV paints in your lure box. Savage have a lovely range of lures and plastic nose cones for rubber baits coated in UV paint, both of which work extremely well. Glowtec Ltd, based in Lancashire, also supply UV Neon and Starglow paints, which can be applied to lures by brush or air spray, and Torch Direct Ltd in Nottingham sell UV torches to test the effectiveness of each colour.

Fluorescent colours also work well for big pike, and the glow effect they give out has led to the downfall of many a big fish. A group of German anglers I know swear by fluorescent lures, especially oranges and pinks, which they use early in the morning or on peaty or murky waters. They have caught huge numbers of big pike from the Bodden, Möhne, Ruhr and Rhine rivers, along with one very coloured water in Sweden, where visibility was down to 0.5 metres and the pike wouldn't touch anything other than fluorescent shads.

UV paints and fluorescent colours can be sprayed or painted onto lures to give them pike appeal.

Savage cut bait herring.

If I had to choose six colours for catching big pike globally, they would have to be red, green, yellow, black, white and silver and, as colours are blurred when a lure is being reeled in, my lures would be painted very boldly using just two or three colour combinations. Stop and start lures that could be hung in the water would be very different, and more detailed scale or body patterns would almost certainly be used, as pike would be able to see them. Apart from this, I would almost certainly have a range of lures coated in UV and fluorescent paint to hand. Lure or bait fishing, as far as I am concerned, should be kept as simple as possible. It's just a matter of ringing the changes, and presenting the fish with the optimal visual colour and size of bait, and at the correct depth.

Once you have managed to crack the colour code for a specific water at a particular time of day and month, make a note of it, as this information will pay dividends when you come to fish similar waters elsewhere. If you are fishing a water with two or more people and one of them starts to catch fish, you can then pool your resources, all fish the same lures, and determine the optimal colour or lure size for those conditions.

Lastly, talk to as many successful pike anglers as you can about what lures or baits have been successful for them, and make a note of it. I have never been too proud to ask questions of other anglers, and nor should you. It's all a learning curve, and we learn something every day. It's remembering what we have learned, and applying it in a simple, thorough and systematic way, that makes the difference in consistently catching big pike. I recently asked two of the best pike anglers in the world about their favourite lures or lure colours.

'Oh, if I had to choose one colour it would be silver,' one said.

The other replied: 'Green, yellow and red. I have over 5,000 lures, but if my life depended on it, I would choose just five of them to catch big pike.'

I think this sums it up. It's we pike anglers that tend to over-complicate things, not the fish!

Rubber UV and fluorescent eels.

Master pike angler Jan Eggers holding a double-figure pike. Note the dark back, green body and bold stripes on the lure.

When you're away for a few days, the trip becomes well worth the effort, and something that can be repeated often enough, providing funds allow, to get fully acquainted with even the remotest of waters.

CHAPTER 13

THE TRAVELLING ANGLER

THE WRITING IS ON THE WALL FOR PIKE ANGLERS EVERYWHERE. More people are turning to pike fishing; fewer gravel pits are being dug, and rivers are shrinking as populations grow. The obvious conclusion is that if you want to continue to enjoy quality fishing in the future, then you need to be prepared to travel. On the plus side, roads have improved enormously in the past ten to twenty years, and with a half-decent car and an early start it's possible to travel over a hundred miles each way for a day's fishing. For a long weekend you could get to a water in an unspoilt part of Britain as much as three hundred miles away, and still have your baits cast out by lunchtime.

The River Wye, just one of many unspoilt waters throughout Britain just waiting to be discovered by the travelling angler.

When you're away for a few days, the trip becomes well worth the effort, and something that can be repeated often enough, providing funds allow, to get fully acquainted with even the remotest of waters. A long-distance trip also means that the cost comes down as you drive away from the crowds. As a general rule, the more far-flung the location, the more likely the ticket price will be a token amount, out of proportion to what's on offer. From the wide open spaces of the Norfolk Broads in the east to the untapped potential of the River Wye in the west, and from the countless lochs of Scotland in the north to the estuaries of the big south-coast rivers, there are a wealth of fishing opportunities for anyone willing to travel.

And if you're prepared to venture abroad, you can fish for pike of a very different size and species from our native British variety. There is excellent pike fishing in the Baltic, Holland, France, Germany, Denmark, Russia and Poland. In America there are muskellunge, which grow to five feet long and can weigh more than 60 lb.

Muskies are found in the northern states of the USA and Canada, where they thrive in the cool climate. The record stands at an ounce short of 70 lb, for a fish caught in the St. Lawrence River in 1957. Even that is dwarfed by earlier monsters, the biggest for which photographic evidence exists weighing a staggering 110 lb. It measured seven feet four inches long and was landed in Michigan in 1919.

TV presenter Chris Tarrant fishing in Manitoba. (Picture courtesy of Anglers World Holidays.)

Jan Eggars holding one of his big Canadian pike.

John Hawsey holding a 20 lb pike caught on a surface popper, Kluane Lodge on Wellesley Lake, Yukon, Canada. (Picture courtesy of Anglers World Holidays.)

North America is a pike angler's heaven. Besides the mighty muskie (*Esox masquinongy*), anglers can also fish for our own species (*Esox lucius*), and three smaller cousins, the chain pickerel (*Esox niger*), redfin pickerel (*Esox americanus*) and grass pickerel (*Esox americanus vermiculatus*). All five species are capable of producing hybrids, the most prized being the tiger muskie – a pike/muskie cross with all of the tackle-straining attributes of both parents. The Great Lakes in Canada are home to big tail-walking muskies, and the rivers of Alberta and Manitoba's Winnipeg River are home to the great northern pike, the same species as our own.

The heart of musky territory is Ontario, where the Ottawa and St. Lawrence rivers and the countless lakes that supply them have some of the biggest examples of this exciting species, while Minnesota is a region with as much water as land, and a reputation for breeding some of the biggest and hardest fighting muskies of all.

But if you feel that America is a little far to travel, then the countries of Scandinavia, with their expanses of brackish water holding huge stocks of pike to a size that would make a British angler's eyes bulge, are an obvious alternative. The only other pike species outside America is the Amur pike (*Esox reicherti*), found in the Amur River in eastern Asia on the border between Russia and China. It grows to just over 20 lb and lives mainly in flowing water, though it migrates to lakes and shallow backwaters to spawn.

Inch for inch, though, British pike are heavier than their American and Asian cousins. A typical 40-inch pike on the other side of the Atlantic weighs in at around 16 lb, while any self-respecting British pike of that length would exceed 20 lb. At 48 inches an average American pike weighs 28 lb, while if you catch one of those in Britain it would be of record-threatening proportions.

What all pike have in common, though, is a predatory habit. They are natural-born killers, and anglers from Boston, Massachusetts to Boston, Lincolnshire use

A sheltered bay on Loch Awe, where perch spawn at a given time each year, attracting large numbers of pike.

similar tactics to tempt them. In recent years there has been a cross-fertilisation of ideas across the Atlantic. Many American anglers are now using our advanced livebait and deadbait techniques to deadly effect, while we in turn have learned how to catch big pike on their excellent plugs and artificial lures.

Be prepared

But before you throw your tackle in the back of the car and set off for somewhere few anglers' feet have ever trodden, it's worth knowing that the single factor that will influence your catches on a remote water more than any other is preparation. The more homework you do before you leave, the more trouble-free and so more enjoyable the trip will be, and the greater the chances of success. If you know where you are going to stay, where you are going to fish, how much the permits are, where you are going to get them, what bait you are going to use, what the weather is going to be, what the usual feeding times are and where the local hotspots can be found, you will have increased your likelihood of success many times over.

If you are going to build up an accurate picture of what is happening on a big lake, you need to establish a contact with someone who lives close by, and is in touch with what is happening on a daily basis. I got to know a salmon and sea trout angler in Scotland, Neil Buchanan, and he tells me when pike are being drawn into one area of a loch because of a natural food source, like a heavy fly hatch or the perch population spawning. This kind of information gives you an enormous advantage, especially if you can only visit that water half a dozen times a year.

The aim is survival

At this point I should make a couple of admissions. First, that the majority of my fishing trips away from home have been to Scotland. I have fished in Wales, in Southern Ireland, in the East Midlands and in Norfolk, but Scotland is

Gavin Harker holding a 26 lb pike caught from the Earn in Ireland.

my first choice, and most of what I have learned has been picked up while north of the Border for a week or two at a time. But the principles apply whether you are spending a fortnight in Inverness or two days in Stoke Poges.

The aim is a dual one: to fish and to survive. If this sounds a little melodramatic, then I should explain that by survival I mean having everything you need to make yourself comfortable, so that nothing will interrupt your concentration and, as a result, your fishing. I'm not suggesting you might not come back alive – only that some anglers come back from trips cold, hungry and too miserable to care about catching fish. If by day two you are dreaming of a hot bath and a big meal, you haven't got it right. There's no reason why you should feel any less comfortable while away than when sitting in your favourite armchair with your feet up in front of the telly.

The second confession I have is that, when it comes to preparation, I'm something of a perfectionist. I used to say I don't do things by halves, but it would be closer to the truth to say I don't do things by three quarters or even nine tenths. It's all or nothing, and what I take with me reflects this. If there's a chance it may be needed, I've got it with me. I don't overburden myself with items I don't expect to need. I know by now what is required, and streamline what I carry to match this. However, my streamlined tackle is more than many anglers take, right down to spares for an outboard motor or tools to repair it. What you consider essential is entirely between you, your bank manager and your conscience. I am simply laying before you what I do, and you must decide whether and where you wish to cut corners. But I should point out that hardly a trip goes by without me having to help someone who's stranded miles from anywhere without some vital outboard motor part, and less than a snowball in Hell's chance of finding somewhere in the Glens likely to stock one. One forgotten or overlooked crucial item can ruin a trip. Like the best boy scouts, I like to be prepared.

Problems are multiplied

If the water you are travelling is bigger than the one you usually fish, or you are spending longer there than you would normally, you need more gear. For two days, you need twice as much bait as for one, twice as many rigs and twice as many leads. If the water is a loch rather than a gravel pit you will need bigger floats, stronger line and hooks, and tougher wire. Everything is different, and you must realise this at the start. If you're catering for yourself – and believe me, it's the best way – you will need twice as much food for two weeks as one, twice as much fuel and twice as much money. And if you are sleeping under canvas on the bank, you'll need twice as many spare clothes for the times when the weather makes you wet through.

THE GOOD FOOD GUIDE

Anyone who's ever been out for a Chinese meal and felt peckish on the way home will know that there's food that gives you a quick burst of energy that's soon over, and food that will keep hunger at bay for hours.

Meals eaten in between fishing sessions are best described as refuelling. You need something to satisfy your hunger and provide you with energy until the next fishing break, but you don't want to spend your time peeling spuds and scrubbing pans.

No self-respecting traveller will leave home without his tin-opener. Forget Delia Smith and her little squirt of lime juice and her sprinkling of fresh herbs. Tinned potatoes, easy-to-cook rice and tinned ravioli or spaghetti are what you want. You need carbohydrates for energy and plenty of them. You can mix in some tinned meat if your taste buds require it, but the important thing is to have something hot and filling. If you can raise your body's core temperature or at least keep it constant, this will greatly add to your feeling of well-being after a cold day spent fighting the elements.

Fred J. Taylor once wrote that the only use for a frying pan was to bang someone over the head. A couple of saucepans is all you need for cooking food, as fried items will take too long to digest and cause cleaning problems. I save on the washing-up by using a metal cup and brewing up with it directly over a flame.

Cooking will become less of a chore and more of a pleasure if you've got a stove you're proud of. I've tried a few, and the Coleman Multi-fuel I've settled on is a joy to use. It will run on leaded or unleaded petrol, meths or turps, making it easy to replenish and very reliable. The price is about £30 to £35 for a single burner; and I wouldn't use anything else. Oh, and take a lighter rather than matches, as matches and water don't mix.

Despite what the adverts say, a bar of chocolate won't help you work, rest and play, and neither will junk food like crisps and biscuits. They will give you a boost of energy, but not the sustained flow over several hours that you need. If this is starting to sound like an edition of *The Good Food Guide*, then I should say that I can't emphasise strongly enough: if you aren't well fed, then you won't be able to concentrate, you're more likely to lose a big fish, and will seriously reduce your chances of success. If you are going to fish for 13 or 14 hours a day, you need to look after yourself better than you would at home, where you have all the comforts of familiar surroundings. It's hard work to be alert and fishing at 4 a.m. and still be concentrating at 11 p.m. for one day after another, no matter what you do in between.

One corner I do allow myself to cut is in never taking fresh water with me, but just boiling up the water I am fishing in. I can imagine people wrinkling their noses as they read this, but I've been using the same method for twelve years now without ill effect. The water that comes out of the taps here in England has probably got more nasties in it than a fresh scoop of water from an unspoilt loch, and until I experience problems I'll carry on. Perhaps in built-up areas or near heavily-farmed land it wouldn't be wise, but in Scotland, at least, most of the water is just melted snow that's come down from the hills, and provided it's boiled, there's no reason why you and I shouldn't drink it. I've no wish to carry a gallon container of water around with me unnecessarily, but if you don't like the look of the stuff where you're fishing, then it would be wise to err on the side of caution.

No self-respecting travelling angler will leave home without a tin opener. A metal cup allows you to brew up directly over a flame, and a Coleman Multifuel is a joy to use.

I rarely spend two weeks away nowadays. One week I can prepare for comfortably, but two weeks brings logistical problems that start to reduce the chances of fishing effectively in the second week, and make calculations unnecessarily complicated. By the time you've loaded up all the essentials you look more like the driver of an aid vehicle on a mercy mission to a war zone than an angler going fishing. I try to keep it simple now, having learned the hard way.

The problem with guest houses

Why not simply stay in a guest house, with meals and accommodation laid on, and a place to dry out when the weather turns bad?

Unfortunately, pike and landladies don't keep the same hours. When the sun rises at 4 a.m. in mid-summer, pike will be feeding as the first faint rays penetrate the water, and that spell may only last for about twenty minutes. You will need to be up before 3 a.m. and in place before they start. Try asking for your breakfast to be served at that time of the morning and you're more than likely to find your bags on the front drive. The motto is, choose your guest house carefully, in the case of Ireland with advice from Paul Harris, who is angling adviser to the Irish Tourist Board. That way you shouldn't have a problem.

Having achieved the ideal of getting up in the dark and enjoying the excellent sport that first light can bring, I like to come off the water for breakfast and a wash and brush-up and maybe even a couple of hours' kip, just at the time when bed-and-breakfast owners want you out so they can clean the place and make the beds. I don't need to tell you that fishing on into the first hour of dark, and getting in after 11 p.m., tired and hungry, isn't exactly popular with non-angling landlords. Find a place run by an angler if you can, as tourist guest houses and successful pike fishing do not produce a marriage made in Heaven.

Bedding down on board

There was a time when I used to sleep under canvas, but the kind of weather Scotland can dish out, and the problems created by packing up and moving, as well as the security aspect, have persuaded me that the best way is to sleep on a boat with a cabin. It's the perfect answer to all the problems created by tents. I now have a sixteen-foot Quayline with a proper cabin, complete with bed and cooker, and with this I don't need to leave the water at the end of the evening, or take shelter from continuous, heavy rain. I used to use a cuddy with an awning thrown over it, but this arrangement was far from ideal. With a boat that has a cabin you can sleep in, you're totally self-sufficient. You don't have to rely on shops and garages, and if you get cold there's a door you can use to shut yourself in where it's warm in the cabin.

However, if you do opt for sleeping under canvas, and plenty of anglers do, don't be tempted to take a bivvy. Faced with seven days of heavy rain, you will realise you can't mess with Mother Nature. A proper tent's the thing, and a strong well-waterproofed one at that. Those of the dome design are light and compact and can be erected in seconds, which is important when you may move from one area to another, or even from one water to another, several times in quick succession.

The two essentials when choosing a tent for fishing trips are enough room to store everything and also sleep inside, and a sewn-in groundsheet to stop water from creeping in underneath. The stove makes a very effective heater inside a tent if used with care, especially just before going to sleep on very cold nights. It's important to be warm when you climb into your sleeping bag. I always have a hot drink before turning in, to raise my body temperature.

Peg it down

The best tent in the world won't keep you dry if it gets blown away in the first gale. Bivvy pegs are vital, and you should try to get the ones that are nine or ten inches long to achieve a secure hold, and push them in as far as they will go. A friend of mine had his tent and its entire contents hurled into a loch after he failed to peg it down in strong winds. Everything was soaked through, and it took him two days to dry it all sufficiently to be able to get back to his fishing. I helped him sort it out, but drew the line at his request to share my sleeping bag because his was still wet. Angling comradeship can be taken too far.

When fishing from the bank you can sit beside your tent, but when you set off in a boat each day and leave the tent behind, it's worth taking steps to ensure nothing gets pinched. You may think that when you go to a place like Scotland to fish you will have the loch to yourself, but Loch Lomond in high summer can become extremely busy with sightseers, and boats will be going to and fro all day. If you are camping, try to set up somewhere where you can see your gear from where you will be fishing, and if possible store it on an island, which is a little more secure than the shore. Even then, it's worth hiding valuable items like spare tackle in nearby bushes, for if someone is snooping around, the first place they are going to look is inside your tent.

And on the subject of hiding tackle, when you go to the shops to stock up on provisions, never leave rods on view in the back of your car. If you haven't got a sealed boot, buy some one-way security film and stick it over the back windows so that people can't see in, or at least cover things with blankets. Valuables have been stolen from the most remote and beautiful places, and many a trip has been ruined by the loss of large amounts of tackle.

The best sleeping bag

A good bag is worth its weight in gold. The one I use is a minus-20, down-filled model with sewn-in waterproof groundsheet and built-in pillow. You can get them from army surplus stores for about £40, or made by the same company for anglers and sold by Fox. You need more than a standard sleeping bag for everything except high summer if you are going to get a good night's sleep and be able to stay awake the next day.

I never used to bother with bedchairs, but that wasn't because I'm one of those Crocodile Dundee types who can sleep on bare ground. I used to use a thick Israeli closed-cell-foam sleeping mat, which doesn't absorb water, and cut down on the amount I had to carry in my days of sleeping under canvas.

Warm, dry clothing

Clean, warm, dry socks are for me the basis for fishing in comfort. All the other warm and waterproof clothing is just as important in principle, but until I've got my feet happy I don't feel comfortable.

WATCHING THE WEATHER FORECASTS

Weather forecasting is something else that has made great strides in the past decade. Now we are offered a far more accurate picture during periods of settled weather than we used to get, and the movement of high- and low-pressure fronts bringing changes in conditions can often be predicted up to a week ahead.

My trips to Scotland happen mainly in the summer because the weather is so unpredictable once winter sets in. I see no point in spending days at a time battling through heavy rain and gales and water whipped to a fury for what is usually a meagre reward under those conditions. What I'm looking for is a period of settled weather with overcast skies, even light drizzle. I don't want the weather to be too bright, as pike tend to shun strong sunlight, which tends to restrict feeding spells to dawn and dusk, whereas we want pike to be on the lookout for food throughout the day. The longer the feeding period, the greater the chances of catching a number of fish.

Settled weather is the key to success in Scotland.

Modern waterproof materials have brought outdoor clothing on in leaps and bounds in recent years. Gone are the days of heavy waxed-cotton raincoats, or nylon overalls that made us sweat so much we might as well not have been wearing waterproofs in the first place. Now we have Aquatex, Ventile and Gore-Tex garments that are light and very waterproof, and don't make a noise like a bag of crisps being opened every time you move in them. They're not cheap, but are worth the outlay for the freedom and comfort they offer. Best of all is the bib and brace, made by Abu in Gore-Tex or Ventile, with several warm layers beneath. It is the ultimate combination of lightweight, warm, waterproof clothing that doesn't restrict arm movement, yet covers you from ankle to chest.

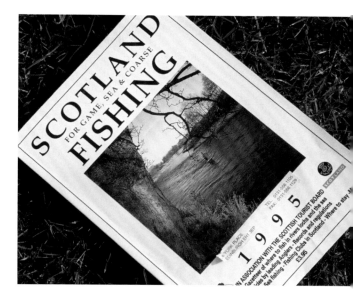

All you need to know about waters north of the Border.

The warmest way to dress is with several loose layers under a waterproof outer one, which has an added bonus that if the weather warms a little you can take off a layer or two until you feel right, as you can't do in a one-piece suit, or straitjacket as I call it. You won't find me in one of these. I can't move freely in them, and I think they could be dangerous if you fell in, because their weight when soaked with water could pull you under.

Spare sets of clothing are a must in case of an accident. Even when you wear waterproof tops, heavy rain can still find its way in, and there can be few more certain ways of feeling uncomfortable than having to brave the elements.

Just the ticket

Ticket information is something best sorted out in advance, and here a phone call to a local tackle shop should help. It's useful to buy the licences and permits you will need on the day you arrive, for the length of time that you need, to avoid losing a day's fishing while you go into town. With an early start when travelling, the shops should be open when you arrive.

I used to have problems finding out who controlled what fishing in Scotland until I discovered an excellent booklet called *Scotland for Game, Sea and Coarse Fishing*, published by Pastime Publications in association with the Scottish Tourist Board. This will tell you all you need to know about waters north of the Border, including maps, details of which club controls what, where you can get tickets and how much they will cost. It is available from the Scottish Tourist Board, 6 York Place, Edinburgh EH1 3EP.

Transporting livebaits

If your pike fishing success depends upon the quality of your bait, then it is worth spending some time putting together a means of transporting them that gets them to your destination in good condition. Getting enough live fish to last you a week from one end of the country to the other in the height of summer without them keeling over is quite an achievement, and it has to be done if you aren't going to risk wasting your time.

On the trips I have made to Scotland, a lot of the fish I've caught have been on deadbaits, but I always take livebaits for the odd times when pike won't look at anything else. Trout bought from a trout farm, which are free from disease, are what you want. I favour brownies of 3 oz to 6 oz. If I can get some chub of 4 oz to 8 oz as well, I will also take these. You may need as many as forty if the fishing goes well, and the pike seem to prefer them to deadbaits. Even with forty baits I've been known to run out within two days. There are times when you must have livebaits, so it pays to know somewhere you can catch them to order in an emergency. I take a float rod and a pint or two of maggots in the cool box, and head for one of the burns that flow into the loch or one of the boatyards. These potential livebait sources are among the things I look for when scouting around for new waters in the close season.

All hands to the pump

To transport livebaits successfully, air pumps are a must. Get one that will plug into the cigarette lighter of your car – Shakespeare makes one, and an American firm makes another called Bubbles. I run the aerator cable from the dashboard to the back of the car and, provided I use it while driving, it won't flatten the battery. The fish are kept in two big plastic fermenting bins with snap-on lids, ideally with trout in one, and chub in the other. The water level should be about three-quarters full. I stick the aerator to the lid of the chub bin with Velcro to stop it sliding around, pushing the air pipe in through a tiny hole punched in the top, with no room for water to splash out. Air stones are fitted at the end of the tube. Make sure all of the connections are secure. A friend of mine had an aerator pipe come away from a pump, and by the time he got to Scotland all of his baits were dead.

The water in the trout bin is kept fresh with a cylinder of oxygen, which you can rent reasonably cheaply from British Oxygen and which will last a long time. Trout need a lot of oxygen to survive, and it's worth the investment if you want baits to stay healthy.

A good tip before setting out is to put a lot of ice in the water, which brings down the temperature. When I reach the loch, I put three quarters of my baits in a keep sack in a couple of feet of water, and the other quarter in a bucket with a battery-run air pump. If I'm going out in a boat, I will put them in an American wire bait bucket, which is G-clamped to the gunwale and dropped over the side.

Fish-moving orders

When transporting livebaits to any water it's as well to obtain a fish-moving order in advance from the Environment Agency. Great damage has been done to individual waters' ecology by the illegal introduction of species which do not belong there. I certainly wouldn't tip any live fish left over at the end of a trip into the loch if they weren't indigenous to the water. It's one of the advantages of using brown trout for livebait. Anglers have no idea how much damage they can do by the simple act of releasing non-indigenous species into a water.

Transporting deadbaits

Keeping deadbaits frozen can be as much of a problem as keeping livebaits alive if you haven't got the right equipment. The best invention from the deadbait user's point of view is a mobile freezer that plugs into a car's cigarette lighter, and runs off a twelve-volt battery when I am out on the water. Cool bags and boxes are an alternative, fairly cheap and will keep baits frozen if well lined with ice packs. Wrap the baits very tightly in layers of newspaper and bubble-wrap plastic to insulate them. However, you can't expect baits to stay frozen for more than a couple of days in the summer. It pays to take plenty with you because they help keep each other frozen. I take four kilos of sardines, a couple of dozen mackerel and a couple of dozen eel sections. They're cheap, and you can throw them away or re-freeze them if you don't use them.

Go on a recce

Some anglers would turn up their noses at travelling hundreds of miles just to look at a water and not wet a line. They'd happily stroll down to the local river in the close season to look for fishy features and hotspots, but they draw the line at a full-blooded trip. But the truth is, the more homework you do, the better your chances of success will be. Whether it's combined with a family holiday or a detour en route to somewhere else, reconnaissance trips can provide a wealth of valuable information, provided you know what to look for.

   If I'm looking around a loch that I've never fished I will try to find where the main feeder streams come in, and see if there are signs of bait fish. Fishy-looking features can be sought out and pinpointed for future attention, and tackle shops, garages and boatyards can be found, saving time when there's fishing to be done.

   One of the richest sources of information can be the local pub. It's surprising how much you can learn over a pint. I like to talk to the salmon anglers who troll the loch and often hit big pike. Usually they are fully prepared to divulge information on the whereabouts of pike, as it's a species that doesn't interest them.

Locals know about the runs of game fish, the routes they take through the loch and where and when the coarse fish, like perch, spawn, and they can save you a lot of time for the price of a couple of pints of heavy or a few wee drams. This will give you an intimate knowledge of what is happening on the loch throughout the year, and put you in an excellent position to make the most of your time on the water. But no matter how much you learn from a close-season trip, you will need to back this up, and get to know the water and its changing moods by making regular visits.

The head of Loch Awe pictured at sunset in high summer.

The daily routine

Most things in life are made easier with a regular routine, and fishing away from home is no exception. The pike and their feeding spells dictate what you do and when, and you will need to monitor these so that you can pace yourself and take rests and catch up on necessary chores in the slack periods in between.

On the lochs in the summer when the weather is warm the majority of the pike feed early and late. I like to get up before dawn, have a quick cup of tea and have the rods cast out ready for the dawn feeding spell. This can be very short-lived, so it's worth making the effort and being there before it starts.

When the feeding stops I make breakfast and have a quick clean-up. This could be still early or it could be mid-morning, but even if the fish carry on taking baits until lunchtime, which is rare, I will have a break at midday. Lunchtime is the chance to get a hot meal down me, and maybe have a siesta if the evening looks like being a long one. Afternoons can produce sport, but generally the fish are not over-active then, so I use that time to get myself together. I'll sort through my tackle, checking the line and trace, tidy up the boat and get ready for the evening session.

A couple of years ago I was determined to make the most of every minute, and fished so intensely that I was down to having one meal a day. I wouldn't recommend it. Sooner or later you have to take a break, no matter how ambitious you are or how many miles you've travelled to be there. It's better to force yourself to have a rest even when you want to carry on, than have to come off the water because you've overdone it.

And you will find that the first couple of days of a trip are usually the best in terms of catches. If someone else has just fished the bay you intended to try, it won't be worth fishing there, because that bay will have been disturbed, and won't produce fish until it has had several days' rest. And the longer you fish in one spot, the more disturbance there is in the water, and the more wary the pike become.

So it pays to take a break, and if you know that the biggest pike will be around at dusk, you can time your evening meal for about 6 p.m., and that way you will be in place and alert when they go on the rampage.

Fishing from a floating platform brings its advantages and disadvantages, joys and woes, but is, even at its worst, a unique experience.

CHAPTER 14

BOATS

M ANY READERS WILL SKIP OVER THIS PASSAGE as soon as they see the title. They're as likely to buy a boat and tow it hundreds of miles up the motorway as they are to emigrate to Australia and start farming armadillos. Which is a shame, not because I dislike armadillos particularly, but because boat fishing can add a new dimension to your angling. Fishing from a floating platform brings its advantages and disadvantages, joys and woes, but is, even at its worst, a unique experience akin to walking on water, and no one should turn their nose up at it until they've had a go.

Whether you hire a boat to see how you get on, or cajole a friend, angling or non-angling, into letting you join them for a day, I would urge everyone to try it once, just in case you find it as wonderfully liberating as I do. If you enjoy the experience enough to want to own your own craft, that enthusiasm should see you through all the preparation and expense involved in boat ownership, which I will be discussing in this chapter, along with how to approach fishing from boats. Owning a boat can be costly and inconvenient, but it can also be as liberating as getting a car.

What boat to buy?

There's never been a better range of suitable boats available to the angler, from glass fibre to the traditional wood.

Glass fibre, or GRP, is my first choice. It combines strength with lightness and is virtually maintenance-free. Wooden boats are very heavy,

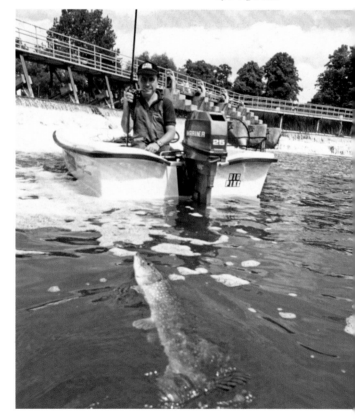

The 16-foot Orkney Strikeliner has a deep draught, and the size and strength to weather any storm that whips up a big water.

Boat fishing is a unique experience akin to walking on water, and no one should turn their nose up without giving it a try.

take a lot of looking after and are not as towable because of their weight. Someone once said wooden boats are like women – they need a lot of care and attention – and I wouldn't argue with that.

I have two boats for different conditions. I have a 13-foot Orkney Dory with a cathedral hull – three keels close together – making it very stable. This is used for most of my slack-water fishing, from navigating the Thames and anchoring in weir pools to fine-weather fishing on Scottish lochs. It's the ideal boat for fishing sink-and-draw style, which calls for a mobile approach.

I used to have a 16-foot Orkney Strikeliner, which has a simulated clinker hull and a much deeper draught than the Dory, but I've recently changed it for a Quayline Reefrunner of the same length. It has plenty of floor space, a deep draught and a self-contained cabin that sleeps two people. Orkney produce a range of fishing boats, in particular the Spinner, the Coastliner and the Strikeliner.

You need a boat with plenty of clearance above the water for when strong winds whip up huge waves. It's ideal for fishing static deadbaits, when a solid platform is needed. I can tow either on a trailer behind my diesel four-wheel-drive, which I can also sleep in, if necessary.

I prefer the Dory because it's flat-bottomed, which makes it easier to stand in, and very manoeuvrable, but it's not good in strong winds, and certainly not the boat to be in when a storm is brewing. You need a bigger boat, one that is capable of getting through waves three or four feet high and crossing from one side of an expanse of water to the other.

To tackle the big Irish and Scottish lochs you need a boat of no less than 13 feet, and if I knew it was going to be rough, or I was going there at a time when the weather could be bad, then it would be a 16-foot craft every time.

Flat-bottomed dory boats are easy to stand in and very manoeuvrable.

To make fishing halfway passable, any decent boat should have a cuddy – a fibreglass shelter bolted to the bow, under which you can sit and be dry and warm, out of the wind and rain, while watching rods mounted on outriggers. If you're out of the wind, you won't suffer from the chill factor, and you can stay out there longer and be more alert if something happens.

Thirty horse-power Mariner engine will get you out of trouble in rough weather.

Choosing an engine

Until you have experienced a storm blowing up out of nowhere on a big water you can't imagine how quickly the weather can change. Water can turn from flat calm to a raging sea in ten minutes, and when that happens you need to get yourself to the lee shore or onto an island and out of trouble very quickly.

To do this you will need a reasonably powerful motor. I have a 30 horse-power Mariner engine, which gets me out of trouble, but I always take a back-up motor slotted on the back of the boat in case the main motor breaks down. I can think of few things worse than being stuck on a big loch in bad weather, miles from where you started, and faced with the prospect of having to row home. I've been known to motor fifteen miles to reach a good spot, and if I break down, I've got this distance to cover to get back.

You may think the chances of something going wrong are slim, but you would change your mind if you looked off the front of a boat into the water of a big loch or lough. The bottom can be fifty feet deep one minute, and a foot down the next. I've damaged props, motors and hulls when I've been caught unawares, because these features – called skerries – are so unpredictable. Some of the Irish and Scottish waters have pointed boulders jutting almost up to the surface that can tear a hole in the bottom of a boat with ease. When you're exploring new lochs, accidents are going to happen to even the most experienced anglers.

But the Scottish countryside isn't exactly over-endowed with specialist stores selling spare parts for various makes of outboard motor. One bad bump, and you could be going home early, or fishing for the rest of your stay from the shore.

The sort of size of engine needed on a big loch can get through a lot of petrol. I take two tanks of fuel and plenty of oil – enough for several days' use. Large, remote pike waters are desolate places when you are stranded. Rarely does a trip go by to one of the more popular lochs without me ending up towing back anglers who have run out of fuel. Others have to cut short their session to come ashore to refuel. The very least you should do is find out in advance the whereabouts of the nearest place that sells it.

The second engine that I carry is 3 to 4 horse-power, which doubles as a trolling motor. It has an integral petrol tank, and is very compact and light.

Also, I always carry a basic tool kit with a spare set of spark plugs, so that if the fault is minor, I can tinker with the engine and maybe fix it.

Extending the handle

My own, personal contribution to boat fishing comfort is an outboard motor extension arm. I offer you this information without any attempt at personal gain, as the item is not sold by a tackle firm under a fancy name, but by DIY stores in the form of lengths of plastic tubing.

The idea came about because I found that when I was trolling, I was continually reaching back, and sitting at an uncomfortable angle. To watch the rods, check the echo sounder and see where I was going meant looking in three directions, one after the other, for long periods of time, which was literally a pain in the neck. The problem was that the standard-length tiller handle on the motor was too far back to reach. But with a two-foot length of plastic tube slotted over the handle of my trolling motor, I can sit facing forwards, watch the rods in front and the echo sounder to the side, while steering, without looking round.

Two types of anchor

Anchors come in two sorts: heavy, flat-bottomed mud weights for holding on smooth bottoms of silt or sand, and traditional lightweight folding hooks, like giant trebles, which grip debris and rocks.

I have home-made, non-folding anchors like grappling hooks, with four prongs slotting into a two-foot length of scaffold tube half-filled with lead. These

Anchors come in two types – flat mud weights and ones with prongs that grip.

Left: An anchor with plastic cable tie enables an angler to pull snagged anchors free. When the cable tie breaks the anchor can be dislodged, as the claws fold in on themselves.

are the only design capable of holding a big boat in a powerful swell. A specially-built anchor is needed to keep a boat still on a big water.

Mud weights are only used to stabilise the other end of the boat, or to anchor up in a very sheltered bay. You can't present baits properly if the boat is yawing, or not stable. My mud weights weigh 50 lb to 60 lb and have large surface areas to stop them dragging along featureless lake beds. I've customised mine by gluing carpet on the bottom to stop them clattering against the front of the boat on the way in and out, and scaring fish.

The drawback with any kind of anchor is that it can get trapped in snags and be difficult to get out. If this happens, you will need to wrap the rope around a cleat and back the boat up until you have pulled it free.

Each rope needs to be 40 feet long, as you could find yourself fishing in 35 feet of water, but more importantly it needs to be at least 3 cm in diameter so that you can get a grip on it without it cutting into your hands. I use polypropylene yachting rope, which floats, a useful feature if you're absent-minded and prone to dropping anchor without attaching the other end to the boat. I carry two shorter lengths of rope, about 10 or 12 feet, which I use when I'm fishing shallow water, so that I don't have lots of coils of spare rope trailing around my ankles. To change over I use karabiners, which are sturdy, snap-on metal links used in rock climbing.

Some people believe a length of heavy chain is a substitute for a well-designed anchor, but no amount of chain will hold an anchor that is prone to slipping when a strong wind gets up.

Always anchor with the bows – the pointed end, for anyone not familiar with such complex nautical terminology – facing into the wind. Anchoring across the wind is asking for a bumpy ride, for waves to break over the side and the anchor to be dragged out of position. And be prepared to change position when the wind changes, as it can do frequently on a big water, or you could find yourself facing in the wrong direction despite having anchored with care a little earlier in the day.

OUTSMARTING LIVELY FISH

The problems don't end with a securely-anchored boat. Once you have presented a bait properly and hooked a fish, anchor ropes become a liability, as does the propeller. I like to get the prop up out of the water in advance, but if a fish goes around an anchor rope, you've got problems.

You can't stop a fish from running under a boat. Believe me, I've tried. I've broken rods sinking the tips and holding on while trying to turn a pike. There is a way of outsmarting a fish, though. The best way to beat them if they've gone under the boat is to put the multiplier on free spool. The fish will carry on for a while, but when it feels no resistance it will stop. You can then pass the rod under the anchor rope, tighten up, and you are back into the fish.

The more you pull against a strong fish, the more it will go away from you. If you slacken off you can

usually get away with it, and the hook hold is usually strong enough to let you do this because you've already tried stopping the fish with rod pressure. Slack lining isn't an infallible technique, though. The odd fish hasn't read the rule book and just keeps going.

All hands to the bilge pump

No matter how hard you try to keep it out, water has a habit of finding its way on board. It could be rain or spray or seepage during overnight mooring, but hopefully it's the regular use of a landing net laden with one big fish after another. However it gets in, though, it needs to be got out. I have an electric in-line bilge pump, and I've known it rain so much I've had it going all day to keep the boat dry.

Electric pumps are very compact – mine is about 20 cm long – and will clear out any water that has collected inside overnight in minutes, through a length of plastic piping. You can use a bailer, but this is much simpler. I attach mine to the battery I use to power the fish finder.

Lost without a fish finder

Maybe it's a slight exaggeration to say I'd rather leave my rods behind than my fish finder when out on a loch, but it comes a close second. Loch Lomond, for instance, is over twenty-five miles long and five miles wide. It comprises thousands of acres of water, and you don't need me to tell you that represents an awful lot of man hours of depth-finding with a float rod and a plummet. If you are trolling without a fish finder, you are working blind. Looking for needles in haystacks doesn't come close when compared to one angler pulling a pair of baits aimlessly behind a boat in a vast loch in search of pike. Lochs are huge sheets of water, more akin to the North Sea than a gravel pit or a big river. They have dramatic fish-holding features that are invisible from above the water line, and you need a fish finder to pinpoint these underwater contours.

But they won't find you pike, and will work against you if you try to use them in that way. Use them as contour finders and feature finders, or to locate shoals of food fish, and look for drop-offs and shelves, holding areas and stream beds.

A 20 lb pike caught from a feature found with an echo sounder. Big blank waters, like the Wiltshire gravel pit that produced it, really require a fish finder to do them full justice.

Anglers caught pike before they were invented and will probably always succeed without them, but against the odds. I only know that I wouldn't be without one.

I run the sounder off a large, 12-volt leisure battery, which is about 18 inches long. This also powers my small-water trolling motor, which is a little Minn Kota electric outboard, which trolls at just the right speed and is almost silent. But for bigger waters I use the 3 horse-power petrol motor mentioned earlier, because it copes better with the larger waves and longer distances involved. If the leisure battery needs to be recharged after prolonged use it can be taken to a boatyard, many of which will charge it overnight for a small fee.

Outriggers make things easier

Like fish finders, outriggers aren't essential for trolling, but they make the job a great deal easier. Mine are bolted on to the sides of the 16-foot boat.

Outriggers are front and back rod rests all in one, that will hold the butt of a rod securely and in a position that keeps the line well away from the boat. They are also useful as rod rests when not trolling, as they get the rods out of the boat to leave plenty of room on board. There are two varieties: under-and-overs, which should have a deep U-rest, because lochs can be choppy places and rods have a tendency to bounce out and get lost; and the American sort, imported by Bob Carolgees, which are more sophisticated, and grip the rod so that there is no chance of it coming free. Both types allow the rods to be spread further out to cover areas away from the boat. They're well worth having.

On my under-and-overs, which a friend made for me, I have plastic tubing covering the rear U to protect the rod handle from damage, and a length of rubber over the top of the front U to prevent the rod from bouncing out and sliding into the water.

On the subject of rod-holding devices, I use lengths of two-inch-diameter tubing bolted to the boat, pointing upwards, to hold my rods upright when I'm moving from one bay to another. This avoids a tangle of rods in the bottom of the boat, that can get trodden on if you should trip over, or tips broken because they protrude beyond the end of the boat.

Splendid isolation

At this point it's time for another confession: I don't like fishing with other anglers in the same boat. Call it selfish or anti-social, but I don't believe there's room for more than one angler in one boat. With another person on board I have to consider them all of the time.

For instance, I'm very meticulous about keeping everything in the right place. When I put something down, like a pair of forceps, I expect it to be there when I go to pick it up again. I like to have everything to hand, and when I fish with

*Left: Savage
Outriggers make
useful rod rests,
taking the tackle
clear of the boat.*

*Below: A Canon
Downrigger and
weight enable
you to hold baits
down at a given
depth.*

*A Minn Koto electric outboard makes an excellent small-water
trolling motor, moving the boat at just the right speed to present
the baits attractively while remaining almost silent.*

someone else they put things down in another place and I can't find them. To
some people it's an acceptable nuisance – the price you pay for having company.
To me it's just annoying.

Besides this, two people create twice as much disturbance in a boat as one,
no matter how quiet they are, and that reduces the chances of success. I know
people are going to say I should be more tolerant, but I just don't find two in a
boat conducive to catching quality pike.

Floor space is another reason. It's important to have plenty when fishing, so
one less angler means double the space. With this in mind, I also make sure I leave
everything I don't need on the shore. The less clutter in the boat, the more room
I have for manoeuvre.

Covering the floor

Having claimed the space in the bottom of the boat as my own, I like to kit it out for maximum comfort – the pike's and my own. I Velcro three big Wychwood unhooking mats to the floor, cut to fit the bottom of the boat, to protect the fish and help keep noise and vibration there to a minimum. By way of a bonus, if you feel like a lie-down then they are just the thing – warm to the touch, being made of closed-cell foam, soft and springy, and offering complete insulation from cold coming through the hull of the boat and up through your feet.

I customise my boats whenever there is a feature that is unsuitable for my needs. The bottoms of many big boats are curved, so they are uncomfortable to stand up in, but that can be solved by putting flat boards in the bottom. And on the Dory I've taken out the big bench-seat storage area so I can walk the length of the boat without tripping over it. It's now possible to buy the boat without that seat, for a considerable saving.

I allow myself one rucksack of non-essential items, which will hold spare clothing and valuables, and this goes in the stowage compartment along with engine spares and tools. The main bag carries the Coleman stove, food, bait, my favourite metal cup for brewing up, trace tidies, forceps, tackle box, scales and weigh sling, plus my camera in a watertight box packed with foam. This is so that if it goes overboard it will float (I've tested it) and it should stay dry. It keeps out the rain as well. I used to rely on the maker's camera case to keep out water, until one £500 camera began to sport mildew and the man from Nikon examined the circuitry and declared it a write-off. I vowed it would never happen again.

Docking arms are a great asset on a trailer, as they help guide the boat when it is being winched out of the water.

The much-neglected trailer

If I had to name the biggest mistake boat-owning anglers make, it is neglecting their trailers, and the biggest area of neglect is wheel bearings. They are forever getting wet, as the trailer gets rolled into the water, and if they aren't greased regularly, they can give out at any time. I do mine with a grease gun every time it has been in the water, and I use marine grease, which stands up to high temperatures and being submerged in water, unlike standard car-axle grease, which turns thin and milky. The bearings take an incredible amount of weight, as even the Dory weighs more than a Mini and takes four or five people to lift. Every time you go over a bump in the road they take the full force.

It's surprising how many people expect it to be easy to tow a trailer. They picture it trundling along the motorway behind the car and don't give the matter another thought. But when the trailer needs to be backed down a narrow jetty at a sharp incline, perhaps in the dark, it's a very different story. It looks easy when it's done by someone experienced, but if you haven't done it before you'll find out it isn't. It's well worth practising reversing your car with boat and trailer attached through narrow gaps before the day of the trip, daft as it may feel. And take it round a few corners while you're at it. Also, make sure the vehicle you use to do the towing is man enough for the job, if you don't want to get stuck on a hill in the middle of nowhere.

Trailers should be as well made as the boats that go on them. If you're getting one, make sure it's galvanised and has waterproof lights permanently attached. A trailer board is too much trouble.

A Berkley Tube rod rack is a must for all boat anglers.

Everything should be welded on so it can't be stolen or fall off. Wheels should have locking wheel nuts, and the spare should also be locked on, and the trailer should be locked to the car. I carry a spare set of keys in case of an accident, and these are attached to a small plastic bottle so they will float if they should go over the side.

On the subject of time-saving, always load the boat with gear while it is still attached to the car, to save walking back and forth into the water. It's surprising how many anglers do it the hard way. When travelling between waters I stash the rods on top of the car, full length, tied to a rod rack.

A trailer with docking arms, which guide the boat on when you are winching it out of the water, can be a great asset, especially when the flow on rivers or the tow on lochs pushes the boat out of position.

Mooring overnight

There are two types of disaster to avoid when choosing a place to moor your boat overnight: natural and man-made. Natural disasters take the form of holes worn in the bottom by sharp rocks as the craft shifts at anchor. The others involve people with designs on your property.

If someone is going to pinch my boat while I'm away, I'm going to make them work for it. I put it somewhere where it's necessary to wade out to get it, right up to their chest. But even when there's no security risk, never moor a boat in shallow water or near any rocks, as that's asking for a hole in the bottom if the wind gets up. Choose as sheltered a spot as you can, and always moor the boat at both ends to keep it from swinging.

If something goes wrong and the boat gets a breach, I carry a tube of fibreglass marine filler for small holes. If you put a big hole in your boat there's not much chance of doing anything out in the wilds. The advantage of the Dory is that it has a double skin of fibreglass, so you can puncture the outer skin and carry on fishing. You just take it to the shore at the end of the day, empty out the water from the chamber between the skins, and fill in the hole. Some bits of a boat's hull are more vulnerable than others, and if you get to know which these are you can built them up with fibreglass to protect them. Best of all, fit stainless steel skid rails under the boat so that if you do hit rocks or are regularly pulling your boat on gravel they will reduce wear and double the lifespan of the hull.

I like to moor where I intend to fish the next day, so that when the new day dawns, I can just climb out of bed and I'm ready to fish. If the boat needs to be moved a little I will sidle gently into position using an electric motor or oars to avoid disturbing the swim. I then drop anchor slowly, without any clattering.

Sleeping on the boat means you are on the spot and can catch pike unawares in the bays where they have been sheltering for the night, or as they come in to feel the sun on their backs.

Essential extras

A life jacket is a must. If you make regular trips it's inevitable that sooner or later you will have a mishap, and if you want to be around to tell the tale you'll need a life jacket. I never go out without one, having witnessed a near-fatal accident.

A friend of mine was fishing alone in a boat in Scotland, when he lost his balance while leaning over the side in very rough conditions. He fell into extremely cold water without a buoyancy aid. Fortunately, I was fishing within earshot and heard him go over. I pulled up anchors and went and got him out. He was an experienced angler and boat user, and a big strong chap, but it was still quite a shock for him. He was having a job struggling back on board when I got to him: his clothing was saturated and weighed him down, and the cold was numbing his arms and legs. He would probably have made it even if I hadn't been around to help, but it was still a predicament he wouldn't ever want to be in again. He also wears a life jacket on the water now.

The best garments I have come across look no different from normal fishing jackets, but have a gas capsule that makes them inflate on contact with water. They also have a whistle to alert other water users. But whatever the make or type, any buoyancy aid is better than none.

Waders or a wetting

Launching a boat is a wet business, even in the height of summer. You need to go into the water to get it off the trailer, and if the water is very shallow close-in, you may have to walk out quite a way before you can get the boat afloat. Thigh waders are no good, it's chest waders every time. I've even tried wearing wellies

I never go boat fishing without a life-jacket under my bib and brace, having seen a friend come close to losing his life after falling overboard. Even strong swimmers can soon get into difficulty.

and standing on the trailer, but the water always comes over the tops and gives me wet feet. Once you're in the boat, of course, the chest waders should be taken off, for safety reasons, in case you go over the side.

When to go

I used to think that you could go pike fishing in Scotland or Ireland at any time of year in any weather, and it was just a matter of having the right clothing to overcome bad weather. But I've since learned from the example of friends who went to Scotland in open boats at the wrong times, and were drenched day-in, day-out until they came home early, vowing never to go at that time again.

Spring can be a wonderful time of year, and pike are catchable on their way to or from the spawning grounds, but when their time comes they are very reluctant to take a bait. When they are grouped together to spawn and preoccupied with the urge to reproduce, I won't fish for them. And when they have spawned they are in the poorest condition they will be in all year, and at their lightest weight. Sport can be hectic as the newly spawned fish replace lost energy by taking advantage of the natural larder of salmon smolts on their spring migration downstream, but I'm just not interested. I don't want to catch them when they are out of condition, but by May and June they are fighting fit and well worth the angler's attention.

Also, the weather is very unpredictable in spring. By early summer the air and water temperatures are higher, hours of daylight are at their maximum, and fish have reached a feeding peak.

My favourite month is June, when pike have a faster metabolic rate and are more active, so are feeding more frequently. I'm convinced the critical factor is the increased hours of light. The longer the hours, the greater the amount of feeding. And it's a bonus that the weather is at its most pleasant at that time.

Where to go

Vast areas of Scotland, which is a honeycomb of fresh water from north to south and east to west, have yet to be explored by pike anglers. Doubtless huge fish lurk up there, and the easiest ones to catch will be the ones that have never seen an angler.

Multipliers are the first choice for boat anglers for bait control, superior presentation and an ideal rate of retrieve.

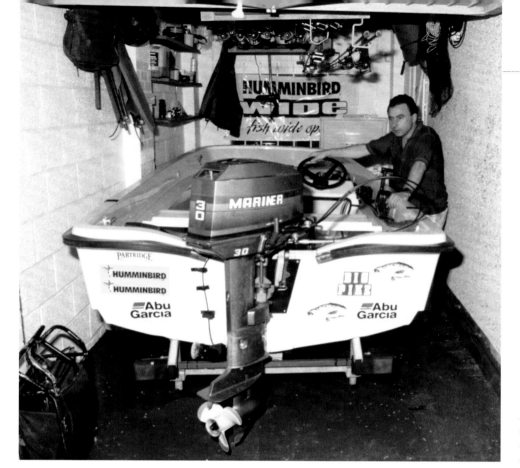

A spare garage makes an ideal boat store for between trips.

When searching for new waters I look for a location that will suit pike and has a suitable environment in which they can find sufficient food, and in which they can go undetected for many years. I look for a water that has extra riches being brought in from the sea, a good run of game fish and a head of Arctic char, a native population of brown trout, and perhaps a fish farm where rainbow trout and salmon are reared and from which a number escape. All of these factors tip the scales in the pike's favour, and increase the chances of such a water holding an extremely big pike. If the water is prone to flooding, making feeding by sight impossible, or without extensive shallows, then the potential is reduced. I want to find somewhere where pike can live out their lives without disturbance, from man or from nature, and then the chances of a fish growing to a big weight are very much increased.

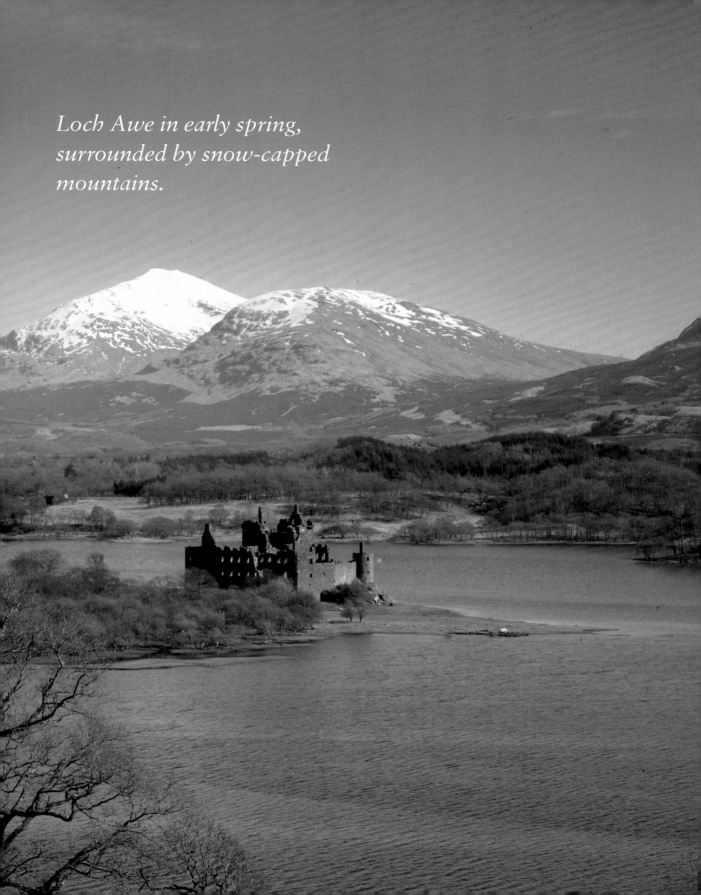

Loch Awe in early spring, surrounded by snow-capped mountains.

CHAPTER 15

LOCHS & LOUGHS

To stand on the shore of a vast natural expanse of water in Scotland or Ireland is a breathtaking and daunting experience for a pike angler. You cannot fail to be moved by the rugged, unspoilt beauty of the landscape, but at the same time as you are marvelling at the scenery a voice inside you is asking, 'Where on earth do I start?'

But the truth is that as much as two-thirds of the waters in some of these locations can be ignored without greatly reducing your chances of success, because it is far too deep. And by concentrating on the few areas that will produce fish, and approaching them with the right tackle, tactics and bait, success is almost guaranteed, weather permitting.

The weather, of course, is the one big drawback to these huge, beautiful expanses of water, for when it decides to rain or blow out on them it can do so with such awe-inspiring fury and persistence that survival, and not catching fish, becomes the prime concern. But go there in high summer, when even the locals can look tanned, and you can experience the countryside at its most welcoming.

A stable environment

The great advantage that lochs and loughs have over rivers and gravel pits is their stability. Loch Lomond is twenty-six miles long by up to six miles wide. In a water like that, pike can live out their lives without being disturbed.

Natural catastrophes are much less likely to occur on such a vast volume of water than on a river that flows through towns and cities, being

The view across Loch Lomond is breathtaking – and the prospect of catching pike from there daunting.

Gord Burton holding his personal best pike of 34 lb 14 oz, caught on suspended perch.

drawn off in one place and pumped back in another with waste products and chemicals added along the way. Gravel pits, too, are vulnerable, being artificially created and often located close to towns, where some people see them as rubbish dumps, or near to industrial estates, where oil and other waste products get into the water table.

The pike in Scotland and Ireland have access to rich feeding at intervals throughout the year, helping them to grow quickly and stay healthy, and unlike river fish do not use up energy fighting a fast current. In the right environment, with as much food as they can eat, no anglers around and no current to work against, a pike can wax fat in a wild water in one of the more remote parts of the British Isles.

I've fished north of the Border and across the Irish Sea, but originally it was to Scotland I went when I felt the urge to fish further afield. It was there I learned to fish wild waters, though most of what I learned and have written about here will apply equally well in Ireland. For Lomond, Tay, Ken and Awe substitute Conn, Corrib, Mask and Derravaragh and you won't go far wrong.

The stuff of legends

The Scotland I went looking for was the one described in Fred Buller's classic book *Pike*, in which he recounts the most desperate moment of his angling career. While fishing with Dick Walker at Port Nellan Bay on Loch Lomond he hooked a fish in excess of 50 lb, and after playing it for several minutes lost it when the trace knot broke. He says he has relived that day in his mind countless times over the years and slowly come to terms with what happened. The pike was found dead a few weeks later, his trace still in its mouth.

I went up there to fish from those places he talks about: the Endrick Bank, Rossdhu Bay, where the Falloch enters the loch, Ardlui, Port Nellan Bay, the mouth of the Finlas Water, Fruin Bay and Balmaha. Lomond is the pike angler's Mecca, and no self-respecting pike enthusiast can drive past without stopping and standing on the banks and thinking of other anglers who have made the pilgrimage. Places like Lochs Garry, Woodhall and Loyne have great potential and are well worth exploring.

But I soon realised that every angler who heads for the Highlands visits the famous-name places, and these popular haunts were being fished too heavily to ever produce anything spectacular. They still provide anglers with 20 lb pike, but I realised that if I wanted really big fish – I did and still do – I would have to explore and find new areas. There are still places that are fished very sparingly, and with a loch as big as Lomond, there's no excuse for not breaking new ground.

It's not a bad idea when you first go up there to start with the famous haunts until you've familiarised yourself with the surroundings, and get a feel for the type of fishing that you will be doing. Many an angler has headed off into the mist on the loch, lost his bearings and spent a long time finding his way back to base.

There are at least nine separate genetic strains of salmon that run through Loch Lomand each year, which bring in extra riches from the sea. If targeted at the right time, the mouths of the rivers Endrick, Leven, Fruin or Luss could turn up a real surprise.

Below: Loch Lomond's Port Nellan Bay on the south-east bank, where Fred Buller hooked and lost his legendary big pike, and where big fish lurk to this day.

First find the food fish

To find pike in untried areas I knew I would have to understand why pike are attracted to one place, so I could seek out areas that offered the same advantages. That's where the really hard work starts. You need to build up a detailed knowledge of the water on reconnaissance trips. I still go up just to have a look at a few new locations and assess the potential of other, less popular, lochs. And you have to find yourself local contacts and get close to the people who live on the loch, and get them to trust you. My salmon-fishing friend Neil Buchanan has a friend who nets the loch regularly for eels, and when he's doing that he's catching powan, important food fish for pike.

I contacted the fisheries improvement people at Pitlochry Freshwater Fisheries Laboratory, who were able to tell me which lochs had decent runs of salmon, sea trout and char, and also which held good numbers of perch, roach and other food fish. That gave me a head start. Find the food and you'll find big fish. Loch Lomond Angling Improvement Association, who are based at 29 Vincent Place, Glasgow, operate tagging schemes which monitor the movement of all fish through the loch, and their work is still going on. I got to know game anglers on Lochs Awe, Lomond and Tay who encounter big pike when they are trolling. The information they passed on over a pint or two gave me a pointer as to where pike may be at different times of the year.

Getting to know these people provided me with location information for several different lochs, and by corresponding with contacts made during visits I was able to build up a picture of where to be and when. Without their help it would have been a very long and drawn-out affair of trial and error, and, being six hundred miles from the waters, I wasn't prepared to waste precious time. The more that can be achieved in advance of fishing in terms of location, the greater the chance of catching the fish you are after.

Pike with a purpose

By breaking the loch down into small areas, the task is made a great deal less daunting. A lot of people try to fish too much of one water at once. Even before I leave for Scotland, I have decided where I'm going to fish and why. To fish blind and decide what to do as you go along is a mistake.

Once you know what draws pike to an area and when, you know where to find them. Pike know they need to be in one place at one particular time to take advantage of a food source when it becomes available. They don't swim around haphazardly, and aren't spread evenly throughout a loch like currants in a bun. There's a deep-seated purpose in all of their movements. They have an intimate knowledge of everything that goes on in the loch, and they know when and where to be to capitalise on any situation from which they can benefit.

Salmon and sea trout smolts run back to the sea about three weeks after pike have spawned, when the pike are desperately in need of a rich food supply to replace the energy they have lost. It's perfect timing. You can plot the movement of the pike to take advantage of this, and if they are there one year, they will, more often than not, be there the next, depending on the weather.

Where two rivers run into a loch close to each other, like the Orchy and the Strae at the head of Loch Awe, pike sit in the mouths of them and wait for salmon smolts to come down, picking them off as they pass. When runs of salmon and sea trout are held back at the mouth of rivers in autumn, due to lack of rain, pike will be there looking for a free meal.

On Loch Lomond there are many well-known islands, such as at Inchcruin, but there's also a submerged island at the McDougal Bank that many pike anglers don't know about. In late May and early June there is a massive fly hatch on the loch, and the trout and coarse fish know there are rich pickings over that island. And anywhere there is a gathering of food fish, pike will be there to pick them off.

And in May, Loch Tay's perch population comes out of its deep water haunts and moves into the same area of shallow water in the same week of the year.

I got to know game anglers on Loch Awe, and their information about the movements of other fish gave me a pointer towards the location of pike.

For three or four days the water comes alive with pike from every corner of the loch, hounding the huge numbers of perch collected in that one area. I've seen it countless times, but it still amazes me that in a sheet of water perhaps twenty miles long, pike know the exact place and the exact week perch will be there, year in, year out, without fail. It must be passed down through the generations, and become something akin to an internal alarm clock that tells them the time has come round again.

Survival of the smartest

It's not just pike that are opportunists. In Windermere the eels wake up from their winter hibernation just as the char spawn. They feed on this rich and plentiful food and then go back to sleep until the spring. Pike are there as well, feeding on the char and the eels, both of which are preoccupied enough to be vulnerable. The fish in these wild places owe their survival to their instinct for where the next meal will come from. They are in tune with the movements of the food fish because they have to be, and they have honed their knowledge down to finely-developed intuition as to where these opportunities will arise. I have located perch in 40 feet of water at another time of year, using the fish finder, and the pike have been close by. Success on these lochs is very much a matter of location, and if you know where there is going to be food for pike, the hardest part has been done.

Make a note of where and when these things happen, because until there's a marked change that upsets the loch's ecology, the general pattern will persist. Loch Lomond pike are very long-lived, and they've been visiting these locations for many generations, and will continue to do so for at least the rest of our lifetimes.

Visible signs of pike

Very early in the morning, Loch Awe pike sometimes come to the surface and swirl, showing their back, dorsal and tail fins. Often they will do this over exactly the same spot for several mornings running, in close proximity to a drop-off, always at first light. I really can't say why they do it but, whatever the reason, they provide anglers with a visual sign of their location, so it pays to keep an eye on what's going on. There's a place on Loch Awe where the depth of water drops from four feet to seven feet, and in one small spot down to fifteen feet, and it's there you see this swirling activity occurring. Loch Awe pike are very mobile, yet this behaviour takes place in this spot more often than anywhere else.

Another visual sign happens when pike come up out of deep water over a shallow sandbank to move into a bay. As they do this their dorsal fins come out of the water. I have sat in my boat and watched them and know from experience where they're going. I've caught them on the drop-off, and I've taken my boat round the back of a nearby island and caught them in the deeper bay.

A WORD OF WARNING

As you'll have gathered by now, to fish large, wild waters and do justice to what they contain you need a boat. If you don't own one you need not despair, for they can be hired from the Portsonachan Hotel on Loch Awe, or at McFarlane's boatyard at Balmaha on Loch Lomond, or at Ardlui.

Some of the best bays are bordered by private land, as in the case of Rossdhu Bay on Loch Lomond, which is surrounded by a golf course and the country estate, putting the banks out of bounds. A boat will take you to areas inaccessible on foot.

A map of the water you intend to fish is well worth the small outlay. Trevor Moss at The Tackle Shop in Gainsborough, Lincolnshire, sells an Admiralty one for Loch Lomond, the best map you can buy. It has everything from depths and contours to bays and islands, sunken and visible, and is essential for anyone with serious designs on big pike from this water.

And when you're fishing big waters, the tackle you use should reflect the terrain – 30 lb to 35 lb trace wire, 20 lb main line, 3 lb to 4 lb test curve rods and float fishing, rather than legering. Too many times I've seen bank anglers new to Scotland legering on the lochs in standard gravel-pit style, and every run they get wraps their tackle around so many boulders they end up playing the bottom and having to pull for a break. Conventional deadbaiting is a nightmare, and losses are all too common when that method is used.

On the subject of being prepared, don't leave home without the insect repellent in summer. Scottish mosquitoes are as pleased to see you as the local people, only the small Flying Scotsmen's welcome carries a lot more bite.

But I'm sure that if I hadn't seen them breaking the surface one day as they moved over that sandbank, which is so shallow you'd have expected them to beach themselves, I would never have known where they were going.

Sun-loving species

When the sun is warm, loch pike like to bask. At midday, when its rays shine directly into the water, though, they will be at their most vulnerable from attack from above, and are inclined to take cover or drop into deeper water. But early in the morning and in late afternoon, when sunlight is slanted and not straight into the water, pike move into shallow areas. They usually stay there for the night, as they don't feel in danger because they can't be seen.

All lochs have shallow bays, the most famous on Lomond being Rossdhu Bay and Port Nellan, and pike will visit them to get the sun on their backs. I once caught a pike which had a lighter back than the rest of its body from basking in the sun in a shallow bay, and I've caught mid-twenties that were lying in just eighteen inches of water.

Pike are not lovers of deep water, but prefer to be in areas that are at least close to somewhere shallow with weed for cover. The Endrick Bank is a flat, sloping, sandy bank that has been made shallow by the constant lapping action of the waves.

A fish of 23 lb 12 oz caught from deep water in the heat of the day. At midday, loch pike are inclined to take cover in the safety of the deeps. This one took a sardine on the bottom in twenty feet.

The waves put colour in the water, and pike are so well camouflaged that they can sit happily in it. But they will move out into deep water to plunder the depths, and return to the shallows in the late afternoon to spend the night sheltering in the weed. I have caught them in just two feet of water on plugs cast to the edge of these beds of potamogeton weed. On Loch Lomond this is broad-leafed, with runners branching off underwater, and keeps pike covered through the day.

Pike still have an instinct for avoiding places where they feel vulnerable to attack from birds, even though the species most likely to pose a threat, the osprey, has long since ceased to do so. Only the odd dorsal fin breaking the surface in the weed or a sudden splash of water gives these pike away.

The most exciting way of fishing for them is to cast a float-fished or float-legered deadbait against one of these dense beds of potamogeton from a moored boat, and wait for something to happen. I have sat twenty or thirty feet from the weed and seen a pike come out and take a bait and move back into cover.

To do battle with a big, hard-fighting fish in shallow water, and to see it break surface through the long strands of crisp, green weed on a bright day is as exciting as anything in pike fishing. Loch pike are known for their tail-walking and powering out of shallow water down into the deeps in one unstoppable run. Their reputation for fighting qualities goes before them, and it is well deserved.

My best catch while fishing next to one such weed bed was made while returning from a fruitless trip to another water. I was a little downcast after a blank visit, and only dropped in for a day on Lomond on the way back on the off-chance of a fish. It just shows you what can happen when you least expect it. The total catch weighed 137 lb, and included three twenties and lots of double-figure fish, all from what I thought would be a brief distraction from my earlier disappointment.

*Above: The dense potamogeton beds in
Loch Lomond's Port Nellan Bay.*

*Below: This Loch Lomond twenty took
an eel section tight to the potamogeton
weed.*

If they won't come out of the weed to take your bait, then a wobbled trout, which is much more visible and easier for them to detect, can be an excellent alternative. The method used is the same as described in previous chapters, perhaps with a lighter wobble bar inside.

High-water hunger

High water is a stimulus for pike to feed. They realise it will bring salmon and sea trout up from the sea, and they seem to relish the total transformation of their environment that high water brings.

With the water level now regulated by power companies, it can be raised or run off artificially at night, creating fishing opportunities or leaving boats moored in shallow water, or high and dry at a whim. You can never be quite sure what you will find in the morning, no matter what the weather conditions. But when the level is raised there is something different happening in the lives of the fish. Their world is expanding, and this encourages them to feed.

Be sure to explore bays, because that is exactly what pike will be doing when the level is higher than normal – finding their way around places that were previously out of reach, and searching for food among vegetation reclaimed by the rising water.

High water is a welcome sight at spawning time, too, because it creates more spawning areas, which can be in short supply in even a large loch. In years of high water at spawning time good numbers of pike are born, providing another plentiful source of food in a year or two's time when the offspring are big enough to make a meal.

The Quayline 16 fishing boat provides an ideal means of exploring lakes for pike.

When to fish wild waters

I've said that I prefer to fish the lochs in summer because of the weather, but another reason is that feeding reaches a peak in mid-summer, linked as it is to light and temperature. I would rate June as the best month to catch a big loch pike. By then they have got over the exertions of spawning, the water temperature is high and the days are at their longest. The longer the daylight hours, the more time pike have to feed in the rich areas of deep water and then in the warm shallows at night. When winter arrives they are unlikely to move into the shallows because the water is too cold, and the shortness of the days means they are feeding less in deep water as well. It's easy to see why summer is a better bet from the angler's point of view.

Having said that, there are other times of year when you can catch big fish, the next best being spring, when smolts migrate to the sea and pike move off their spawning grounds. On Loch Awe I have had bumper days as pike have come off the shallows at Kilchurn Castle.

How to tackle them

Most of my fishing in Scotland is done by float-fished or float-legered deadbait, as mentioned earlier, but trailing a livebait under a float behind a boat or trolling a dead trout is also successful, especially over deep water. Both are good ways of covering a lot of water if you are having trouble finding fish, especially if the pike have moved out from the margins into the main loch. I often have a trout or coarse bait on one rod and a deep-running plug or spoon on the other. An Abu Toby or Hi-Lo, particularly a fluorescent one, or a Kuusamo spoon seem to

work best. Fluorescent lures are particularly good in water with poor clarity but, taken overall, a trolled fish seems to produce better pike.

The difference between trailing and trolling is that trailing involves the use of a float to set the depth at which a livebait will work, and is best suited to water of up to 15 feet deep. Trolling has no float, but uses a downrigger to hold a deadbait at the right depth. The main problem with trailing on lochs is in getting a float big enough to cope with the waves, and in finding a weight heavy enough to hold the bait down and stop it riding up to the surface. A downrigger, with its 5 lb lead, will take a trolled deadbait down to the desired depth and keep it there.

Pike drop into deep water through the day, and I have caught them in over thirty feet of water while trolling. Any area with a drop-off into deep water and

A downrigger, with its 5 lb lead, will take a trolled bait or plug down to the desired depth – and keep it there. I have caught pike in over thirty feet of water while trolling.

nearby rocks and boulders and petrified tree stumps washed down from feeder streams is particularly good, and so is a narrow channel between two islands.

Trolling also helps you to get to know the loch a little better. Sometimes I just drift around with the fish finder and have a look at contours. Even now, after I've been doing that for many years, I still come across features I didn't know were there.

A fish finder is essential for this type of fishing, and an outrigger and downrigger very useful for regulating depth. But all in all I don't do a lot of trolling, preferring to fish less speculatively. I believe the best way of catching a big pike is to find the fish and then sit it out with a deadbait. It's very slow and laborious, but it's what the pike want, or the biggest fish do, and it's those that we're after.

Pestered by eels

Trolling a large expanse of water in Ireland. This method enables the angler to cover a lot of ground, and is an excellent method of locating big pike.

Scottish lochs have a vast eel population, and because there's so many of them and they're so rich in protein I'm sure they play an important part in a pike's diet. But the smallest ones can be a real nuisance to anglers when they rip soft deadbaits like sardines to shreds in minutes on days and nights when they are active. It's usually when the weather is overcast and wet, and then they are everywhere. I've even had them come into the shallows and take livebaits, following them in as I retrieve.

But the problem can be solved by using eel sections for bait, brought with you frozen or caught by putting an eel rod out. Balmaha Bay, on Loch Lomond, is particularly productive. One small eel will make five or six baits. I've caught plenty of Scottish pike on them, though I won't use them over 1 lb 4 oz because eels are so slow-growing. A fresh trout or roach will also get around the problem, but put a soft salt-water bait on and the eels will have it, spinning the trace into a knot in their efforts to tear the flesh, and leaving just the bare bones.

Things ain't what they used to be

Unfortunately, Loch Lomond is not as good a water as it was in the 1950s and 1960s. Powan numbers have dropped dramatically, though they have made a comeback in the past two years since eel trappers started returning ones they caught by accident. But runs of salmon and sea-trout are not as good as they were three decades ago, so the loch we fish today is a different and much poorer water in terms of the resources available to pike, and this has an effect on their size. To catch a pike in excess of 25 lb these days is an excellent angling feat.

Anglers have only themselves to blame for part of the problem. They have taken ruffe and other non-indigenous species from English waters to use as livebait and, without intending to do so, have enabled them to colonise the loch, upsetting the water's ecology. Vast shoals of ruffe now swarm all over Loch Lomond, where there wasn't one to be found a couple of decades ago, and pike are eating them instead of the richer, natural food fish, the powan. And the ruffe population explosion has had its effect on powan stocks, as they are probably responsible for eating powan eggs.

It doesn't take an expert in fish ecology to realise the damage that a non-indigenous species can have on a delicately balanced ecosystem. I'm strongly against the releasing of non-native species of fish into these lochs, because the effect they have is, at best, unknown. Take livebaits back with you or knock them on the head, or better still, take only brown trout and those coarse fish already present, rather than species that don't belong. And if you can catch livebaits while you are up there, use these wherever possible. Considering how successful deadbaiting can be in Scotland, there shouldn't be any need to take so many livebaits that you have to resort to transporting ruffe.

Loch Lomond now attracts thousands of boats each year, particularly in the summer when the holiday season is in full swing. The

Anglers pestered by small eels should resort to using eel sections for bait. One small eel will provide five or six portions, and be left alone in a way that fish baits like sardine and mackerel never will.

oil from their engines and the rubbish from their occupants can't be good for the loch, and water quality isn't what it was twenty or thirty years ago.

Litter strewn around the islands from picnickers who don't clear up after them is a sad sight on such a beautiful water, and an indication of the pressures now facing these once-remote places and the creatures that live there. Scotland used to be a world away from the south of England, but motorways and railways have meant that someone living in London will think nothing of travelling there to spend a long weekend on the loch. The roads that brought these places within our reach have done the same for other water users, and all we can do as anglers is try to leave the place as we found it, and hope others will be responsible enough to do the same.

Fish farms – friend or foe

Rainbow trout and salmon farms have had a marked effect on the ecology of Scotland's lochs in the decade or two since they first appeared. Thousands of 'inmates' have escaped over the years, and in some cases this has led to the spread of disease to the native fish population, and interbreeding with wild salmon that have navigated their way back to their birthplace to spawn. But on the plus side, pike have had an extra source of semi-tame food.

From the pike angler's point of view, when looking for a rich water capable of producing a big fish, cages for rearing trout and salmon for the table should be considered for what they are: a feature that will enhance pike size, along with good runs of wild salmon and sea-trout. Anywhere with either is worthy of attention, and somewhere with both should be worth a great deal of time and effort. But avoid lochs with high mountain ranges that drop off steeply straight into water, creating deeps close to the shore. Unless a loch or lough has extensive shallows it is unlikely to yield big pike, no matter how plentiful the food sources.

Conservation, not annihilation

The more nets that are bought by salmon angling interests to allow migratory fish largely unhindered access to their spawning grounds, the better for pike anglers, so long as estate management doesn't involve coarse fish culls. The benefits of reduced poaching and regular game fish restocking programmes will be enjoyed by pike anglers on lochs adjacent to game rivers, but on certain waters where pike are seen as vermin, whole populations may be all but wiped out in pike removal operations.

In Scotland, I'm pleased to say, the message that pike bring people who want to catch them and who spend money trying to do so is slowly filtering through, and the species is beginning to get the respect it deserves, if for reasons of tourism rather than informed fishery management. But in Ireland the thinking seems to be less well advanced, and tales filter through to me of huge fish culls on Lough Corrib, wherein a dozen or more 30 lb-plus fish are slaughtered to protect the trout, which is what, it is said, the visitors come to catch. The local people there know when the pike spawn, and so by longlining and gill-netting at this time in Cushlough Bay they can almost rid the lough of pike in two or three days.

Surveys have proved that most of the time pike feed on perch and roach, much slower-swimming than agile game fish, which take a lot of energy to catch. The only time pike feed heavily on game fish is during the annual run of smolts towards the sea through narrow river mouths. But even then nature has arranged for the rush of fish to happen in a short space of time, ensuring a large number get through safely.

Yet pike are still trapped and culled because they are believed to be killing game fish. So long as local people with influence labour under this misapprehension, then wonderful, wild waters with healthy populations of pike and some very big fish will continue to be plundered at regular intervals in the name of fish conservation, or fish extermination. And while this happens, fisheries in Ireland, and the few where it still happens in Scotland, will be much the poorer.

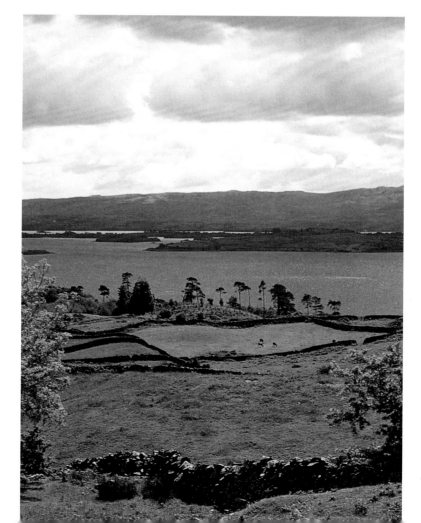

Looking down on Lough Corrib in Ireland, a home of great pike.

Starved of food around our coast, cormorants have moved on to our rivers, lakes and reservoirs, where they have settled in colonies as large as 600 on a single water, breeding successfully and working their way through the population of fish of takeable size.

CHAPTER 16

ANGLING,
ETHICS & THE FUTURE

Pike fishing is under attack from all sides: two-legged, four-legged, six-legged – you name it, all are having a strong influence on the sport and will slowly change the face of fishing as we know it.

The major threats

They say the best way to win a battle is to know your adversary. We ought to be aware of the major threats to our sport, so that we can speak out against them when the opportunity arises, and recognise them when we meet them face to face. The afflictions endangering the future of fishing generally, and pike fishing in particular, should not be underestimated for the threat that they pose.

Abstraction

It's become something of a cliché to say so, but there are streams where I fished as a boy that are now no more than dry beds of stones and weeds. We hear of water supplies to households being cut off, and people having to use standpipes at the end of the street in winter and summer, but it is perhaps only when we go back to somewhere we haven't fished since our youth, and see how dramatically the river has changed, that the full force of how much less water we have is brought home to us. The stark fact is, there are more of us demanding our share of a resource that can never increase. Pesticides and nitrates trickle into the river from adjacent farmland with the first rains in September, adding to the colour and the weed growth. It has become a regular feature for the

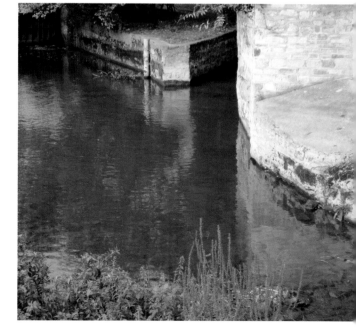

The Castle Stream in the centre of Oxford, reduced to a trickle by abstraction. Yet licences continue to be granted, when what we need is more water, not less.

Thames to fish badly straight after the heavy rains of autumn, as the summer's accumulated agricultural pollutants pour into the river in one foul slug, choking the fish with chemicals.

Cormorants

That cormorants have moved inland from the sea says a great deal about how commercial fishing has destroyed the ocean's resources. Starved of food around our coast, cormorants have moved on to our rivers, lakes and reservoirs, where they have settled in colonies as large as 600 on a single water, breeding successfully and working their way through the population of fish of takeable size. They even attack fish as big as 20 lb, spearing them in the side, often fatally, in their frustration at not being able to eat them. I have seen scientific figures which indicate that an adult cormorant will consume in one year the equivalent of the entire edible fish population of one mile of river. If this is true, there could soon be little left that a pike or angler could want.

An archipelago in Sweden. (Courtesy of Lars Bygdemark and Alvkarleby Municipality.)

Mink

Also here to stay are mink, another of nature's least loveable creations. Even someone with a seriously underdeveloped sense of irony cannot fail to appreciate what an own goal animal liberationists scored when they gave hundreds of captive mink the freedom of the Great British outdoors. Having spread and bred successfully for a couple of decades, they have wiped out moorhen populations on some stretches of river and canal. They are not averse to taking on the odd human being, either, and possess a bite that any ferret would be proud of.

How long can we carry on livebaiting?

Considering the amount of good that anglers do in getting polluters prosecuted, and caring for Britain's waterways and everything that lives in and around them, we still have a poor reputation in the eyes of the public. Their image of angling comes from occasional documentaries about swans and lead shot, pictures of dead birds tangled in discarded line and debates on whether angling is cruel and fish able to feel pain. But it must be said that we don't help ourselves. As pike anglers we are responsible for one of the least easy practices to defend, namely livebaiting. There may well come a time when mounting a live fish on treble hooks and casting it out to catch another fish for sport is outlawed, if not for humane reasons then at least to limit the spread of disease – and we will be unable to argue a case for avoiding a ban.

Artificial livebaits

Perhaps the ever more sophisticated world of electronics will provide us with a suitable substitute, in the form of an artificial lure capable of swimming on its own and sending out high-frequency impulses that mimic a fish in distress. If such a lure could be devised, I for one would welcome the passing of the need to carry buckets of baits, in favour of a small box of realistic, rubbery creatures and batteries to bring them to life.

Mink, cormorants, signal crayfish, mitten crabs and now otters are all having a drastic effect on our pike stocks.

Above: An otter swimming with a double figure pike, which was later eaten on the bank.

As lures become more lifelike, and soft rubber plugs as common as plastic ones, there could soon be a suitable artificial alternative to a deadbait for wobbling and sink-and-draw. Some American lure patterns have semi-permeable membranes you can inject with a scent and retrieve to leave a trail. Lure fishing could be a major beneficiary of the march of new technology.

The first fishing reels with alarms built in are already being manufactured, and the ultimate in rod rings that are strong, light and won't wear, no matter what, are available now. They are made from titanium by Hopkins of Holloway, and at the moment sell for well over £100 for six.

Electronics will play an even greater part in fishing in the future, with fish finders getting still more sophisticated. There may come a time when they can tell you what species of fish you are looking at. But really all I want in the way of improvements is for a manufacturer to produce a large reel with a Baitrunner facility, with a nice big handle that takes the knocks. When they do this, I'll be happy.

Anti-anglers

Anti-anglers are now as much a part of the face of modern fishing as national rod licences and echo sounders. With regular reports of attacks on fishermen, we ought not to be surprised to find them bobbing about in the water in front of us in frogmen's suits.

NORTH AMERICAN CRAYFISH

But perhaps an even greater threat to fish stocks is posed by the six or seven separate varieties of non-indigenous crayfish that have found their way into Britain. Armies of the creatures are spreading across southern England unseen by anyone except anglers, and wiping out whole year classes of the fish population as they devour the eggs laid by coarse and game species. There are few natural waters the interlopers have not penetrated. Northern Britain now has its share, and they have found their way over the Border into Scotland. On some stretches of the Thames and many southern gravel pits it is no longer possible to fish with bottom baits, as they get torn to shreds soon after being cast out, especially at night, when crays are most active. On other waters, pike that were once plump are now painfully thin, because crayfish mop up any dead or dying fish that fall to the bottom, and then wipe out a whole year's spawn. When eggs aren't allowed to develop into fry, it's the predators at the top of the food chain that are the first ones to suffer.

Foreign crayfish could one day make legering impossible.

Retaliation is never the answer, as huntsmen have found out in the courts, but we ought not to be afraid to point out that as anglers we are unpaid watchdogs of Britain's waterways, performing a quality-monitoring service and ensuring food and shelter for the birds and fish that live there, completely free of charge. Thanks to our vigilance, ordinary people can enjoy a walk by a river without the smell of sewage, and can see kingfishers and herons at the water's edge, not shopping trolleys and mattresses. We do it for our own ends, of course, but everyone else benefits as well, including anti-anglers, whose spare time is not spent making the countryside a better place but hindering the work of conservation.

Close season – friend or foe?

Only time will tell whether removing the close season on still waters has cost us dear among a number of influential friends. We certainly can't have endeared ourselves to conservation groups by scrapping the annual period when we left the birds and fish in peace and gave the banks a chance to grow back.

You could say that the close season doesn't affect pike anglers much, because the best of their fishing is in the winter, Scotland and Ireland excepted, and many pike spawn before mid-March anyway, so they have always been catchable. But before spawning, the females are in a delicate state and in need of protection from anglers for the sake of future pike stocks, for if they are mishandled there is more than one life at stake. And after spawning they have used up an enormous amount of energy, are thin, vulnerable and in the worst state they have been in all year.

You may have gathered by now that I am in favour of a close season, but it is not just concern for the welfare of fish and nesting birds that has swayed me. I fish very hard during the eight or nine months of the open season, and when it closes, the break gives me time to spend with my wife and son. I need a break to look back on the season just ended, and to re-trace my steps, evaluate my strengths and work on my weaknesses. There will be reconnaissance trips and days spent sorting out tackle and carrying out essential close-season tasks. In short, I need the break as much as the fish, and was sorry when the change was brought about and the magic of 16 June was lost. I would like to see the close season reinstated. This has happened in Europe, where some countries, including the Netherlands, scrapped it and then brought it back. Maybe we should learn from their example.

Commercial fisheries

You have only to look at how popular heavily stocked man-made carp waters have become to realise that they are going to play a big part in the future of fishing.

A commercial pike fishery, however, is surely a contradiction in terms. Yet there are already large waters that get stockings of pike netted from trout reservoirs. Perhaps we will see more of this practice, and in smaller waters, where pike can

Above left: Darren Willingham holding a pike of 45 lb 15 oz caught from a trout water in Oxfordshire. (Picture courtesy of Gerald Straford)

Above right: A 30 lb pike from a trout water caught by Steve Kilbee. Jaws would drop if some of these waters opened their doors in summer.

be fed artificially. And when the supply from trout waters runs out, there may be farm-bred pike.

Improved fish-rearing techniques have already enabled fish farmers to offer fishery owners carp and rainbow trout of well over the British record. Perhaps pike won't be far behind. Given a rich diet and careful temperature control, a 60 lb or 70 lb pike may be possible, to be sold to the highest bidder to boost ticket sales on his water.

Why wait for a fish to grow to that size, though, when they are already available from other countries? It can only be a matter of time before we follow the example of the carp and catfish people, and bring muskellunge or Baltic whoppers into the British Isles. Whether they would be suited to our waters is another matter, but that is hardly going to trouble the sort of people who legitimise the stocking of alien species as commerce. The trade in illegal imports is one of the few growth industries in angling.

I can't help wondering why import laws and fish movement regulations are not upheld in the UK. Every week, according to the angling press, fish are brought in and stocked illegally, and moved from water to water; illegal sites for crayfish farming are set up – but when do you hear about a prosecution? Yet the Environment Agency will happily hand out a summons to an angler without a licence to fish, or fine him for standing too far from his rods, which is an excellent way of driving people away from the sport.

Piking on trout waters

If there's one development that pike anglers can truly look forward to, it is the opening-up of more trout waters to coarse fishing. It will have to come about, as revenue from a dwindling number of trout anglers falls below acceptable levels and those in charge seek income from other sources. When you consider that the British record pike and its predecessor came from a trout fishery, you begin to realise the untapped potential many of these waters represent.

Alternatively, pike anglers after a Red Letter Day can venture abroad. Every year British anglers catch huge foreign carp, catfish and exotic creatures like Nile perch and mahseer, but so far pike haven't figured much in these holiday catches. Before long, though, British anglers will become more adventurous and visit the Baltic, for example, to get to grips with outsized Scandinavian pike.

So much for the future. If I seem a little pessimistic, then I apologise. My intention is merely to forewarn, not to deter. I hope I'm proven wrong, for if not, we could lose what little unspoilt fishing is left in a country where concrete and tarmac are taking over. If there was nowhere left to go pike fishing except commercial fisheries, where all the fish have names and turn up on cue like performing dolphins, I for one would hang up my rods and find some other way to spend my evenings and weekends. I wouldn't want to fish if commercialisation was all there was, and neither, I believe, would you.

All forms of fishing for big pike with lures offer enthralling excitement, be it searching out deep water with heavy sinking lures, or eagerly anticipating the sudden thump of a bone-jarring strike.

CHAPTER 17

THE LURE OF THE BIG PIKE

BY GORD BURTON

A HUGE FISH EXPLODED FROM THE WATER in a wild, head-shaking fit of madness, lashing across the surface in a vain attempt to shake free of the lure it had chomped just a few seconds before. This is the kind of pike fishing scene I have experienced hundreds of times over many years of hunting big pike with artificial lures: hair-raising and tremendously exciting – and do I love it? I reckon so!

FISH THIS SIZE DO NOT COME ALONG THAT OFTEN! ONE DAY A FISH OF THIS SIZE WILL BE CAUGHT IN THE UK. *(Courtesy of Blinker Anglers.)*

Right: Christian Stuck holding a huge pike weighing 22 kilos 120 grams/48.78 lbs. The fish was caught on 1 May 2013 in Biggesee, a huge reservoir in Germany.

Below: Austrian angler Engelbert Leibetseder holding a fish of 22 kilos 220 grams/48.98 lb. The fish was caught in a backwater of the River Danube on 13 July 2013.

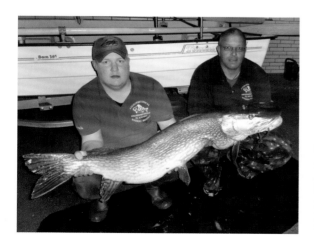

All forms of fishing for big pike with lures offer enthralling excitement, be it searching out deep water with heavy sinking lures, or eagerly anticipating the sudden thump of a bone-jarring strike. Working lures in clear-water situations where fish movements or follows can often be observed right up to the lure being engulfed – wow! Watching the pulsating throb of the trolling rod tips as the boat is steered on its chosen route, and the sudden shock of a rod-wrenching take ... What about watching a thirty-pounder slowly home-in and close its mouth over a swaying crankbait? For a pioneer of lure fishing it is always a pleasure when a new lure development or idea crops up.

Going all the way back to the start of the seventies, when I started to take it very seriously, it has been my good fortune to have caught big pike from nine countries on my lures, from the great lakes of America and Canada to the loughs and lochs of Ireland and Scotland; from gravel pits and reservoirs and the large waters of the English Lake District to across the North Sea and Holland, Scandinavia and Sweden and the mighty Baltic Sea. During the course of these fishing adventures some of the most incredible sport imaginable has come my way – hundreds upon hundreds of big pike to over thirty pounds in weight. These sessions have had me whooping with delight. Big pike have hammered my lures, and just about every structural element encountered when fishing such a diverse range of waters has been well and truly exploited casting or trolling artificial lures.

Way back when I first began to pursue big pike with lures there wasn't a great selection to choose from in tackle stores. In complete contrast, today the number is huge, and the variation of artificial lures at hand is simply incredible. There are lures at hand today that will do just about everything – small lures to giant ones, light lures of 1 oz to heavyweights up to 4 oz, fast to slow sinkers and suspenders in between, wobblers to gliders, jerk-baits, crankbaits and top-waters too, plastics and bucktails, spinners and spoons, jigs and spinner-baits as well. In other words, there is a lure available to cover every conceivable situation on the water! When I first began lure fishing it became my priority to find out what any big pike was caught on. In this chapter I will reveal many names of some of the greatest big pike-catching lures ever made.

Let us take a look through the whole range of tackle I use to combat any situation I'm likely to meet. Starting with the rod, reel and line combination, it is very important this set-up is a balanced one and suitable for the lures being used. From the smallest lures up to giants over a foot long, one rod cannot do it all.

For most of my lure casting I opt for short, powerful trigger-grip lure-casting rods and multiplier reels. These rod/reel combinations cover most of my fishing situations. For casting sessions that can be hours long, day after day, it is of upmost importance that the rod/reel set-up is comfortable to use. My preference is for rods of 6 ft 6 in. to 7 ft 6 in, and which are capable of casting lures in the

Left: A tail-walking pike.

Below: My lure carrier.

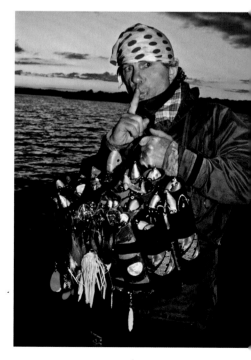

1 oz to 4 oz weight range. My shortest rods are what I use to cast and work heavy lures such as jerkbaits and Bulldawgs in the 3 oz to 4 oz range. The rods of 7 ft or more are used for casting most crankbaits, spoons, bucktails and such-like up to about 3 oz. In all instances, my preference is for one with a forgiving action that will enable me to impart a good action to the lure, and not one with a stiff, poker-like action, not even for jerkbait fishing. There are many suitable rods available in both one- and two-piece. The E.T. Lure Series, Andy Lush Series or my own personal Normark 'Whopper Stopper' and 'Superhog' are models that fit the bill. These rods will cast lures long distances effortlessly, and have the power and backbone to set the hooks into the jaws of big pike when they slam onto a lure.

For many years my first choice of multiplier reel was from the ABU range, in both left- and right-hand-wind models. For heavier lures, and with the shorter, more powerful rod, I opt for the 6501-C3 from the 6000 range. To go with my longer rods and lighter-weight lures the choice is for a smaller model of reel from the 3000 range – the 5501-C3. Both are super reels that have served me very well indeed. Recently I have been using a Shimano Calcutta 251 for my lightweight lure casting, and it is a really superb piece of equipment. This rod and reel combination is very comfortable to use, as it sits easily in your hands.

Although I have fished extensively with a long rod and fixed-spool reel, nowadays I only use this set-up when casting spoons. I feel it is more advantageous to use a longer rod of 9 ft with a casting weight of around 60 gm. I use an E.T. Tormenter, which is a powerful rod perfectly suited for handling big pike, teamed with a Shimano Stradic FA 4000 fixed-spool reel, for casting large, broad spoons or lightweight spoons. A longer cast is attained more easily with this combination, especially in wild, windy conditions. A sudden gust of wind hitting a spoon can severely affect the distance it will fly on the cast, and with a multiplier this can cause a backlash on the cast, which can lead to a bird's nest tangle in the reel. This doesn't occur with a fixed-spool reel.

The only other method of lure fishing for which I employ a longer rod is trolling, and this is simply to spread the width of the lines trailing behind the boat. The only option here for me is for a 10 ft rod with a 2½ lb test curve, combined with a Moocher centre-pin-type reel, which has a super drag system. As well as loading this reel with braided line I also use it in conjunction with lead-core line and wire line for trolling lures deep in the water. When trolling among or close to very jagged rocks on Ireland's Lough Mask, I use 30 lb test trolling wire to combat these rough, tackle-busting hazards, because mono or braid was getting cut through, and lures were getting lost regularly.

Lines

To cover all casting and trolling options, the multiplier reels are loaded with three different breaking strains of braided lines. Modern low-stretch lines are best because of their fine diameter and direct contact with the lure. Due to the low stretch factor, the slightest touch from a taking fish is felt immediately or seen on the rod tip. My number-one choice for fishing in rough and rugged surroundings casting and trolling big lures is 30 lb test smoke-coloured Berkley Fireline, which is a very high-abrasion-resistant line. I use olive- and smoke-coloured 30 lb Power-Pro, which is softer and more supple than Fireline. I use this for casting small to large-sized lures such as plastics, spoons, crankbaits and so forth. The strongest line, 65 lb Power-Pro, is used for casting heavier jerkbaits and MagDawgs and for trolling large, heavy lures. These are the breaking strains I have used extensively for all my fishing for big pike worldwide, and for big muskies in the USA and Canada. They have never failed me on fish or casting, so I don't see the need to step up to heavier tests of line.

It is vital that the correct knot is used to tie leaders to the braid, and the Palomar knot or the five-turn Grinner knot are the most reliable. I pass the braid twice through the eye of the swivel when tying Grinner knots.

Wire leaders

The choice of wire leader has come under discussion in angling literature numerous times in recent years. In my opinion many anglers do not give enough consideration to the quality and make-up of a leader. Even today there are still few leaders available in tackle stores that satisfy my demands. For this reason I almost always make up my own, simply because all the necessary components are available from pike angling suppliers.

The wire leader is a very important and serious piece of lure-fishing gear. It has to withstand not only serious cutting and abrasive contact with crunching jaws and very sharp teeth, but also the rigours and stresses of constant casting of big, heavy lures and the endless jerking and twitching of them. Having spent so many years casting lures, I now use what I consider to be the very best of leaders, which have never let me down. For this reason, the leaders must be made up using only top-quality components. For all my lure fishing I use two types of wire: seven-strand and single-strand, either bronzed or green. I use seven-stranded for all casting and trolling with spoons, crankbaits, jigs, bucktails, spinner-baits and plastics, etc, and make up two different strengths of bronzed or green-coloured seven-strand leader. When casting the smaller lures up to half an ounce, a twelve-inch leader is made up using 40 lb test wire. When fishing with the heavier lures, the wire strength is upped to 60 lb test. There are numerous brands available on the market, so there is no problem obtaining spools of this excellent wire.

For attaching lures, I have found small- and medium-size Stay-Lok snaps to be the most reliable of all lure-connecting links, and so far they have never failed me, either casting or on a fish. When it comes to swivels I only ever use one type, and

A big one on an Ernie lure.

that is a black ball-bearing swivel made by both Berkley and Sampo in 50 lb and 100 lb breaking tests. To connect the clip and swivel, turn back about an inch or so of the wire, make a small loop in the end, then take the loop through the eye of the swivel, or clip and back over it to form a hitch lock. The short end is then wrapped neatly around the main wire and the job is done.

During the course of long, arduous casting sessions it is of utmost importance to check the reliability of the wire and scan for broken strands or kinks, looking over the swivel for bent rings and testing the lure-attaching clip for weaknesses. A leader can gradually weaken, and at the slightest sign of any defect it must be rejected. If you don't, the result could be a snap-off when casting a large, heavy lure or, worse still, what once happened to me. I over-used a leader and lost a big fish when it failed under the strain of a violent tail-thrashing tantrum. For jerkbait fishing it is necessary to use what is termed as a solid, straight wire leader of around twelve inches. This is where single-strand wire comes into use. My choice is single-strand Stealth wire from Tooth Proof American Fishing Wire, or Seven Strand Tackle Corp's single-strand, bronzed stainless wire in 95 lb and 131 lb breaking strains, which combat the strain of casting the different weights of jerkbaits I use.

The Stay-Lok clip is fitted onto one end of the leader using a haywire twist, and to the line-tying end I simply make a haywire loop and the job is complete. The lighter test wire is used for small jerkbaits such as the Titchy Jim, Titchy Darter and Piglet, or if fishing plastic baits in a jerking, erratic manner. The stronger of the two leaders is what to use when casting the heavy jerkbaits such as the Reefhawg, Eddiebait, Suick, Big Hedgehog, Hog and Hogseeker and such like.

Big fish such as this test tackle to the limit.

These are the lure leaders I have used for many years, and they have accounted for a huge number of big pike. They are absolutely reliable and have never let me down. Now let's look at the lures for *big* pike.

Crankbaits

The crankbait in particular has long held a great attraction for me, right from the very beginnings of my serious pursuit of big pike with lures. Crankbaits such as the Creek Chub Pikie, Cisco Kid, Gudebrod Sniper and the Heddon Vamp Spook mesmerised my thoughts. My beloved old boat is named *Creek Chub*, out of respect for this legendary crankbait.

Right from the outset of using crankbaits I began to catch specimen fish. When catching big pike on Loch Lomond I used to whoop out, 'Give 'em a Creek Chub, they love 'em!' The crankbait has produced big fish for me from every type of water. I have now taken pike of over twenty pounds on thirty different diving crankbaits. I have taken pike in every twenty-pound bracket to over thirty pounds, so you see why I have such a craving passion for using these deadly and versatile lures.

Crankbaits are amazingly versatile. They can be used in so many ways that there are few situations in lure fishing that cannot be exploited using one. The range of different types of crankbait available to the pike fisherman is truly immense. There are literally hundreds and hundreds of them in all shapes and

A giant high roller caught on a crankbait.

*Crankbaits.
Left column
(from top):
Depth Raider
(perch);
Depth Raider
(tiger);
Jointed Depth
Raider;
Invincible.*

*Right column
(from top): Eight-
inch Mirrolure;
Shallow Raider;
Super Shad Rap.*

sizes, and in an unimaginable range of colour patterns. The number of different sorts of crankbait on which I have caught pike is almost endless. Although I have taken some very big pike on little crankbaits, it is the larger sizes that give me the best results with big fish, and all the lures revealed are super big-fish lures.

For hunting big pike I favour lures in the five-to-eight-inch range, though I have taken some heavyweight pike on lures over a foot long. There are large-vaned deep-divers like the Depth Raider, Ernie, Hooker, Monster Shad, Mann's Stretch and Thunderstick, which are perfect for working along deep weed edges, down sharp sloping drop-offs or bumping over deep rising humps from the bottom of a lake. These are also tremendous trolling lures.

Small-vaned, shallow-running minnow baits such as the awesome Whopper Stopper Hellcat, Original 18 cm Rapala, Bang-O-Lure, Rapala Husky Jerk, Bomber Long A, Gabb's Grabber, Nilsmaster Invincible and Rebel Minnow are all around seven inches in length, weighing up to 2 oz. These lures have a tight swimming action and are truly dynamite for fishing across plateau shallow weedflats and twitching over pike lies in sub-surface weedbeds.

In Com Mhin Bay on Lomond, Esthwaite Water in the Lake District and Lough Derravaragh these tactics brought amazing hauls of jaw-snapping big pike, with many topping twenty pounds. Sometimes a lure with more action may be needed to stir up the pike. Crankbaits like the Shallow Raider, Rapala Magnum, Big M, Pikie Minnow, Jake and Grandma Lure have a wider swee-sway movement when pulled through the water, and give off more of a flash to hopefully stir up a strike. Indeed, the Shallow Raider will really zig-zag and flash when given a good jerk with the rod, and this trick often proves irresistible to pike.

Above: A big one from the Baltic Sea.

Below: Another big one caught on a Depth Raider crankbait.

*More crankbaits.
Left column
(from top):
Believer;
Hellcat;
Grandma;
Bomber Long A.*

*Right column
(from top):
Jointed Shallow
Raider;
Super Shad Rap;
Shallow Raider;
Windcheater.*

Fast sinkers like the Countdown Rapala, Countdown Depth Raider and CD Super Shad are great for working along very deep ledges, deep trenches or simply combing through deep depth levels. There are shallow and deep-diving lures that will suspend and hang in the water when a pause is put in a retrieve. They will then begin to rise – a deadly trick for catching pike that may be a little finicky and not up to chasing a fast-moving lure.

Jointed crankbaits like the J Shallow Raider, J Depth Raider, J-13 Rapala, Hi-Finn Scamper, Pikie Minnow, Jointed Pig and Reefdigger are lures I use in low light conditions, coloured water and in wild water weather, and have accounted for fish way over twenty pounds. These lures really stir up the pike. I said crankbaits are versatile! A buoyant floating lure like a Super Shad Rap, Pikie Minnow or Believer can easily be used as a top-water lure when retrieved slowly – the tail of the lure will wiggle on the surface, creating a wake that will make enough disturbance to bring about explosive action from striking pike.

The action of so many crankbaits can easily be altered by changing the weight and size of the hooks, or even cutting down the size of diving vanes to change the depth they will dive to. These are ideas I have experimented with so many times to make a lure more compatible with a specific situation. It is possible to make lots of floating, hollow plastic lures into sinkers, simply by drilling a hole into the body and injecting water or cooking oil inside, then sealing the hole with candle wax.

Be sure to check all lures to confirm that the hooks and attaching split-rings are very strong and will not open out or buckle under the strain of a wild, tail-thrashing pike. Failure to do so could result in the loss of the fish of a lifetime. Throughout the course of my lure fishing career I have altered so many lures that my friends have called me the 'Lure Butcher'!

Jerkbaits

Originally designed to catch big muskies in the USA, this type of lure caused a sensation when it first became available, because it proved to be a fantastic big-pike lure. What amazes me about it is that I had a black Suick jerkbait stored in my tackle box since 1969, and didn't think it was any good, simply because it had no action when it was reeled in. It lay in my box for a further fourteen years, until I found out it had to be jerked in order to impart any action into the lure. Jerkbaits can be bought in all sorts of shapes and sizes: divers, gliders, flippers and those that zig-zag through the water on the retrieve; fast sinkers, slow sinkers and those that hover and suspend when a pause is taken in the retrieve. It's what is termed 'hang time' by those in the know.

For fishing in shallow, clear water of less than ten feet, diving lures like the Reefhawg, Hogseeker, Bobbie and Suick are very good jerkbaits that can be worked down in the water and suspended, especially for working slowly over submerged weedbeds. Buoyant slow sinkers such as the Darter, Hedgehog, Dolphin, Jackal, Zalt, Magic Maker, Manta and Flipper are super lures for fishing in shallow

A big pike caught on a jerk bait.

water. These baits have an erratic, zig-zagging, keeling-over type of action when fished with constant twitches on the rod. The Zalt in particular comes in a variety of suspending and sinking models. The other baits can be obtained in weighted, fast-sinking models, making them ideal for working over most deep-water situations. Using these heavy baits I have taken big pike lying deep down in over forty feet of water. Other baits like the Eddie, Big Hedgehog, Easy Glider, Jerko, Powerglide and Slipslider have a wide zig-zag left-to-right swimming action, and can be fished very slowly if the tactic is needed. Most of these lures are around seven inches long. There are times when a smaller jerkbait can produce the goods, and lures like the Titchy Darter, Titchy Jim, Piglet and Little Reefhawg are an excellent choice. Even adding plastic grub-tails to jerkbaits is now very popular, the Squirrely Burt and Squirko to name but two, and just another aid to tempt the pike. Jerkbaits are indeed most versatile lures.

Spoons

Spoons are great pike catchers, and have given me my largest ever hauls of pike, topping a hundred fish in a day. When fishing on a fly-to lake in Canada there was a time when, as fast as I could cast out the spoon, a pike would smash onto it. These lures come in all shapes and sizes, and I prefer them in the four-to-six-inch bracket. Spoons like Kuusamo Professor, a lure I was the first to use and publicise in the UK, the Gator-Back, Gator-Spoon, Daredevle, Lizard, Red Eyed Wriggler, Doctor Spoon and the Thompson Spoon are just a small selection of the very best. Spoons are yet another very versatile big-fish lure that cover so many situations. When a

A selection of good, fish-catching spoons.

Bucktails.
Left column
(from top): Russ's
Big Buck; Three
Russ Bucktails;
Bucktail; Whahl's
Eagletail.

Right column
(from top): Three
Rizzo Wizs; Two
Bucner Tails;
Musky Killer.

Bottom centre:
Spinner bait.

flashing bait is required, the spoon is always a good choice. A good tip when using brass and copper spoons is to carry metal polish to keep them shiny when the water tarnishes their sheen. On Wollaston Lake and a fly-to water called Ahenekew Lake in Northern Saskatchewan, Canada, I experienced unbelievable sport as a whole host of big pike slammed onto spoons fished in shallow bays.

Spinners and Bucktails

Many pikers use much bigger baits these days, and spinners are a much-neglected lure in the armoury of today's big-pike hunter. However, I have caught plenty of big pike on them, and I know of some real heavyweight fish caught on spinners, including a one-time British record holder of over forty pounds. The Ondex 5 and 6, Mepps Aglia and Lusox are some of the best. The Bucktail is an amazingly popular muskie and pike lure in the USA and Canada. Before they became available in this country I had my own made for me by fly-tying friends. Then I went to North America to fish for the mighty musky and used a whole variety of bucktails, and it didn't take long to find out that they also caught lots of big pike. Lures like the Buchertail, Russ Borst's bucktails, Musky Killer, Harasser, Willowbuck and Rizzo Wiz and Rizzo Tail are just a few of those that have given me top catches. I use these lures mainly in water of ten feet or less.

Spinnerbaits

These lures are very good all-rounders, and ideal for fishing in coloured water, low-light situations and into the dark, and very good for weedy and snaggy spots, because the hook and trailing hook are up-turned and pretty well snag-resistant. They are available in single- and dual-bladed versions, and I have taken twenty- pound pike on both types. I use them to cover all situations, but rarely in very clear water. I have done equally well with both plastic and bucktail-dressed spinnerbaits. My son Walker has taken over a hundred pike on a chartreuse/ sunrise pattern dual-bladed spinnerbait. Again, I have done a lot of altering of these lures. For instance, I have removed both of the large blades from a Bagley's Brute and fitted a small Brass Colorado blade to the chartreuse model, or a nickel blade to the rainbow model, and this has proved to be a great idea. The big pike just love to chew them. Bionic Bucktail, Reed-Runner, Grinder, Slopmaster and the M&G are top catchers. Another good tip is to add a curly grub to the tail hook as an added attractor.

Soft plastics

At times it seems anglers have gone plastic-crazy, as so many are seen casting these lures. The curly-tailed BullDawg and SpringDawg are amazing, and after my initial successes they began being imported to Britain. They catch with all types of retrieve, and I have seen big fish hammer onto a MagDawg fished jigging-style thirty feet down below the boat! Similar lures like the Ugly Joe and Super Sandra have curly tails and are truly dynamite fish-catchers. The plastic Shad, Castaic and Reaper Tail are also super catchers. The Sloppee Pig Jnr is a fine top-water lure. I first experienced the surprise of using a jig with a nine-inch plastic worm with a plastic skirt on the front to catch big fish in North America. These lures will cover all sorts of structures, from shallow- to deep-water jigging. Most plastics are 'must have' lures.

Topwaters

Fishing for and catching big pike on surface-working lures can range from frustration to mind-blowing excitement. Just imagine seeing a huge fish cruising slowly behind a dancing Jackpot lure right to the boat side and not take, yet continually come back in consecutive retrieves, and still not strike. Well, there are tricks I will reveal that will provoke a violent reaction from big pike and produce jaw-crunching responses. Now imagine a big twenty-pounder suddenly exploding onto a lure at the end of the retrieve, rearing up out of the water in a tail-lashing frenzy and bouncing off the side of the boat. Or how about the big fish that almost takes in slow-motion when it rises up, opens its mouth and engulfs a Magnum Jitterbug?

I have experienced both. Two of my best surface lures have just been mentioned, but there are a few others that big pike love. The Top-Raider, Musky Jitterbug, Timebomb, Hogwobbler and Creeper are other great surface lures. Even a large, broad spoon can be used as a top-water lure when twitched and skittered across the surface in a tactic I termed 'show-boating' – one I used to great effect on Canada's Wollaston Lake.

Lure colours

Colour choice crops up in many lure fishing debates, and could fill a whole chapter. Make no mistake, what pattern you use at certain times can have a tremendous effect on your results and the numbers of fish being caught. For example, fish may be taking a silver mackerel pattern crankbait in bright sunlight and clear water, but suddenly turn off when cloud cover comes over. A quick change to

Right: A big fish caught on a BullDawg.

Below: 'Mouse lures' have also accounted for some very big pike.

fluorescent orange/green in the same model of lure, and the pike are on the prowl again. The colour change is enough to turn fish on again, and is something I've done many times.

In my tackle boxes there are lures in a multitude of patterns – perch scale, pikie, shad, silver, gold, roach, ciscoe and trout finishes. These are used most in water clarity that varies from very clear to slightly tinged, with a visibility to five feet or so. One time I fished a lake and discovered a trout finish was the hot pattern. I took a whole string of big pike topping twenty and thirty pounds on a Hellcat crankbait.

In more stained water situations I will often switch lures and work through a hotspot with more and more bright and fluorescent gaudy finishes – like the Psycho Perch, Master Blaster, Firetiger, Hot-Tiger, Hot-Perch, Crazy Clown, Orange Bandit, Chartreuse Bandit and many others. Fluorescent orange is a very important colour and very effective in both stained and very deep water. I use lures with this colour feature a great deal. Black is a much-neglected colour, and one I have talked about for many years, because it will catch in all light and water clarity situations at some time or other, though I don't know why. I have learned lessons using this colour and seen huge fish caught from deep-stained water, clear water and on topwater lures.

Well-worn lures. Left column (from top): Z180; Jackpot; Noz's Timebomb.

Right column (from top): Creeper; Jitterbug; Top-Raider.

Blue is the most neglected colour of all. Yet when fishing the Baltic Sea off Finland, blue mackerel Rapala Magnum and Rebel Windcheater crankbaits caught a whole string of big pike to over twenty pounds from what most would term quite stained water.

Casting

Obviously the most important element in hunting big pike is to fish the best types of place they inhabit, and this can range greatly from water to water. Always ensure that the boat is positioned in the best strategic position to cover the whole of a hotspot. Now I will reveal some of the techniques and the top lures to best exploit these situations, working lures through all of the depths from around forty feet up to the surface.

The deeps

Big pike can often be found moving in very deep water, as far down as forty feet or more. This could be off a rocky shelving point reaching out in a big water, a steep sloping drop-off or maybe a deep-lying hump or a bowl in the bed of a lake. In these situations I will commence casting lures that will sink down to the bottom quickly. A bright-coloured jerkbait or a BullDawg is a good start. Long casts cover most water, so I use this approach and make pinpoint casts across and alongside a point or slope, letting the lure sink to the bottom. A heavy jerkbait or large spoon is a good choice, because it can be fished slowly or twitched vigorously and will still stay deep and close to the bottom. The heavy plastic lures are also best

Right: A 23 lb Canadian pike caught on a plastic worm.

Below: Trolling deep using a wire line.

retrieved slowly when fished deep down, until the line is at a very steep angle downwards. Be ready for a take at any time in the retrieve. A fish may follow a lure up from the deeps and strike, or a high 'cruiser' may smash onto the lure as it ascends towards the surface. I have taken plenty of fish that have nailed the lure close to the end of a retrieve, so beware!

Also, making parallel casts along a sloping drop-off with these same baits is a very good approach for picking up fish as they patrol along a route. To begin with, I cover just the deepest area, and if no fish show then I change to a more buoyant bait and start working up in the water for fish moving along a different level. The same tactics and lures can be used over a deep hump, though I have taken many big fish using a countdown sinking crankbait. A long cast along or across a hump, bumping a lure across and off this feature, is a deadly method. One second the lure is crunching the structure, and then just as it lifts off – boom! A big pike has hammered its jaws onto it.

Deep bowls and trenches can be tackled in the same way, and it is very pleasing to catch big pike in such places because they fight hard to stay deep. In windy conditions a drogue will slow the boat down and enable you to cover plenty of water as you drift slowly over deep water. A large copper spoon or heavy sinking crankbait are ideal lures to use. Cast the lure as far as possible and let it sink to the bottom. Then simply retrieve and twitch it in very slowly, keeping it as deep as possible the whole time. This was a tactic I used to catch big pike from depths below forty feet on Ballyquirke and Cloonahee Lakes in Ireland. On all the big waters I fish, even when anchored in deep areas of around thirty feet, a constant look-out is kept for big pike moving on the surface. 'High rollers' are what I call them. A rod fitted with a shallow running lure is kept at the ready. A crankbait is the best choice, as these are aggressive hunters willing to chase and smash onto the bait. I shudder to think of the numbers of big pike I've caught this way.

Hand-landing a big one.

In shallow water down to twenty feet a whole array of lures can be used, and a lot more pike-holding features can be covered. In shallower water if two anglers are fishing it pays to use different types of lures, with one working faster lures in the hope that fish are raised quickly. A big fish can catch a lure as fast as it can be reeled in. Fishing is more exciting because many big pike are actually seen. Their reaction to a lure can be worked out, along with what trigger-trick to use to bring a strike. Use a variety of lures and varying retrieves, and work through the depth levels until fish are raised. Take note of how pike are reacting and striking lures to see if a pattern can be worked out. The moods of big pike constantly change. When a biggie is sighted coming in slowly to a lure, a sudden change in its movement can bring about an arm-wrenching strike. Sometimes a big fish may follow a slowly worked plastic shad or Dawg and decline to take and turn away. A change of lure to a crankbait or fluttering spoon and a cast back in its direction could bring about a pulverising strike. Sudden changes in lure selection often bring sudden pike. In clear water it is not vital to get a lure close to the bottom, as lots of anglers think, because with a lash of its tail a fish will roar up and hit a lure worked several feet above it.

Hunting big pike with artificials in shallow water lakes, or 'rogues' cruising shallow weeded flats, is the most straightforward approach of all. I like to fish such locations in low light conditions, or when a good wind is putting a wave on the water. The lure choice is varied. Twitching crankbaits and shallow diving jerkbaits, or buzzing a bucktail or fluttering a spoon over the top or around submerged weeds, can be electrifying. I was catching so many pike on Lake of the Woods, which straddles the US and Canadian border, that the fish were shredding the hair from bucktail lures. Pinpoint casting and the speed of retrieve can be vital when fishing such areas. Pick up weed on the hooks and the cast is wasted.

Topwater

You like excitement? Well, this is it! Yard after yard it came, its nose barely inches behind a surface-crawling Top-Raider. A sudden change in pace brought about a body-lunging strike, and a giant, jaw-snapping *Esox* went skywards. Using a surface lure demands concentration at all times or fish will be missed. Be alert for pike that continually follow. Look for signs of aggression in fish and be ready to change lure direction. Putting a sudden pause or a jerk or speed in the retrieve are tactics that provoke takes. A big pike has struck at a Creeper several times in a retrieve before finally chomping it. Sometimes a big fish may follow deep and not be seen, so be ready for a shoulder-shaking strike from a boatside beast. Many

One fat Hawg!

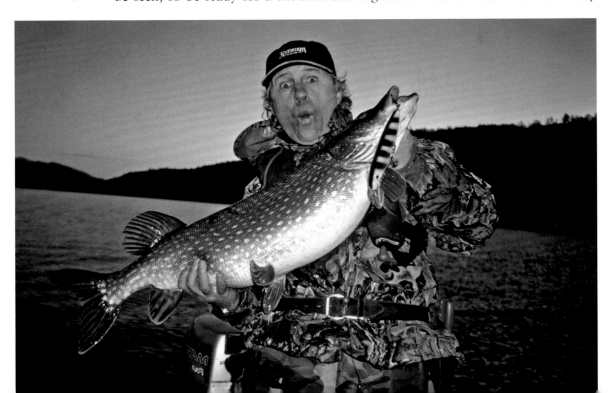

anglers think topwater fishing is best done in calm water. Not so. Even in quite rough water topwater lures can be very effective, and it pays to use a lure with a more surface-disturbing action, like a Top-Raider or Hogwobbler. Finally, when watching a following pike, do not strike until you actually see its mouth close over the lure and the fish turns away. Then hit it hard and whoop with delight!

Trolling

When limited on time, this is my favourite method for seeking big pike-holding areas on vast expanses of water. I have very wide experience of using this approach. It is a method that keeps lures in the strike zone at all times, as the boat is steered along a specific depth contour and covers large expanses of water much more quickly than a casting approach. I have been on charter boats on Lake Vanern in Sweden and Lake Ontario in Canada, fishing down-riggers using more than ten rods at a time. I have used downriggers to take pike from the depths of Scotland's Loch Lomond and Ken and Stor-Treen in Sweden as deep as fifty feet down. The use of a downrigger allows for precision trolling and keeps lures exactly at the chosen depth. When flat-line trolling lures behind the boat, the most important thing is to know the amount of line out behind the boat and the speed the lures are moving. This will seriously govern the depth the lures will dive to.

A specific crankbait can only dive to the depth its diving vane will allow it to go, and it is vital that it works to the best of its ability. It pays to pre-locate an area to be trolled, and check out the depth contours along sloping drop-offs and off rocky outcrops from shallow water, down to depths in excess of thirty feet. I may start off trolling water shallower than ten feet in the search for fish. In shallow water be aware of large sunken boulders or reefs – such hazards wreck your gear. Also, have an anchor ready to lower to prevent drifting onto a rocky

Below: A fish caught trolling with lead-core lines.

Bottom: Controlling down riggers on Sweden's Lake Vanern.

Unhooking a big pike caught on a jointed crankbait.

shoreline when a big one is hooked. If no fish are forthcoming, I will begin the 'step down' approach and work through the twenty-foot band and deeper until fish are located. For most of my trolling, I work lures at distances of forty and fifty yards, though in calm, shallow water I will troll lures as far as eighty yards astern. If you don't have a line-counter reel, it is simple to put a distance mark on light-coloured braid using a black or red indelible marking pen. On black or dark green lines I tie on a stop-knot at the chosen distance. To get the trolling rods into action, motor out over water deeper than you intend to fish and clip on the chosen lures. Pay all of the lines out, then steer the boat in and along the chosen depth contour. Steering a boat along meandering and rising contours, in-turns and rising humps takes a long time to learn to do effectively.

A shortcut to success is to go afloat with somebody who is very experienced at doing it. Speeds of one and a half to three mph are the main speeds I troll at, and I have caught a hell of a lot of pike this way. At first, trolling and getting to know how deep lures will troll involves a lot of trial and error, but many lures are similar in the depth they dive to, so a pattern is quickly picked up that will cover many types of lure. If a lure bumps the bottom, then it has dived too deep,

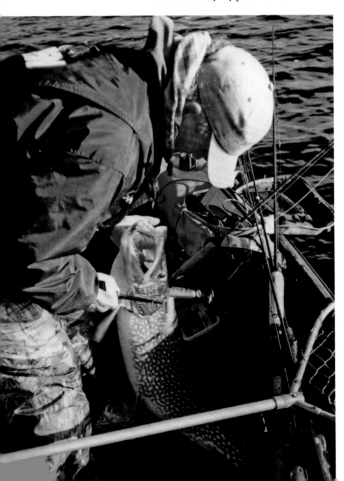

so make adjustments. Slow down, take in line or move into deeper water. Keep a close watch that the rod tips are vibrating when trolling. If one suddenly deadens, the lures have picked up debris, so reel in and clean it off. Trolling at 3 mph at 50 yards on 30 lb test Fireline, a standard Depth Raider will dive 30 feet down. A Rapala Super Shad Rap or 18 cm Nilsmaster Invincible will swim down to 12 feet. The Gabb's Grabber and small Grandma Lure are ideal even for shallow water.

These crankbaits have given me lots of twenty-pounders. I often troll with three or four rods, and many times a lure furthest astern will produce most fish, especially in water around twelve feet deep. On Scotland's Loch Ken and Last Mountain Lake in Canada, pike often took spoons twenty yards behind the other lures, in what I term a 'tail gunner' style. Pike turned on by lures just passed by struck the next thing they saw. Constantly change speed to vary the action of the lures. Make certain the drag on the reel is set just right. Too tight could result in a broken

THE LURE OF THE BIG PIKE · 271

rod if a lure gets snagged or broken under the strain of a big fish. The forward-moving boat could even rip the lure from the fish's mouth. Ensure the drag is set so that hooks are pulled into the jaws of the taking fish. There is a lot of pressure exerted on the line and rod when a big fish hammers a lure fifty yards astern and thirty feet down in the water.

The strike

When a big fish smashes onto a lure, it is vital the strike is solid and hard pressure is put on the tackle at all times in the fight, keeping a very tight line on the fish. Big pike are real experts at head-shaking, and any easing of strain on the line could result in a lost fish and the lure being thrown free.

Unhooking

The best tools for removing the hooks from the mouth of a big pike are long, slim-nosed pliers. I have ground little grooves into each point of my pliers, which allows for a better grip on the shank of large treble hooks. Mini bolt-cutters are also a vital piece of equipment. There could be a time when it is necessary to cut hooks from fish – for example, if they become badly tangled in the mesh of a landing net. A large-meshed net is best for landing pike caught on lures.

Finally, try to land all big pike as fast as possible, and get them back in the water quickly. A tail-lashing returned fish is a healthy specimen. Keep them lures pushing water!

Right: Bucher Depth Raiders – variety of models and colours. Nos 3 and 8 are Gord's Specials – Psychaperch and Masterblaster.

Below right: Popular Lures – top to bottom: Mean Conqueror; Halo Conqueror; Rapala Supershad; Muskie Mania Jake, Creek Chub Pikie (jointed); Heddon Lucky 13; Heddon Meadow Mouse; Lucky Strike Lizard; Northland Reed Runner; Mepps Aglia.

Below: Mean Conqueror Premier – an example of a high-quality holographic finish.

Possum Pioneer and Prospector – an example of a hybrid lure (hard/soft plastic).

Kuusamo Professor spoons.

Arbogast Jittersticks and Jitterbugs – a 'family' of surface lures.

Rapala Supershad and Deep Rap.

Bucher Mogambo Combo – very large spinner with large soft plastic tail.

Mean Reef Shark – jerkbait.

Microlure Whalike Jambed Minnows.

Mepps Aglio Spinner in Brown Trout and Rainbow Trout pattern.

A selection of QED soft plastic lures.

Creek Chub Pikies.

Muskie Mania jerkbaits.

Mean Shimmy vibrating lures.

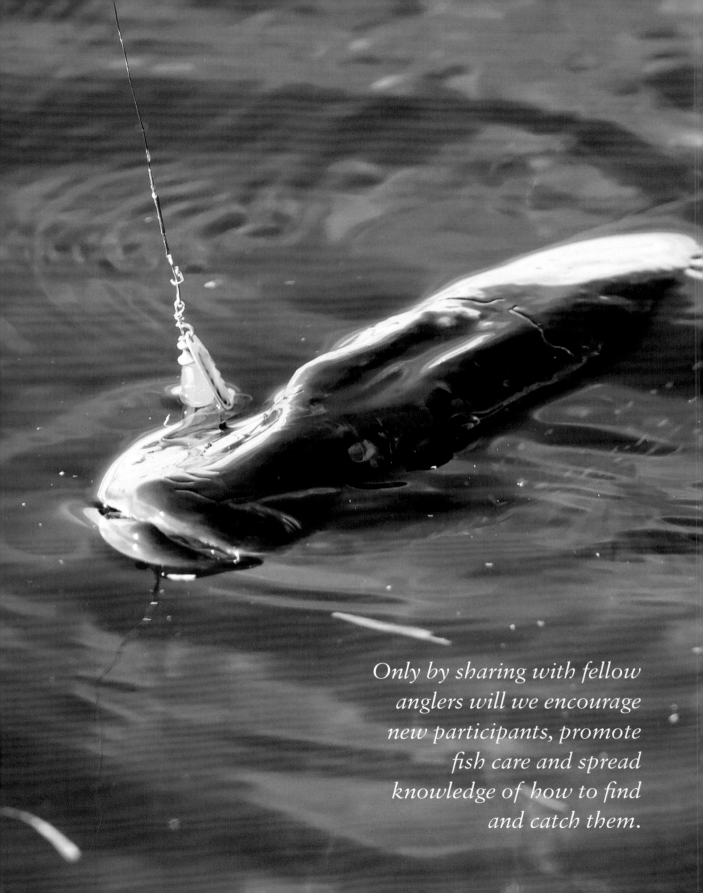

Only by sharing with fellow anglers will we encourage new participants, promote fish care and spread knowledge of how to find and catch them.

CHAPTER 18

FLY FISHING FOR PIKE

A PASSION FOR PIKE FLY FISHING BY MICK WILLIS AND BOB CHURCH

I HAVE ALWAYS BEEN FASCINATED BY THE DIVERSE BEHAVIOUR of different types of fish. Some lurk in the margins while others swim in open water; some are bottom feeders, while others find their food on the surface. It is a knowledge of these differences and why they occur that separates a good angler from an excellent one.

Angling is a lifetime's preoccupation. You never stop learning when you study fish and their habitats, and it is this constant accumulation of knowledge that brings success and gives an angler with a little extra knowledge an important edge.

I design specialist fishing tackle, and having a naturally inquisitive mind and an eager eye when on the lookout for new ideas and materials is essential to successful innovation. My engineering apprenticeship and business have proved invaluable when designing and manufacturing fishing tackle. The knowledge that I have of different materials and how they will or will not work together is a great asset, and without these skills some of my inventions would never have made it past the design stage. But even the finest ideas can be spoilt by cheap and inferior materials, which shorten the item's lifespan greatly.

My fishing days began back in 1950 when I was seven. A neighbour took me with him one day, and that was it. I was hooked, and my enthusiasm has never waned. The same neighbour gave me my first rod, reel and other tackle, because he saw in me the potential for a lifelong love of angling, and how right he was.

The same gentleman also set me on my own trail of what I needed to learn to fulfil my angling ambitions. He showed me what signs to look for when fishing, and to think about what equipment I needed to use for different species and different waters and conditions. He showed me what to look for in the habitat of these fish, and how these signs changed, but, more importantly, he taught me never to be afraid to pass on knowledge to others. Only by sharing with fellow anglers will we encourage new participants, promote fish care and spread knowledge of how to find and catch them. He passed on to me the accumulated knowledge of years of fishing, and I owe him a debt of gratitude for a lifetime of angling pleasure.

In those early days I began to design and make items of fishing tackle for myself, including new rods. Some who saw them asked me to design items of tackle for them, and I enjoyed doing this so much that I obliged, without any financial gain. My design and manufacturing business grew out of that, but I always found time for fishing. For thirty years I have fished for pike, even managing third place in the European Pike Fishing Championships in Southern Ireland in 2001, but for even longer than that I have fly-fished. It was inevitable that the two would eventually come together.

It was when accidentally catching pike on fly when fishing for trout that I first began to consider setting out to catch them that way intentionally. It was obvious that substantial tackle alterations would be needed to cope with sizeable pike, since some of those I hooked accidentally felt as if they might break my trout rod.

The rod for the job would have to be strong enough to beat a big pike, but light enough to cast a fly line and give good sport. The reel would need to hold sufficient line and to match the rod, and then there was the matter of fly size and a wire trace, and how the fish would be landed. The conclusions I came up with were as follows:

Below: The selection of pike flies available is now greater than ever.

Bottom: Fly lines made by Cortland – probably the best there is.

The rod – this needs to be strong but with a good action and be long enough to cast large flies. After several attempts I settled on one of 9 ft with a fly line rating of #10/11, two large 'stripper' rings and a big tip ring.

The reel – my preference is for a large-arbor fly reel with a good disc drag. The bigger the arbor, the less likelihood of line 'memory' or coiling, and the faster the rate of retrieval. It could be that I am biased, though, having designed the first large-arbor fly reel for trout fishing back in 1974, as far as I know the first in the world. The size of the reel makes it suitable for heavier fly lines, which are slightly bigger in diameter than lighter versions, but necessary for catching big pike.

The trace – I wanted a 9 ft leader, but not made all from wire, because wire of this length would be prone to kinking. I decided to have an 8 ft length of braided mono fly line backing with a needle loop at the 'butt' end and splice 1 ft of supple, 49-strand wire on the business end.

On the end of the wire I crimped a high-quality snap link to enable easy changes of fly pattern and give the fly more movement in the water.

The fly – when I started there were no purpose-made pike flies, so I made some myself. I used size 4/0 long-shank sea hooks tied with brightly-coloured feathers extending about five inches long, and enhanced their appearance with a marker pen. Having made my pike fly-fishing set-up I was eager to test it, and the anglers who saw me trying my hand for the first time back then were certainly intrigued, and perhaps more than a little amused. Many years later, having learned a great deal by trial and error, I had an opportunity to demonstrate the fish-catching power of fly fishing for pike that was too good to miss. The British Pike Squad, whom I sponsored at that time, had invited me to one of their lure-fishing practice days, and when I arrived they had all tried a variety of plastic and metal artificials without success. I set up my pike fly tackle and announced, to widespread disbelief, that I would catch them a pike. With my very first cast I landed one of 7 lb, after which I was banished from the lake for showing them up.

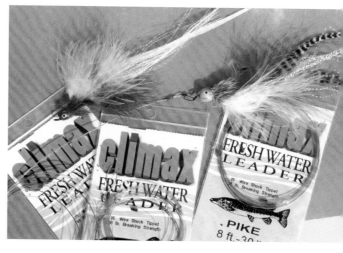

Fly-fishing leaders for pike.

Later I was asked why this method had been more successful than their lures, and I told them it was because a fly has an action that is closer to the pike's natural food, though it is by no means infallible. A fly can be made to move at high speed or it can lie prone in the water, drifting down through the layers with an occasional twitch to imbue it with life. A plug or spinner is without life when not being retrieved, but the feathers of a fly have a life of their own, and one that predatory fish of all kinds often find irresistible.

I made several converts that day, and two of those anglers have since gone on to win the annual Mick Willis British Open Pike Fly-Fishing Championship, which brings me back to my original point about the pleasure you can gain from helping others to succeed in angling.

If you would like to try your hand, here are a few tips on how to get started at fly fishing for pike:
- Get some lessons in fly casting. This will save hours of frustration and wasted time while you are still learning the basics.
- Match the fly line you use to the depth of water – floating for shallow (up to 6 ft), intermediate for medium (6 ft to 10 ft), and sinking for deep (10 ft plus).

A selection of purpose-tied pike flies.

- Fish to features, just as you would for other species, whether they be overhanging trees and bushes, weedbeds or islands.
- Experiment with different rates of retrieve. Fish that want a fly stripped back on one occasion will be in the mood for a gently twitched fly on another.
- Chop and change the fly patterns you use. Light levels and water clarity have an important bearing on whether or not a fly works, and a seemingly empty piece of water can suddenly come alive with activity when you attach the fly they want to the end of your line.
- Persevere if at first you don't succeed. Attempting something new is always difficult, but all of the unsuccessful outings will be forgotten when you hook your first fly-caught pike.

Mick Willis.

SPECIMEN COARSE FISH ON A FLY ROD

BY BOB CHURCH

CATCHING SPECIMEN COARSE FISH on fly-fishing tackle is poised to become a very popular side of the sport. Most trout anglers who visit large reservoirs have caught coarse fish by accident from time to time, many of them to specimen size. But a trend is emerging of catching these fish by design, and many of the pioneers are enjoying impressive results. There is a world of difference between catching coarse fish by accident when after trout and doing it intentionally. When you deliberately catch coarse fish on fly – and they are usually sizeable – there is a tremendous feeling of satisfaction.

I am lucky in that I have six of the country's major reservoirs between five and forty minutes from where I live in Northampton. They all hold a good head of coarse fish, as well as prolific numbers of trout. My personal favourite is Grafham Water and, while pike and perch are numerous in other reservoirs, I had heard that Grafham could provide me with a chance to fish for something different, namely zander.

Many years ago the late David Fleming Jones, who was then Grafham's manager, predicted, 'One day zander will get into Grafham quite naturally through the water pumping-in system from the Great Ouse. When this happens I will welcome them, because they will create bonus sport for fly-fishers without damaging the trout. They will also help control excessive shoals of coarse fish, which mature and eat the same food as the trout, i.e. aquatic insects of all kinds.'

I first heard of one or two zander being caught at Grafham in the mid-1990s. This was always an accidental capture by someone using a fast-sink line and a lure. But now there are serious zander fly-fishers, attracted by the fact that the species has established itself firmly at Grafham. When these stories of good zander and pike catches being made at the reservoir began to spread, I decided to ignore the trout on my next trip, and try for something different. It was early September when my boat partner, John Emerson, and I set out in search, and at the back of our minds was the hope of a good perch, or even a big bream. Past experience has taught me that big bream will take a six-inch tandem lure at this time of year, when their predatory instincts seem to be aroused.

Armed with a 10 ft 6 in IM8 Alaskan fly rod and weight, forward-eight and double-taper-eight fast-sink fly lines, plus a good selection of big, feathered and Flashabou-based lures, link-swivelled to wire traces, we set out on our mission. We headed for Hill Farm Bay and kept well out from the shore, over twenty-five to

Bob Church holding a 20 lb pike caught on fly.

thirty feet of water. I have caught plenty of zander up to double figures from the Fens on bait, and a few by accident on fly from a lake at Dreux in France. I have also caught a pike of 21 lb on fly, from Gaynes Cove at Grafham, so I had some idea of what to expect.

We dropped anchor and started fishing, and straight away began to catch perch, some as big as 2 lb. About a hundred yards away there was another boat anchored, and we could see the lone angler on board using a very specialised shooting-head outfit and a massive pike fly, which he was casting some considerable distance. I said to John, 'This guy knows what he's doing.' We watched him catch a couple of pike in quick succession, and two zander of about 6 lb each. He later introduced himself as Andy Goram, from Suffolk. He and his fishing pal, Jim Woolnough, are specialists in fly fishing for pike, which they have done for several years, mostly on the Norfolk Broads.

John and I moved away from our perch spot because we seemed to have fished it out. I had lost two good fish, which fell off on the way in and, judging by the way they fought, we believe they were zander. We found a new spot in thirty feet of water, and John put on his tandem size-6 Appetiser lure with a wire trace. I tied on a seven-inch pearl tube fly, and as the eye of the swivel on my wire trace wouldn't go through the thick plastic tube, I decided to take a risk. I threaded the 12 lb main line through the tube and tied the size-4 salmon double hook on direct, sliding the shank back into the tube so that only the hooks were exposed at the rear. We both made our first cast and left the lures and line for thirty seconds, so that they sank right down and laid on the bottom, before starting the retrieve. As soon as we began recovering line we both hooked very heavy fish, which we were sure must be pike.

After fifteen minutes of steady pressure both fish came up and showed themselves at the surface. We nearly had kittens, as both were over 30 lb. With only one specimen landing net between us we had a problem, but within seconds it was solved as my fish dived deep again and was gone. It was entirely my fault, as it had bitten through the plastic tube and then easily through the 12 lb nylon. Some lessons you have to learn the hard way. I set about netting John's fish and got it first time. I was glad we had a net with 42-inch arms as the fish was enormous. I took the Appetiser from the scissors of its jaws with my forceps, and we left it in the folds of the net over the side of the boat to recover from the fight.

With a fish of this size, John was naturally keen to weigh it without harming it and have his photograph taken with it. We called over to Andy for help and he had the proper equipment, along with a cushioned mat to lay the pike on in the bottom of the boat, so it couldn't knock itself. He also had a large hammock-shaped weighing sling. I did at least have the correct scales, which weigh up to 60 lb. John's pike took them down to 30 lb 8 oz, and swam away strongly after the pictures. The capture brought home to me the importance of having the right gear to deal with these big pike in a boat. If you don't, you are likely to end up with a dead fish on your hands. Big pike need handling with great care.

After the capture we couldn't help speculating on the chances of hooking two pike of 30 lb at the same time: they must be one in a million. We saw mine before it bit through, and it was of a similar size.

After a further hour at the same spot with nothing to show, we decided to move. It seems that keeping on the move is a good policy when searching for coarse fish, and if the wind is not too strong it is worth trying 'back drifting', or fishing with lines out of the back while being carried by the wind. This is a good way of covering a large area of water.

My luck changed at the next spot. I started with a 6 lb 8 oz bream on a tandem Appetiser. Bream have a reputation for being lacklustre fighters, but this fish provided good sport on fly tackle, putting up a dogged fight. Big bream definitely feed on fry in the autumn, when prey fish are in abundance and are big enough to make them worth chasing.

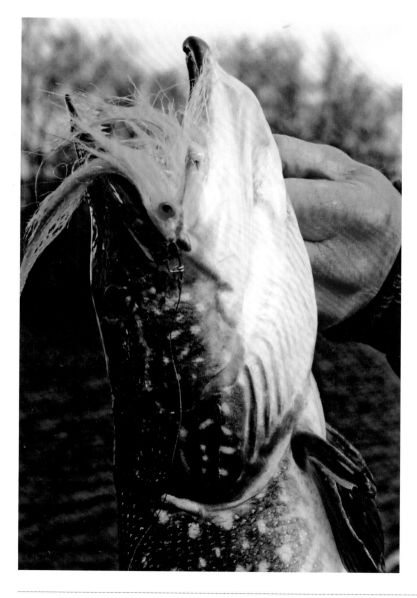

This is my favourite pike fly. They love it. Called the 'Canary' fly, it has produced scores of pike to 20 lb-plus. The big single 610 hook is better than a treble for hooking right in the scissor of the jaw.

After losing another zander I decided to give the next one a couple of extra-firm strikes, to set the hooks more securely. John gave me one of his large Boobies, which have pieces of buoyant foam tied in at the head to make them rise in the water after being pulled down by the weight of the sinking line. He had tied them up especially with zander in mind. I put one on the link-swivel of my wire trace and at last boated a zander. It wasn't big, at between 4 lb and 5 lb, but it was good to get one on board. David Fleming Jones's words rang true – they are a second sporting species for the reservoir, and one I am certain will become popular with the majority of Grafham's visitors.

We returned for a second trip the following week, to see if we had just been lucky the first time in having such a memorable day. Andy was there once again, this time with his friend Jim, and there were two other boats with anglers obviously fishing for pike and zander. They all caught several zander and double-

Bob Church with a well-marked 15 lb pike from 60-acre Patshull Park Lake, near Wolverhampton.

figure pike, the best 18 lb 8 oz, while John had perch to 2 lb 10 oz and two 6 lb bream, and I had a lovely young pike of 19 lb 4 oz. That convinced us that this first trip was no fluke, and we looked forward to many such days in the future. And to my amazement, not a single trout was caught on either trip!

If you are serious about taking up this new and exciting side of the sport you will need to get the right equipment. Andy and Jim use number 12 shooting-head lines on specially-built fly rods for pike. You need this extra power on reservoirs because most of your fishing is deep down with big lures, and you need to be able to cast long distances and set big hooks. For zander, perch and bream our outfits were more suitable, and we just about got away with them for pike.

Once you can handle a fly rod you can take your tackle along to any coarse water. I accompanied Mike Green from Northampton, who has specialised in this for a few years, on a trip to a shallow lake in Buckinghamshire, fishing from a punt. We drifted using a drogue to slow us down and caught several good pike. Mike has had as many as five over double figures in one session, and his best on fly is a fish of 18 lb 8 oz, from another, more difficult water. Fly fishing often gives you the edge over spinning, in that it allows you to slow down your retrieve without fear of forever hooking submerged weed beds.

So popular is fly fishing for coarse fish becoming that Anglian Water fisheries manager John Marshall has had to introduce new rules at their four waters to cater for the extra interest. Many coarse fish were being killed, especially at Grafham, so now only one zander and one pike of not more than 12 lb can be retained. This will go some way towards safeguarding stocks. After all, you can't have anglers removing the fish that an increasing number of people are only too willing to pay good money to try and catch.

CHAPTER 19

THE MENDIP RANGER'S FINEST HOUR

BY PETE CLIMO

This is a story about a pike fly, a fly that was conceived in my head and born in my vice. It has accounted for many fine pike over the years, but on a wet April afternoon some years ago, it was responsible for a catch of considerable rarity.

The story begins in the autumn of 2001, when the management of the famous Somerset trout water Chew Valley Lake invited pike anglers to fish for the pike that had appeared in the water. The event was a great success: lures and deadbaits accounting for substantial catches of big pike. After the event, the fishery manager wrote to the participating anglers inviting them to try fly-fishing for the pike during the trout season starting the following spring. My boat partner, Bob Jones, and I decided to try our luck. We had fished Chew and its sister lake, Blagdon, extensively for trout during the 1970s and 1980s, so we had a great deal of experience on which to draw. We had no specialist pike fly gear, so we decided to use our trout tackle to see whether it would cope with the more substantial pike. It didn't! We had a fair bit of action and hooked a number of fish, all, save for one twelve-pounder, which got away due to the inadequacy of the tackle. I decided not to try again until I had sorted out some better equipment.

At the time there was little available specifically for pike fishing, so I turned to the American salt-water market for a suitable rod. I settled on an Orvis no. 11-weight rod at 9 ft, designed for tarpon and permit. Most pike fly-fishers use full lines, but I wanted to use a shooting head, which proved so effective during my trout-fishing days. A shooting head would deliver a long line across the wind from a drifting boat with the minimum of effort. I bought two no. 12-weight forward-tapered salmon lines, one fast-sinking and the other slow, and I cut out nine yards of the thickest part of the lines to make my shooting heads. These were spliced to hollow-braided monofilament shooting line, and a 6 ft fluorocarbon leader of 15 lb-breaking-strain was attached at the business end to nine inches of 49-strand 30 lb-breaking-strain wire, which completed the set-up.

My armoury was now complete save for one vital component – the fly! To use a shooting head effectively demands a light, almost weightless, aerodynamic fly. The commercially-tied pike flies I looked at were hopelessly unsuitable: Bob Jones likened them to trying to cast a parrot! I had always intended to tie my own flies, but the challenge was coming up with a design that was both light and aerodynamic, but also imposing enough to catch the eye of a discerning pike.

The first job was to find a suitable hook, and here again sea fishing came to the rescue. At my local tackle shop I found some Sakuma Manta hooks in size 2/0, intended for baiting with crab and squid. They were round-bend, thin in the wire and very strong. More importantly, they were much lighter than the hooks used on the commercially-tied pike flies.

Next job was to design a fly using lightweight materials that would look like something a pike would want to eat. The most prominent bait fish in Chew Valley was roach, and countless thousands around six inches long seemed to be everywhere. So I based my fly on a six-inch roach; not an exact replica, as a mere caricature would suffice. Where possible I used synthetic materials, as these resist absorbing water and so are lighter than traditional fur and feather. I experimented at the vice and eventually came up with a very simple design I was happy with. The head of the fly extended the full length of the hook shank and was tied with black Fritz. The tail of the fly, which represented the body of a roach, was tied with a sparse bunch of red bucktail, topped by a slightly more generous helping of Angel Hair. The finished fly measured six inches from hook eye to tip of tail, and displayed three characteristics

Pete Climo's Mendip Ranger. Note the red, white and green on the tail of the fly.

of a roach: the dark head, the red bucktail underbody, suggesting fins, and the white and silver Angel Hair, suggesting scales. A visit to a local pond confirmed that the fly performed beautifully with the shooting head. The Mendip Ranger was born; all that remained now was to seek the pike's opinion!

April 2003 was my first opportunity to fish Chew with the new set-up. I had named the Mendip Ranger after the range of hills that sweep down to the lake from the south. It was early in the month, the wind was raw, the water was cold and the pike were unobliging. We had made a number of drifts across the shallows, but no offers were received. Then we noticed some movement in the reeds and took the boat in to investigate. Sure enough, pike were spawning in the reed beds. We began to drift along the reed line, dropping our flies as close to the stalks as we dared. As the boat passed a small bay in the reed line I noticed a swirl in the bay. I dropped the fly into the fading ripples and just one draw of the line provoked a savage take. After a frenetic tussle in the shallow water, a 15 lb 8 oz female was lifted into the boat. First blood to the Mendip Ranger!

The following week the weather was kinder. A gentle southerly breeze was coming across the Mendips, a strengthening sun was warming the shallows and the pike were showing a keen interest in our flies. Almost every cast produced a take or a follow, and after the umpteenth jack was unhooked at the side of the boat, I had the take I was waiting for.

When it came, I barely realised it. At the end of a long draw of the line I felt a faint pluck. I wasn't sure whether it was a take, so I started another draw and was immediately into a fish. It took off like a scalded cat, burning my forefinger as I gripped the shooting line against the cork handle. This happened four or five times before the fish was finally brought to the net. She was long and lean, having recently spawned. Her weight was 2 oz short of 21 lb: she had tested the tackle to the full, but it passed with flying colours, and the Mendip Ranger had claimed an important scalp.

As the month progressed, the temperature continued to increase until it became unseasonably warm for the end of April. We fished on the last day of the month, the noticeboard in the lodge warning of possible thunderstorms, but there was no sign of these as we loaded our gear into the boat on a glorious spring morning.

We motored down to the southern shallows and began a drift, starting at the two small islands near to Herriot's End. The warm southerly breeze was just enough to make steady headway without being too strong to interfere with casting. We were employing our normal tactic of positioning the drogue at the stern, one angler at the bow end casting to the left and the other at the stern casting to the right. This enabled a wide band of water to be covered as the boat progressed down the wind. At the end of each drift we would change positions, to allow each angler a fair share of the easier casting position at the bow end. We had learned this method of drifting during our trout fishing days at Blagdon, where it had proved deadly. It was to prove equally deadly for the pike.

A low double apiece was the reward for our first hour's work, but then the weather took a dramatic turn for the worse. I first noticed an inky black cloud creeping up the valley from the south-west. Then the wind increased, and in no time at all the storm was upon us. Cloud enveloped the lake, taking away our visibility; the landscape just disappeared! Thunder roared overhead and forks of lightning probed down towards the lake. Then came the rain, torrents of it! We decided rapidly that being out on the lake in a boat in these conditions was not a good idea, so we quickly motored to Wick Green point, beached the boat and dived into the bird hide for shelter. When the final storm departed it left behind warm, steady rain on a gentle breeze under a sullen sky. On the first drift following our return, I boated a hard-fighting 16 lb 8 oz pike, which had snaffled the Mendip Ranger close to the boat. I took us back upwind and commenced a drift on exactly the same line as before. Halfway through the drift, Bob hooked what was obviously a very heavy fish. He was soon able to bring the pike close to the boat, where we could see it in the clear water.

'It's big,' I said. 'Could be a "thirty". Take it easy.'

Despite this being Bob's first big pike on a fly, his vast experience of playing big fish ensured the outcome was never in doubt. With a powerful flick of its mighty tail, the pike shot away from view. The splice between shooting head and backing line rattled its way through the rod rings, providing accompaniment to the pike's departure. Time and again Bob brought the pike to the boat, and time and again it shot away, accompanied by the familiar rattle! The runs were getting shorter now; soon it was time for me to play a role. Bob drew the tiring fish over my sunken net. A firm, steady lift, and a magnificent pike was swathed in mesh.

We marvelled at her awesome beauty as she lay on the mat at our feet, out of her element but in her prime. These brief moments are the very reason you are a pike fisherman. But, there was work to be done: weighing, photographing, then back upwind for another drift on exactly the same line in the hope of catching another. The scales confirmed my earlier estimate – 31 lb 2 oz. The Mendip Ranger strikes again!

At the start of the next drift I had a remarkable stroke of luck, although I didn't realise it at the time. I hooked a tree stump! When I pulled to free the fly, the line

Bill Jones holding a 31 lb 2oz pike.

parted with a tug of no more than a couple of pounds. The wire trace had broken just above the fly. I then remembered I had failed to check the trace following the capture of the 16 lb fish earlier. The hidden tree stumps on the bed of Chew Valley are a curse, but this one was to prove my salvation.

As the drift proceeded, my confidence was high. Bob and I had swapped places, so I was in the right position to cover the area where the 'thirty' had been hooked. The boat was drifting at just the right speed to put a good curve in the line on the retrieve. A long cast was made at 90 degrees to the wind, the slow-sinking shooting head was allowed to sink for a count of ten, and then the retrieve began. Long, steady draws of the line were made, with a slight pause between each until the fly was beside the boat. The shooting head required one false cast to put it outside the rod, then a final cast with a double-haul to deliver the fly 35 yards away across the wind. The rain was falling steadily,

THE MENDIP RANGER'S FINEST HOUR · 291

but I was oblivious to it; the whole of my being was absorbed in the pursuit of a big pike. We were nearing the end of the drift, and I thought my chance had gone, when I felt a slight pluck at the end of a draw. I struck instantly, and my rod arched down, answering to the pull of a big pike.

The fish was hooked near to the boat, so I had sight of it almost straight away. It looked easily as big as Bob's fish, possibly bigger. I could feel my legs shaking as the pike swiped its tail and disappeared into the depths. The battle followed the now-familiar pattern of short, fast, powerful runs and dogged resistance as line was recovered. The regular rattle of the splice running back and forth through the rings served as a reminder of the frailty of the tackle. So many joins – backing line to shooting line, shooting line to shooting head, shooting head to leader, leader to trace, trace to fly: so much potential for disaster. These thoughts filled my head as I played the fish. I was worried I would lose it, but somehow I knew I wouldn't. I felt a huge sense of relief when Bob engulfed the pike in mesh. Now there was a different pike on the mat at our feet, but one thing remained the same: the Mendip Ranger firmly hooked in the scissors! After a few moments' deliberation of the dial, Bob announced: '32 lb 8 oz.' What a fish, what a day, what a fly! It was indeed the Mendip Ranger's finest hour!

Pete's pike. He passed on to me the accumulated knowledge of years of fishing, and I owe him a debt of gratitude for a lifetime of angling pleasure.

*The River Dalälven,
Sweden, the home of
monster pike.*

CHAPTER 20

SWEDEN

THE LAND OF A THOUSAND LAKES

R ECENTLY I WAS INVITED TO GO ON AN EXPLORATORY FISHING EXPEDITION to find out the true pike-fishing potential of Sweden's River Dalälven, in Gysinge, a little village north of Stockholm. I was pleasantly surprised when I discovered the flight from Heathrow to Stockholm took just two hours: coupled with the superb sport I was to encounter, it made the trip doubly enjoyable.

On arriving in Gysinge I couldn't believe just how much water there was: the potential seemed endless. The opportunities for a pike to grow really huge were all there: vast expanses of water when a pike could live out its life undisturbed, and the stability of the environment, were two crucial factors. The amount of food available was amazing – huge shoals of bite-size bream around the 1 lb 8 oz mark, huge shoals of perch, along with trout and grayling. This endless food supply was topped up by extra riches coming in from the sea by way of salmon and sea-trout. Everything seemed to point to mammoth pike.

Johanna Färdigh holding a big Swedish pike caught on a trolled lure in five feet of water.

The angler seemed to have everything available to him in one place – huge weir pools, rivers and lakes all in one area. The whole environment was in pristine condition. The Nedre Dalälven has one of the largest populations of osprey in the world, their staple diet being pike. This again was an indication of potential. Vast shallow areas mean lots of available spawning grounds, which are responsible for the large number of pike hatching out each year. For once I was completely lost for words. Here was something very different from the desert of popular imagination – a pike angler's paradise. It had been a long time since I had felt this enthusiastic about any water, and that evening I dreamt as I had done as a boy about monster pike and great battles, laying plans for tackling the leviathans I knew must exist.

The following day Thomas Johanson, my guide, and I powered up-river to the pike grounds. The 13-ft aluminium boat really took a hammering on the

The River Dalälven in Gysinge. The home of mighty pike.

boulder-strewn river beds. Bait was our immediate concern, but this posed few problems, for within half an hour we had enough perch and bream to last the entire trip. The fish were transferred into Thomas's wire fish trap, and we set about locating likely-looking areas.

The high water had moved the pike into shallow areas of the lake which lent themselves to sink-and-draw tactics. I cast a small bream tight to some rushes in a bay, and began to wobble and flutter the bait a couple of feet below the surface. Just feet away from the bait a huge bow-wave raced across the water, followed by two others from left and right. My bait was hit at incredible speed and the rod almost torn from my hands. These pike had come after the bait simultaneously, but the largest fish had got to it first. It went round and round the boat, tail-walked and crashed into deep water. It seemed an eternity before we eventually netted her – scale-perfect and weighing 18 lb 8 oz. And all this with one cast; I couldn't believe it. That afternoon we caught eighteen other pike into double figures, and with each cast four or five pike came after my bait simultaneously. The number of fish in one small area was amazing.

Kalle Hedin holding a mid-twenty-pounder from the River Dalälven.

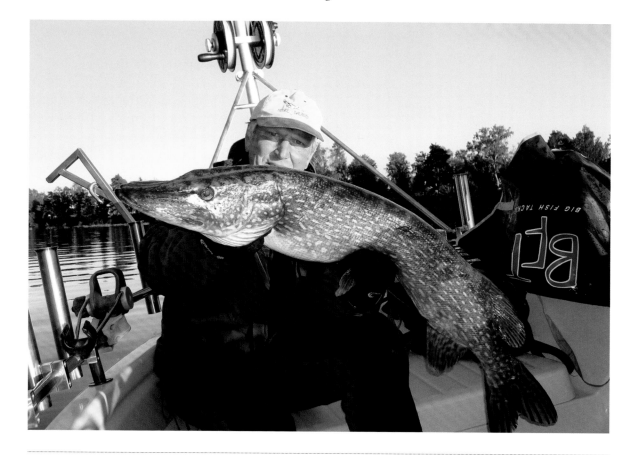

At sunset Thomas and I watched beavers swimming to and fro, along with three moose which had decided to swim alongside our boat. Osprey swooped into the shallow bays and carried off small pike to feed their young, adding to the atmosphere I was enjoying soaking up. This was fishing at its very best.

The following day Thomas and I decided to move from the lake to the River Dalälven itself. The river forked into two just above Gysinge, each branch leading to a weir pool, with an island separating them. I decided to change tactics, and opted for livebait with a sliding float. The average depth seemed to be about 15–20 ft, so I tripped the baits through at 12 ft, allowing them to swim through the fast water, holding them back occasionally to allow them to ride up and down in the current, searching each band of water. I then wafted the bait along the crease, fluttering it downriver for about 150 metres. The process was repeated over and over again without success. Surely any self-respecting pike on the prowl would have taken the opportunity to secure such an offering? I decided to try an 8 oz rainbow trout, and this was sent through the same swim, followed by a roach, but still with no success.

As a last resort I lip-hooked a big perch and worked it slowly down towards the tail of the weir. Suddenly the float vanished, and I was into a very big fish. The boat was up-anchored to avoid the line being torn by the sharp boulders, and we followed the fish downriver. Five minutes later we had our prize, the most beautiful pike I had ever seen. She pulled the scales down to 24 lb, and we placed her gently in a sack and lowered it into the water tied to an overhanging tree.

Thomas suggested that I fish behind some huge boulders and outcrops of rock strewn across the river, each of which had slack water behind it. Another perch was lip-hooked and cast behind one of the boulders. Immediately the bait was taken, and a massive fish tail-walked in front of us

A left and right 24lb and 30lb fish caught from the River Dalälven in Gysinge, Sweden

and swam right into the boiling mass of white water, then turned and powered off downriver. She, too, was eventually beaten, and as she rolled into the net, Thomas's face said it all. I had caught a Swedish river 30. A 24-pounder and a 30-pounder in one morning from a river is something I had always dreamt of becoming reality in the country from which my family originated centuries ago.

For the remainder of the week I fished many different lakes and tributaries of the Dalälven, and the potential seemed never-ending. Six other doubles came to my net over a two-day period, but I was happy and content just to be part of what is a super-rich environment unaffected by man through the passage of time. Yes, Sweden really is a piker's paradise. The thought of returning in October, when the pike fishing is at its best before the ice comes, when the shoal fish are grouped up and location is fairly simple, made my imagination run wild with the possibility of catching a river fish in excess of 43 lb.

Liso, the Baltic.

To catch big pike regularly and consistently I need to be on good waters at the right times. This can and usually does take a great amount of effort, time and money. With fishing you only get out what you put in.

CHAPTER 21

PIKE FISHING IN IRELAND

BY AL RAWLINGS

I MOVED TO IRELAND IN 1994, and have been pike fishing extensively there ever since. Most weeks throughout the winter I would be out fishing for pike, and during this time I would hardly see a living soul, apart from the odd farmer. This suited me fine as I like my own company and felt in harmony with the wonderful Irish countryside. I have always targeted the bigger pike – I mean specimens over twenty pounds, as I have seldom been in a position to target anything over thirty pounds. Basically, I fish for twenties, and if a thirty pops up, so much the better. However, I do try and fish waters where catching a thirty-pound pike is possible, but they are now few and far between in the wild natural Irish waters where I love to pike-fish.

During this time I have learned how to tackle these big natural loughs from shore and boat, and most importantly how to focus my efforts on catching the bigger pike we all crave. Over the past twenty years I have extensively fished a range of different waters, and caught more pike in excess of twenty pounds than any other angler. At the time of writing my record stands at 457 pike over twenty pounds, 134 over twenty-five pounds, and 11 Irish thirties from 56 different venues, including large and small rivers, huge loughs and small enclosed lakes.

Between 1996 and 1999 I decided to find out what made the bigger pike suddenly turn on the feed. Imagine the scenario I repeatedly found myself in back then: bivvied up for a week, my baits positioned in a well-known spot, but nothing doing – not even a bleep from the alarms – despite trying different baits. Then, on the fifth day, at 10.35 a.m., the big pike suddenly came on the feed, and the result was four pike weighing over twenty pounds in three hours. Then, nothing for the rest of the trip! I was delighted but puzzled, and from that day onwards made it my quest to find out why big pike were feeding at specific times.

Timing

Timing is crucial for success. You could be fishing the best thirty-pound water in the country, but if your timing is wrong, little or nothing will happen for days on end. On the other hand, getting the timing bang-on could see several big fish landed in succession. So, what makes the timing right?

I've kept detailed diaries on each of my pike sessions, which have become very useful tools for identifying the distinctive feeding patterns of larger pike. Sometimes I use diagrams of the venue and swims, plotting the bait positions with crosses, and the depth in which they are fished. I had been keeping fishing diaries like this for the past three years, and they were constantly being re-read. In fact I used to take them out fishing with me on longer sessions to have the information at hand.

Back in 1998 I was fishing from one of many islands on a big Irish lough. It was a day in late October: mild, some sun, some cloud, and the wind light from a westerly direction. Water conditions also looked very good. The brown stain caused by the heavy rain running through the extensive peat bogs surrounding the lough had finally dropped out, and the water level was lower at last. The baits were out and the kettle was on. The diary was penned with all necessary data for that day: air and water temperature, general weather and water conditions, air pressure, wind strength and direction – but fishing methods, types of bait

A 31 lb 5 oz pike caught on a small dead roach, which was presented close-in.

used, and where I was fishing each bait type were all carefully recorded. I had scribbled in that the weather forecast was for it to become much colder the next day. The day was quiet enough, but in the early afternoon I had one take on a dead roach close-in, which resulted in a fantastic pike of 31 lb 5 oz. Delighted and buzzing with this catch, I was putting the information into my diary when it suddenly dawned on me: this had happened several times before. A good catch of big pike always occurred just before a sudden drop in air temperature. I quickly got out my earlier diaries to check, and sure enough, every time there was a big temperature drop, big pike came on the feed and superb sport followed.

An opportunistic feeder

Armed with this vital big-pike feeding information, I planned my fishing trips to coincide with these downward temperature changes. Incredibly, every trip was successful. All I had to do was to get out before the air temperature dropped and fish through the change in the hot spots. It was guaranteed big pike success. During this time I was also exploring new areas of the lough with the help of my echo sounder, looking for features such as drop-offs and food fish, then fishing these areas when the air temperature was changing. This was normally a day before the drop, but sometimes a three-day session would be planned in order to fish right through the change. I may have been sacrificing some good pike fishing on my known hotspots at such good feeding times if I got the location wrong, but I loved finding new waters and catching new pike. If I didn't catch going through the change I could guarantee the big pike were just not there at that time, although this might not be the case at a later date. It was more information for the big pike diary. Numbers of twenties were really racking up now, and I remember passing the one hundred mark in 1999 and being contacted by Neville Fickling, who wanted to add me to his list of notable pike anglers.

I must add, however, that although an approaching cold front gives optimum feeding conditions for big pike, they can be caught at other times too. There are prolonged periods when the weather remains mild for several weeks, even months, and during these times, I believe, the pike respond to very small, subtle changes in temperature and atmospheric pressure. A close study of the barometer will show the trigger that big pike will use for a short burst of feeding activity. I have witnessed this several times. Additionally, if I have caught pike over twenty pounds when there has not been any real cold front or cold snap for a while, the pike look thinner and have evidently not fed for some time. Fish can go without food for months, and without a doubt their feeding is totally controlled by weather conditions. Even slight temperature fluctuations will trigger a feeding spell.

Pike feeding times are also controlled by the movements of our moon, giving specific 'start-of-feed' times. This is not the phases of the moon, but what appears to be a sudden change in the force of gravity, which gives *Esox* a wake-up nudge. In my opinion, big pike can be caught on any day of the moon's monthly phase cycle, and a study of all my 20 lb-plus pike catches indicates that equal numbers were caught during each lunar cycle. This just goes to show that it is the weather, and air temperature, which are the critical factors in triggering big pike to feed. The moon's effect gives the specific start time.

What really stands out, though, is that if the weather and air temperature are going to take a plunge and high pressure moves in, coinciding with a full or new moon, I can expect fantastic pike fishing for a much longer period.

A 25 lb-plus pike. This fish was certainly an opportunistic feeder. It was caught at long range on a float-ledgered bait.

Full and new moon phases give far better start triggers. I have studied and plotted these triggers throughout the whole year. The solar system is a precise machine: for example, I know that around the winter solstice of 21 December, the shortest day – nearest new moon, or full moon plus one day – the triggers are running exactly 2 hours 10 minutes apart. Couple this with a good cold front moving in the next day, and, bingo – superb pike fishing! These red-letter days only occur once or twice in an entire season, but when they do happen the results are mind-boggling. One of my best days produced five 20 lb-plus pike in three and a half hours, during a mad feeding spell. I have also had other days when six twenty-pounders and numerous double-figure fish were caught float-trolling during these very conditions. The pike fed all day long, and feeding was boosted every 2 hours 10 minutes by another moon trigger.

So what is this trigger that makes the pike feed or attack bait? I believe it's some sort of gravitational shift making the wind suddenly blow stronger, which fish and animals can feel. These moon triggers stir pike into becoming opportunistic feeders for just a few minutes, especially when the approaching weather is getting colder. Many of us have experienced these narrow feeding windows, when we have been fishing all day and then get three takes within half an hour, with other anglers further down the bank starting to catch at the same time. This is a gravity-shift trigger: the observant ones among you will have noticed a shift in the wind – an increase or decrease, or change of direction, that brings about a feeding frenzy. Obviously you need to be on the pike in the first place. Successful big pike fishing really is a combination of rights: right water, right location, right time, right bait or lure and right presentation.

Weather and wind direction

Wind direction is worth noting around your fishing days. A wind moving from west to north-west to north over a three-day period is most favourable for big pike fishing. Good fishing could be experienced on any of the three days, but usually the day when the wind direction is north-west would be the one to be out fishing. I have experienced this many times. The big pike come on for an hour or so during the day, and then it goes stone dead. Miss this day, morning or afternoon, and you'll be missing out on this big pike feeding opportunity. I cannot emphasise enough how tight these feeding windows actually are.

Successful big pike anglers are tuned into the weather throughout the season, and would instinctively know when and where to go. An angler who is self-employed or has flexible working hours can really take advantage of these good feeding times. For others, it really is pot luck what feeding scale you have on your weekends off, although smaller pike are usually obliging when the bigger pike are not having it, so a bend in the rod is still likely. However, following the weather and temperature is still an advantage to the weekend angler. Knowing what has happened and what has fed during the week before you head off can be a real advantage, and the clued-up angler can fish accordingly. If the weather changed to a cold snap during the week, and the bigger pike have already fed and are resting and digesting their meals, there is no point fishing big mackerel baits to tempt one. A more subtle and thought-out approach is needed.

I have noted over the years that non-oily bait can work wonders at such low feeding times. For example, a small dead perch, a small dried-out freezer-burnt roach, an eel section, a small brown trout, or a pollan would be good choices of bait at such times. In fact any non-oily dried-out freezer-burnt bait is good to catch a non-feeding pike. A lot of confidence is required to fish such baits instead of a fresh mackerel or herring. Try using a burnt-out roach or small brown trout on one rod during an entire season, and you will be pleasantly surprised at how good your catch rates become.

Small ledgered live bait can also tempt a big pike during such times, as can the right type of lure. A fly or a non-vibrating no-noise lure fished over the heads of parked-up pike during the right moon/planet time can trigger or stir the pike to take any one of the above. It is slow fishing, though, and for any success you need to know exactly where the pike are parked up. On such days no non-feeding big pike will move more than a few yards. Patience is a virtue. I love getting out on those big feed-up days, however, when the colder air temperature drives the bigger pike to feed. I call this proper piking, and it's a real buzz to be out when big pike are on the move and actively feeding. They are looking for proper food items, and bigger deadbaits, bigger livebaits and bigger lures can be fished with confidence. Takes on such days can be savage.

In a good pike season, it's possible to have as few as five to eight really good days. It really pays to stay in tune with the weather so you don't miss those good temperature drops. In a poor pike season you are looking at only one to four really good days: the window is that narrow. The entire rest of the winter would consist of low feeding-scale days, with the odd medium one here and there, where the big pike would be mostly non-feeding fish. The pike are not impossible to catch on the right lure or bait during this time, but the fishing is definitely a lot harder and slower.

Wind direction is a great indicator of how good or bad the fishing is going to be. The old sayings, 'When the wind is from the west, the fish bite best,' and, 'When the wind is from the east, the fish bite least,' are so true. East winds generally give poor pike fishing to those who do not adjust their methods. Remember, the pike are not really feeding at such times, and strange behaviour can be observed, like float attacks! Lure fishing would therefore be the best choice. A pike fly-fished in water with good visibility would be the best method. Obviously, if east winds continue for any length of time, the pike will have to feed eventually, especially after spawning. Look out for atmospheric changes during such times, as this triggers big pike to feed.

I was out one winter when an east wind started to blow, and the first two days produced a fish of just over 29 lb as the air temperature began to plummet. I then proceeded to blank for the rest of the week as the relentless east wind blew on.

This particular water was a good deadbait water in its day, and a terrible lure water because it was so coloured: not a good venue during an easterly wind. At such times clear water where pike use their eyesight for hunting is the type of water to head for, as lures can be fished with confidence to non-feeding but possibly interested pike. To catch big pike regularly and consistently I need to be on good waters at the right times. This can and usually does take a great amount of effort, time and money. With fishing you only get out what you put in.

During the course of the season I will fish various waters at the optimum time, and whenever possible fish them through a good cold front to maximise my chances. When I fish waters further away from home, I go in the hope that the right weather and temperatures come along during my stay. If I'm staying long enough at the right time of year, say October or November, cold fronts should be coming in regularly. However, global warming is causing strange weather changes and fluctuations, and nothing is guaranteed any more, which makes the pike fishermen's task of getting the timing right much harder.

Location and tackle

If a water is new to me and I need to find out where the pike are located, and fast, a boat with an echo sounder is used. I usually troll a lure with the petrol engine running slowly, to cover as much water as possible. These pike are more than likely to be small- to medium-sized fish, but that I have located pike at all assures me I'm in the right spot for a bigger one. Now I need to fish the swim at the right time when the bigger pike are on the feed. If a boat and sounder cannot be used on the new water for some reason, then location will be a slower affair.

A 29 lb 1 oz pike caught on a dead roach.

A 29 lb 12 oz pike. This fish was caught on a small dead roach which was trolled.

Here, other anglers' catches can be a short cut to success, although this is not my preferred approach. Another method is to use a bait boat with an echo sounder which looks for drop-offs, food fish, plateaus and gullies. I then fish baits close to these features through a good cold front, and big pike are eventually caught.

Don't be impatient, as learning about a new water can take time, and the bigger the water, the more secrets it will hold. Success in catching big pike consistently could take two or three seasons. Piecing the jigsaw together is never a simple matter, as weather, temperature, water depth, underwater features and food/fish movements all play a part in the movement of big pike.

Your tackle must be strong. I cannot emphasise this enough, as snapping off on a big pike almost certainly results in a dead fish. My advice is to tackle up for a really big fish, say a fifty-pound weight, and you should be OK. Test all knots well. To test my gear before fishing, I usually attach my terminal tackle to the garage door at home and walk backwards, striking several times very hard. You never know: the next take could well be that fish of a lifetime, so fish to that philosophy and you'll be all right. Pike are not tackle-shy, I assure you, even the fish that get caught regularly in British gravel pits. I have carried out several experiments on big pike over the years and used wire of 144 pounds breaking-strain in crystal-clear water, to see firstly if pike were aware of my terminal tackle and, secondly, if they were prone to dropping a bait because of it. My conclusions are that using heavy wire doesn't have any bearing on the number of big fish caught. In fact, I even used the same wire on my float ledger rigs, and up-traces have caught several fish which had been landed previously.

I have, however, noticed different pike feeding behaviour that could be misunderstood for pike being aware of terminal tackle, or recognising the use of the same bait. These fish seem to inspect the bait, look at it for hours, flip it over, pick it up and then drop it. It looks as if the pike is very suspicious of your offering, but nothing could be further from the truth. This type of behaviour is linked solely to the weather and temperature. Consequently, the correct method and bait must be used, otherwise the behaviour will occur time and time again. However, on other days when a pike's feeding level is much higher, the same bait, in the same location, will be taken with confidence.

When fishing the big Irish loughs from the bank, I use powerful ten-foot up-tide rods. Baits are usually fished on a float ledger set-up over drop-offs around 150 metres from the shore. A 5 oz weight is required to anchor the bait, and the rigs are set up as self-hooking bolt rigs, which hook the pike in the corner of the mouth every time. The powerful rods help set the hooks at distance and the main line is really strong, 65-pound braid, coupled with multiplier reels which, unlike fixed-spool reels, prevent line twist. Distance is normally reached by a bait boat or a small rowing boat incorporating an on-board echo sounder. I also use tough 40-pound mono leader about 33 feet long – I find Mono far tougher than braid and slightly more abrasion-resistant.

When I launch my boat I always wear a lifejacket, as the weather on these big Irish loughs can get really rough and dangerous. I also check the weather forecast for the day, and tend to launch my boat on the lea wind side of the lough. I find a decent-looking area to fish by keeping an eye on the echo sounder, looking for drop-offs down to about 20 feet in the winter, with food fish shoals present within 150 yards of the shore. I also like flat and grassy banks that are easy to pitch the bivvy on. All the bank and camping gear would be on board, and I would probably have supplies for a few days' fishing, so I could fish before, during and after the cold front pushes through. If my timing was right, I would typically catch on the second day of a trip, and if I did I would pack up and go home, rather than blank the third day.

My baits are fished on float ledger set-ups (see diagram), with 5 oz fixed weights incorporating the essential pike-safe three-foot up-traces, which are rowed out and positioned well spread-out, in or around drop-offs. My stop knots are set at a third over depth. If there are lots of boats on the lough I use sub-surface floats, but for most of my fishing I use big floats, as I can see the bait positions from the camp. One of the main reasons I use float ledger rigs rather than a straight ledger set-up is to avoid the snags and sharp zebra mussels often found on steep drop-offs.

My braid is clipped up tight to heavy 2 oz-drop back indicators, and the rods are placed on Txi Delkim alarms. The sensitivity is adjusted according to the conditions. Rod tips are typically fished high or very low, which helps absorb surface float movement from the waves. I prefer to fish mine high, as I can then drive my bait boat under the lines, and also walk under them. But if the side winds are too strong, the tips are fished in a downward position to keep the lines straight.

If you are after really big pike, then winter is the best time to fish. Water temperatures are much lower and pike survival rates are very high. Big pike are often caught from Christmas time to the end of March. After this you are well

This is Al's float ledger pop-up rig, which has accounted for many of his big pike.

Float Ledger P.U Bait Rig

Stop knot set at ⅓ over depth

To rod and heavy drop back indicator

Large float

40 lb mono leader 33 ft

Swivel

Popped-up bait

Solid Marlin steel wire 90 lb

130 lb plastic-coated up-trace

Swivel

½ oz bomb

Main weight standard 5 oz, or breakaway with weak link

into spawning time on most of the Irish waters. Then the female fish are at their heaviest, and often weigh 20 per cent above their normal body weight. Some pike caught at 30 lb in October could easily weigh 36 lb during the following February or March. The trick is finding a water that has an October 30-lb fish in the first place! Many of the Irish waters simply don't foot this bill, and many October pike are lean and light, and tend to top out later in the season at a maximum weight of 32 lb. There are a handful of waters with the potential to grow very big pike but, unfortunately, the Irish Inland Fisheries still continue to gill-net and kill the pike on them. However, the big Shannon loughs of Ree, Derg and the

A bait boat with sonar is ideal for placing baits over drop-offs. (Note the rod tips in the air.)

Erne system tend to throw up 30 lb-plus fish every now and then. There are some stories of 35-lb pike, but most are exaggerated. Nowadays there are many more pike anglers here in Ireland all looking for and fishing these same waters; add the poachers, anglers that kill their fish, massive pike competitions, and gill-netting, and you feel like you are always fishing for what's left! There may still be one or two special waters dotted around the country with potential, but I feel the good old days here in Ireland are long gone.

I really do live in hope that the gill-netting will cease for good here, and the famous big pike waters of the west will return to their full glory. Wild forty-pounders

A 32 lb 1 oz pike caught from the River Shannon on suspended roach under a drifter float.

are indeed possible from the awesome loughs of Mask, Corrib and Conn. I should add that there are a handful of commercial trout waters scattered around Ireland with the potential to produce pike of over 35 pounds. Some are gill-netted, and their potential fluctuates depending on its success. Some are far better-run but are mixed commercial fisheries, and the fish are not wild.

Most of my pike fishing in the future will take place on the huge Shannon system, where twenty-pounders are always on the cards, and there is also a chance of a real whopper. The system still has that mystery about it, and you never know what's going to turn up next. To me, this type of fishing is the real deal: proper piking. May it long continue.

The 1997 Austin Hogan
Award

is presented to

FREDERICK BULLER

This award is given in honor of the founder of the
American Museum of Fly Fishing's quarterly journal,
The American Fly Fisher, established in 1974

This award has been given since 1985 to recognize
excellence in writing about the heritage of the sport of fly
fishing.

Richard G. Tisch, Pres.   Kathleen Achor, Editor

*Fred Buller with Hugh Falkus holding a
double figure pike in the background.*

CHAPTER 22

LOCATING A WORLD RECORD PIKE

BY FRED BULLER

M ANY FACTORS COME INTO PLAY when considering the most likely location for a really big pike. Years of experience have taught me that we can be almost certain about one thing: the pike we seek to catch is unlikely to be a river fish. Why? Our target fish is likely to be between 13 and 16 years old, and so near the end of its lifespan. During its life it will have enjoyed optimum growth, never retarded by periods of dirty-river flood water, when poor visibility would hinder a pike seeking its prey. Such murky water would also make it more difficult for the pike's scenting acumen to locate suitable food.

Unlike its river cousin, the loch pike, on the other hand, once grown large, lives out its life in a safer environment, since there is little chance of discovery by its only serious enemy – man. The loch pike is safer, too, from the great inundations of storm and flood, which don't blight its appetite or hide its prey as they do at times in the flooded river.

One thing is sure: in order to ensure uninterrupted growth our theoretical superpike must have enjoyed throughout its life a regular diet made up of a range of suitable fodder fish of ever-increasing average size. But even supposing a pike manages throughout its life to prey on readily available fish of the most suitable size, another consideration is its nutritional value. If we look at the modern carp-fishing scene, we can appreciate the significance of the protein used in baits and groundbaits by observing the spectacular growth of carp in well-managed lakes and ponds. The importance of the quality of the pike's diet has been shown up by catches of magnificent pike from trout lakes, where a stock of healthy trout is maintained by regular top-ups with hatchery-bred fish. For example, five weighing over 40 lb have been taken from Chew Reservoir (40.04 lb, 40.06 lb, 40.08 lb, 41.08 lb and 42.04 lb).

So let us look a little closer at some of the most successful pike anglers in Britain, to see where they enjoy their pike fishing. It transpires that they are among those who take the opportunity to fish famous trout reservoirs, the owners of which now look upon the income derived from pike anglers as an important contribution.

However, finding big pike in a trout reservoir is not a new phenomenon. The Dowdeswell Pike was found dead in the Dowdeswell Reservoir in Cheltenham in 1896, and it seems to me that repeating the situation that produced such a fish may possibly produce another one. The pike's true weight is unknown, since it was found in an emaciated condition; its estimated weight is recorded as 60 lb. From *The Domesday Book of Mammoth Pike*:

The Dowdeswell Pike had every opportunity to grow to a large size, for it lived out its life unmolested in a well-stocked trout preserve. Moreover, it competed with no other pike; since, as far as we know, it was the sole representative of its species in Dowdeswell Reservoir.

The Dowdeswell Pike, estimated weight 60 lb. This fish is undoubtedly one of the largest found in Britain.

The head length of the Dowdeswell Pike, i.e. from nose to back of operculum, is 13 in. Now, its head length of 13 in. is really something; it even beats the monster 'Endrick' head by nearly half an inch. The total length of the Dowdeswell Pike at 53¼ in. (nose to end of caudal ray) is the greatest length ever recorded from a preserved specimen in Britain. The Freshwater Biological Association, using a Walford plot [a mathematical device to estimate age/growth data of fish] determined its age as thirteen years, and they were able to make the following back calculations:

Age (in years)	Length (in inches)
1	10
2	16.5
3	21
4	28
5	33
6	38
7	40.5
8	43.5
9	47
10	49
11	50
12	50.5
13	51

Years ago, when I was young, I worked for the Freshwater Biological Association at Windermere, on a scheme to reduce the perch and pike population of the lake, in order to achieve a bigger and locally more desirable population of charr and trout. At some point, I realised that my boss's real interest in this scheme lay in observing the ecological impact on the rest of the flora and fauna of Windermere after several years of trapping and netting activity. So I asked my immediate boss, George Thompson, if he would ask the big boss, Dr E. B. Worthington, a question for me: if I wanted to put myself in front of the largest pike in the British Isles with a view to catching it on rod and line, where would I start?

The answer came at once:

You should go to one of the larger lochs in Scotland, such as Loch Lomond, or to Loughs Corrib, Derg or Conn in Ireland, and concentrate your efforts somewhere on the route taken by migratory fish, such as salmon grilse or sea trout. These fish, during their spring, summer and autumn runs, add a huge bonus from the sea to the diet of larger pike, which wait somewhere on the route to the spawning beds in order to ambush them. Incidentally, the movement of salmon and grilse throughout the nine-mile length of Lough Conn has been well documented by Irish boatmen and fishermen for over a century, and it would surprise many to know that the odour of the fish's natal stream within the confines of the lough is the key to their movements and the deadly ambushing spots – thickets of potomageton weed perhaps, where a pike can hide, waiting for grilse or trout to swim within striking distance.

Proof of the accuracy of Dr Worthington's advice came in dramatic fashion. A year later, in the summer of 1945, Tommy Morgan, a wholesale newspaper proprietor from Glasgow, caught a 47 lb 11 oz pike from Loch Lomond. Although salmon and sea-trout fishing on Loch Lomond had a long history, and fishing for these species had a substantial following, at the time he caught the big fish Tommy was probably the only pike fisherman operating on the loch.

The fantastic news of the catch was much delayed in reaching me. I heard it some years later from my friend Robert Myslik, a Czech rodmaker who built rods for my company, Chubbs Ltd. Myslik, a political refugee during the 1939–45 war, was stationed in a camp near Loch Lomond. Through a mutual interest in fishing, he got to know Tommy Morgan and Morgan's friends Harry Britton and Jackie Thompson, all fishermen who in due course became friends of mine. This was lucky because they told me a secret: another huge pike, at least as big as Tommy's, had taken over the home ground of Tommy's 47 lb 11 oz fish – i.e. Portnellan Bay and its small islands and weedbeds.

A list of nine heavy pike taken from readily accessible waters indicates that, alongside loughs and lochs, man-made fisheries are gradually creeping up the table, and I believe this trend will continue. All these pike come with acceptable capture documentation (although some students of the subject may disagree).

The Endrick Pike. Probably the largest pike ever found in Britain. The weight of the fish when alive may well have been 70 lb.

DATE	NAME	LOCATION	WEIGHT	METHOD	SOURCE
1849	Howill Considene	Lough Derg	65 lb	Probably shot in a spawning drain	*The Field* 20 January 1877
c. 1856	Tonnie Kane	Lough Derg	64 lb	Pitchforked in a spawning drain	*Buller's Domesday Book*, pp. 44–46
1893	Sergeant in Royal Irish Constabulary	Lough Conn	63 lb	Livebaiting	*Fishing Gazette*, 12 May 1900
1895	Tim Clarke	Lough Conn	56 lb	Trailing spoon	*Fishing Gazette*, 26 January 1895
1917	Bernard Brown	Lough Conn	45 lb 8 oz	Trailing Devon Minnow	Letter in author's possession, 1914
1920	John Garvin	Lough Conn	53 lb	Trailing spoon	*Fishing Gazette*, 14 November 1929
1945	Tommy Morgan	Loch Lomond	47 lb 11 oz	Livebaiting	Letter in *Angling*, July 1951
1989	Gareth Edwards	Llandegfedd Reservoir	45 lb 6 oz	Spinning with a large Mepps	Buller was fishing with Edwards
1992	Roy Lewis	Llandegfedd Reservoir	45 lb 13 oz	Spinning with Creek Chubb lure	Mammoth Pike, Fickling, 2004

Conscious as I am of attempting to rule out British and Irish rivers as likely producers of exceptionally large pike, in putting such a statement in print I have a feeling I may end up red-faced. One possibility in particular worries me in that regard, though it still excites me. I suggest that we need to take another look at what I wrote in *Pike and the Pike Angler* (p. 135) about a huge pike found dead at

Meelick Weir on the River Shannon, the longest river with the biggest catchment area in the British Isles:

Of all the stories of big pike, the one that I find perpetually fascinating is the story of the great pike of Meelick – probably because it affirms my long-held view that a location capable of producing one monster pike is likely to produce another. An example of this phenomenon is provided by Tommy Morgan's 47 lb 6 oz [11 oz] record Scottish pike. Within ten yards of the spot where he caught it in an area as vast as Loch Lomond (some twenty-seven miles long and up to six miles wide), I hooked and had the chance to land one at least as big.

The underlying assumption is that a location that produces a monster pike is by definition an exceptionally favourable habitat, which provides the opportunity for a pike's continuous and rapid growth, and which, notwithstanding the passage of time and providing there was no fundamental change, would do so again. So far as I am aware, the first published account naming Meelick as the home of a monster pike began with the publication of a letter in the *Fishing Gazette* of 28 February 1891. The following is an extract from that letter.

I can truthfully state that a very large pike was found dead at Meelick Weir in December last. She was not weighed, but was measured by a German engineer, a Mr Hasey, and she was exactly 1¾ metres, or 5 ft 6½ in.

She evidently got smothered or choked, as she had a salmon partly swallowed and jammed in her gills that had not spawned. The salmon was partly decomposed and, when extracted from the monster's mouth, was estimated at about 15 lb at least before capture by a fisherman who saw it. The monster must have been dead some days, and a strong SW gale landed her dry on the weir wall almost at the end of the sluices.

The upper waters of the Shannon, near Banagher and Meelick, also abound with enormous pike, which have been caught as heavy as 50 lb. This is a great weight, but you will be told that there are even heavier pike in that river. When I was in its vicinity last year, I heard of one that must be – if half the stories told of him be true – the grandsire, or rather great-grandsire, of Irish pike; in fact, the matriarch of the *Esox lucius* tribe. Her favourite haunt – for I am informed that she has not yet been captured – is a deep, large pool below the Queen's salmon gap at Meelick. There she levies blackmail on the shoals of salmon grilse as they endeavour to pass through the gap, besides indulging in occasional trout and other fish. During many seasons, almost every angler who visited Meelick has tried to catch this huge water monster – always, however, with the same result: loss of tackle. Numberless have been the encounters; but, like a giant guarding an enchanted pass, the 'great pike of the gap' has sent back all her assailants, shorn of their tackle and honours.

The Field of 7 April 1927 published a letter from Mr Parker-Hutchinson, who had written to S. H. McGarry, the loch-keeper, and received the following letter about a report of a large pike that had been found dead (*Pike and the Pike Angler* page 136). (In the originals of the two letters quoted, the pike was referred to as male. However, the fish would certainly have been female, and there references have accordingly been changed.

Fred Buller stood close to the salmon gap at Meelick.

Meelick Weir on the River Shannon.

Next page: Fred Buller holding his largest pike, a 32 lb fish.

The reader may be wondering why I believe that pike could grow to a huge size in the Shannon and not in other big rivers. In what way is the Shannon different? My answer is that other rivers do not have a man-made funnel to direct ascending salmon and grilse past hazards. On the Shannon, the salmon and grilse have to pass, or attempt to pass, through the Queen's Salmon Gap, where man-made traps form part of the weir's construction. The funnel device was designed by the river authorities to ensure that a proportion of the salmon and grilse could always progress upstream.

INDEX